The Billy Wright Inquiry.

D1356523

Ulster Unionism and the Peace Process in Northern Ireland

Ulster Unionism and the Peace Process in Northern Ireland

Christopher Farrington

Government of Ireland Postdoctoral Fellow
School of Politics and International Relations
University College Dublin
Ireland

First published 2006 by
PALGRAVE MACMILLAN
Houndmills, Basingstoke, Hampshire RG21 6XS and
175 Fifth Avenue, New York, N.Y. 10010
Companies and representatives throughout the world

PALGRAVE MACMILLAN is the global academic imprint of the Palgrave Macmillan division of St. Martin's Press, LLC and of Palgrave Macmillan Ltd. Macmillan® is a registered trademark in the United States, United Kingdom and other countries. Palgrave is a registered trademark in the European Union and other countries.

ISBN-13: 978–1–4039–9285–7 hardback
ISBN-10: 1–4039–9285–1 hardback

This book is printed on paper suitable for recycling and made from fully managed and sustained forest sources.

A catalogue record for this book is available from the British Library.

Library of Congress Cataloging-in-Publication Data
Farrington, Christopher.
    Ulster unionism and the peace process in Northern Ireland / Christopher Farrington.
        p.   cm.
    Includes bibliographical references and index.
    ISBN 1–4039–9285–1 (cloth)
    1. Northern Ireland—Politics and government.   2. Peace movements—Northern Ireland.   3. Unionism (Irish politics).   I. Title.
    DA990.U46F36 2006
    941.60824—dc22   2005045604

10   9   8   7   6   5   4   3   2   1
15   14   13   12   11   10   09   08   07   06

Printed and bound in Great Britain by
Antony Rowe Ltd, Chippenham and Eastbourne

Contents

List of Figures and Table

Figures

Table

Acknowledgements

It is impossible to complete such a project without accumulating enormous debts that cannot be repaid within any normal space of time. I am grateful to the funding provided by Queen's University of Belfast, and the Irish Research Council for the Humanities and Social Sciences that enabled me to embark on and complete this research. Primarily I owe a great intellectual and personal debt to Richard English and Graham Walker, who have been both supportive and encouraging at every possible turn. Colleagues and friends in Belfast and Dublin also provided help, support and stimulation at crucial moments and I would like to thank Miranda Alison, John Barry, Stephen Bloomer, John Coakley, Aaron Edwards, John Foster, Gladys Ganiel, Karin Gilland Lutz, Adrian Guelke, Ciara Hogan, Albert Hughes, Colin Irwin, Tara Keenan-Thomson, Kieran Laird, Jane McConkey, Owen McEldowney, Marie Moran, Caroline Newell, Margaret O'Callaghan, Catherine O'Donnell, Michael Potter, Bert Preiss, Kieran Rankin, Brian Thomson and Jennifer Todd. I would also like to thank my family, my mother, father and brothers Graeme and Laurence. The usual qualification applies.

Many people assisted with the primary research. I would like to thank the staff at various libraries and district councils, who have been generous with their time and expertise and without them this thesis would have been significantly poorer. In particular, Darren Topping at the Newspaper Library in Belfast's Central Library and Yvonne Murphy, Ciaran Crossey and Kris Brown at the Northern Ireland Political Collection have provided invaluable assistance. I would also like to express my heartfelt appreciation for the assistance of Margaret Kane at Enniskillen Library, Liz Connor at Fermanagh District Council, Barbara Johnston at Ballymena Borough Council and Helen Crozier at Craigavon Borough Council who all generously gave time out of their busy working days to allow me access and guidance to the local government minutes of their respective areas.

As should be obvious from the text, many politicians gave generously of their time and thoughts. I would like to thank Jack Allen, Paul Berry, Esmond Birnie, David Burnside, Gregory Campbell, Mervyn Carrick, Fred Crowe, Joe Dodds, Jeffrey Donaldson, Raymond Ferguson, Sam Foster, Roy Garland, Oliver Gibson, William Hay, Bert Johnston, Bertie Kerr, Gordon Lucy, Robert McCartney, William McCrea, Chris McGimpsey,

David McNarry, Joe Miller, Jim Nicholson, Robert Saulters, George Savage, Duncan Shipley-Dalton, Martin Smyth and Jim Wells. I may not have given the assessment that Jim Wells was keen that I would: 'So basically I want you to write the DUP's all singing, all wise perfection and going forward from strength to strength ... so anyone who reads this will join in the morning!!' But I do hope that I have been fair and representative of all the views that were expressed to me.

Abbreviations

AIA	Anglo-Irish Agreement
APNI	Alliance Party of Northern Ireland
BBC	Ballymena Borough Council
BCC	Belfast City Council
BICO	The British and Irish Communist Organisation
CBC	Craigavon Borough Council
CBI	Confederation of British Industry
CDP	Campaign for a Devolved Parliament
CEC	Campaign for Equal Citizenship
CLR	Campaign for Labour Representation
CSCE	Conference on Security and Co-operation in Europe
DCC	Derry City Council
DSD	Downing Street Declaration
DUP	Democratic Unionist Party
ELO	Electric Light Orchestra
EU	European Union
FDC	Fermanagh District Council
FEA	Fair Employment Agency
HMG	Her Majesty's Government
IRA	Irish Republican Army
MEP	Member of European Parliament
MLA	Member of Legislative Assembly
MP	Member of Parliament
NIO	Northern Ireland Office
NIUP	Northern Ireland Unionist Party
NIWC	Northern Ireland Women's Coalition
QUB	Queen's University of Belfast
PIRA	Provisional Irish Republican Army
PR	Proportional Representation
PSNI	Police Service of Northern Ireland
PUP	Progressive Unionist Party
RUC	Royal Ulster Constabulary
SDLP	Social Democratic and Labour Party
SF	Sinn Féin
UDA	Ulster Defence Association

UDI	Unilateral Declaration of Independence
UDP	Ulster Democratic Party
UIO	Unionist Information Office
UK	United Kingdom
UKUP	United Kingdom Unionist Party
UUC	Ulster Unionist Council
UUP	Ulster Unionist Party
UUUC	United Ulster Unionist Coalition
UVF	Ulster Volunteer Force
UYUC	Ulster Young Unionist Council
VUPP	Vanguard Unionist Progressive Party

Introduction

The conflict in Northern Ireland has consisted of multiple relationships between and within groups (sometimes violent, sometimes merely antagonistic). By extension a peace process necessitates addressing these relationships and transforming them into a mode which is less destructive. The extent to which the peace process in Northern Ireland has accomplished or has intended to accomplish this is debateable but the process has fundamentally altered all of these relationships. Indeed, as the process has developed, it has created yet another dynamic, as the various groups developed a relationship with the process itself. It is that relationship which this book examines and in doing so it seeks to link the study of Ulster Unionism and the study of the Northern Ireland peace process. Too frequently the peace process is considered without a thorough understanding of this relationship and, similarly, Unionism is discussed as if it exists outside the political changes which have occurred since the early 1990s. It seeks to give Unionism a central place in this analysis, to understand the relationship between changes that are initiated and driven by other political actors and the attitudes of the group which is not central to those changes. The focus is on 'formal' politics throughout. In other words, the focus is on political parties, public intellectuals and politicians. However, in studying these institutions and people, the effort has been made to move the focus away from the elite leadership, on which some of the most recent studies have concentrated (Godson, 2004; Miller, 2005). In addition, the focus is on the longer-term processes and how these have interacted and influenced the development of the political parties, rather than on the micro-issues of the process such as when and how a particular deal or trade-off was made.

Two main debates have dominated the study of Unionist politics. The first is a matter of definition. There is no difficulty defining *who* Ulster

Unionists are; they are primarily Protestants who live in the six north-eastern counties of Ireland. The greater difficulty is in defining *what* Unionists are and what they want. The second debate concerns the divisions within Unionism and, more particularly, how these are translated into a political dynamic. In both of these debates there is a certain level of disjuncture between popular understandings of their importance and dynamics and the research-driven academic analysis, although the most interesting developments in Unionist politics have occurred when this interface has been thoroughly explored, such as the discussion on Unionist ideas in Chapter 1. These two questions of definition and division are central to the Unionist experience of the peace process and yet a thorough engagement with these debates has not been central to the analysis of the peace process in general. As we shall see in Chapter 1, Unionists were developing their own ideas about the various salient relationships involved in a resolution to the conflict but at this stage it is worth sketching some of the basic observations that can be made of Unionists, concerning their relationship with British national identity and key aspects of their traditional political arguments.

Unionism is, at core, a political idea which is wrapped in identity politics. Ulster Unionists are British but the manner in which they have expressed their political identity has made them seem curious and odd. National identity has been described as more of an emotional than a rational concept. Benedict Anderson has argued: 'it would...make things easier if one treated it [nationalism] as if it belonged with "kinship" and "religion," rather than with "liberalism" or "fascism"' (Anderson, 1991, 5). Therefore it seems more appropriate to examine it with reference to its internal structure and terms of reference rather than subject it to rigorous academic analysis to find intellectual coherence, as we would with a work of political theory. However, Ulster Unionists have conceived their political environment somewhat differently to an interpretation based wholly on nationalist assumptions. This is partly structural, relating to their relationship with British national identity, and partly the product of their distinctive political thought, which tends to see the political conflict in Northern Ireland in a quasi-legalistic manner. This is neatly illustrated by the title of a pamphlet written in 1981 which was presented by a group of prominent professional and business people who were, at that time, non-party political Unionists, *The Case for the Unionists* (McCartney, 1981). Dermot Nesbitt (UUP) further illustrates this: 'Unionists today need not be despondent: there is an argument to be made, a case to be won – and it *can* be won' (Nesbitt, 1995, 3, emphasis in original). Conceptualising

Unionism as an argument rather than an identity creates difficulties when the nature of that identity is investigated. Thus, Unionism appears either confused or fractured when asked to define itself (Cochrane, 1997) and the range of responses indicates uneasiness with definitions based on a national identity.

The Unionist community has always been more diversified concerning national identity than political options for Northern Ireland. Opinion poll evidence has consistently shown that, while independence has been a significant minority option, the majority of Unionists have chosen political options which keep Northern Ireland's position within the United Kingdom (UK) intact. In contrast, Nationalists have generally been more divided by options which maintain or eliminate the border (Breen, 1996). In a 1978 poll, 39 per cent of Catholics opted for devolution with power sharing while 24.9 per cent chose a united Ireland. Of the Protestants surveyed, 72.1 per cent opted for some version of devolution and 15.6 per cent for direct rule. No other option received more than 5 per cent support (Moxon-Browne, 1983, 24). In a similar poll in 1996, 63 per cent of Protestants opted for direct rule or the British state; 7 per cent chose a continuance of the Anglo-Irish Agreement (AIA) and a further 10 per cent for North–South institutions. Catholics surveyed, on the other hand, were split between an Irish State (32 per cent), joint authority (24 per cent), AIA (14 per cent) and North–South institutions (11 per cent) (Irwin, 2002, 131).

Fifty years of devolved government in Stormont has inculcated an insularity within Unionism. Over this period the Unionist case became implicit, in that it was no longer seen as important to articulate Unionist arguments. Moreover, the end goals of Unionism altered. During the Third Home Rule crisis, partition was a means to defeat Home Rule but, from the establishment of devolved government in Northern Ireland, maintaining partition has become the end goal itself. Nevertheless, Unionists have traditionally utilised a number of arguments in defence of the Union, based on religion, British nationality and economics (Whyte, 1990).

However, according to Whyte, the major weakness in Unionists' traditional interpretation is that it fails to take account of the division within Northern Ireland, and this, for Unionists, makes the conflict incomprehensible (Whyte, 1990, 162–3). Indeed, a recurring critique of Unionism is the absence of a consideration of Irish Nationalism and Unionists' perceived inability to adequately incorporate the minority within their discourse. McGarry and O'Leary identify this as the foremost defect in conventional Unionist discourse: 'The absence in conventional unionist literature of any significant treatment of the Nationalist minority, one which takes seriously its experiences and preferences, suggests profound political prejudice' (McGarry and O'Leary, 1995, 105). Moreover, both Whyte and McGarry and O'Leary argue that the experience of Nationalists, and Unionists' denial of it, during devolution between 1922 and 1972, severely damages the Unionist case (McGarry and O'Leary, 1995, 106–11; Whyte, 1990, 164–9). Jennifer Todd has analysed how this occlusion has had a negative effect on Unionism. Todd has argued that the body of Unionist political thought contained tensions and contradictions but these were not necessarily logically incompatible. Their problem lay in the challenge that they consistently faced in 'the Irish context'.

> The real problem for unionism was always partly occluded within its own self-understanding – the existence of Catholics and Nationalists within the unionist state. Once Catholics asserted themselves, the contradictions between the exclusivist foundations of Northern Ireland and its liberal ideals became clear. (Todd, 1993, 207)

As a slight corrective, infrequently acknowledged in the literature, this 'political prejudice' is not restricted to Unionism (see O'Halloran, 1987) and, indeed, some prominent Republicans are now acknowledging that their political ideas and strategy were based on an ignorance of Unionists and their political options (English, 2003, 312–13). For example, Tom Hartley, a leading Sinn Féin (SF) strategist, has stated: 'In a way we made them a non-people...we didn't even see them as part of the problem, never mind as being part of the solution' (English, 2003, 312).

Many of the Unionist arguments are concerned with legitimising Unionism and its place within the UK. However, full appreciation of Unionist ideology has to begin with a consideration of the peculiar circumstances of Unionism. Unionists are at the centre of two very different and complicated relationships. Unionism has been concerned with Ireland's relationship with Britain and this has been further complicated for Unionists because they have had a parallel, and as problematic, relationship with Irish nationalism. In both relationships Unionism has been the junior and often neglected partner and it is the nature of these relationships that determines Unionism's defence of the Union. Unionism may have no place for Nationalists within its political philosophy but this does not mean that it is, or has been, unaware of their presence; Unionists were all too aware of the divisions within Northern Ireland. However, by the early 1990s it was clear to Unionists that they were losing the battle on several fronts and throughout the decade there was restructuring of a number of substantial areas. Primarily these were concerned with proselytising the Unionist message but there was also a new vehemence about how they tackled Nationalist arguments. This will be addressed in Chapters 1 and 2.

Cochrane has argued that there was an 'identity crisis' among Unionists caused by their insecurities and confusion. However, many of the problems which have rendered Ulster Unionist identity perplexing and awkward have arisen from the tendency to look at Unionism through the prism of an Irish Nationalist framework, which shares some of the assumptions of primordialist approaches to nationality and emphasises certain characteristics of nationhood, such as language, origin myths, culture and self-determination (Connor, 1994), thereby failing to recognise the existence of nations within nations, such as Scotland within the UK or Catalonia within Spain, which do not always seek the same goals or exist within the same statist frameworks (Keating, 2001). Unionists certainly display some of these 'primordialist' characteristics but it is significant that no one has seriously advanced such an analysis of Ulster Unionism and most studies take an implicitly constructivist approach.

Thus, the relationship between state and nation is crucial and has not been thoroughly analysed in the study of nationalism in general (Guibernau, 1999; Keating, 2001) and especially in Northern Ireland. British national identity does not perform the same functions for Ulster Unionism as Irish national identity does for Ulster's Nationalists. British national identity has been described as 'banal nationalism', lying implicit in public discourse (Billig, 1995) and therefore is not articulated in the same manner that Irish Nationalism is and has been. The distinction between an explicit and an implicit articulation of national identity has meant that Unionists have had fewer resources to call upon in the intellectual conflict and therefore the expressions of Britishness seem more crude than those of Irishness. Indeed, this has led Feargal Cochrane to argue that the relationship between Britishness and Ulster Unionism is poorly and incoherently understood by Unionists and is not reciprocated by many in Great Britain who do not understand Unionists and have no particular wish for them to remain part of the UK (Cochrane, 1994, 1997, 372). Overall, Cochrane sees the connection with Britain as a regressive dynamic within Unionist politics, tending towards stagnation (Cochrane, 1997, 373).

However, recent writing on Unionism has dovetailed with a new interest and understanding of the nature and development of Britishness (Kearney, 1989; Colley, 1992) within academia, and much of this work indicates that Ulster Unionists are far from aberrant in their views on national identity (Longley, 1997, 112–13). There has been an increased awareness that 'British history' is not coterminous with 'English history' (Pocock, 1975; Harvie, 2004). The influential historical perspective provided by Linda Colley shows how Britishness was a construct built upon other identities, although never replacing them (Colley, 1992). This has opened new avenues in reflecting how to reconcile the 'four nations' with the 'one nation'. Hugh Kearney argues that if we accept that the UK is a multi-national state then many more phenomena are intelligible than is otherwise the case but is uncomfortable with the word 'nation'. He prefers to see the history of the UK as ' "multi-cultural" rather than "multi-national" '. To use the term 'multi-national' is inaccurate because it 'ignores the unifying factor of "Britishness" ' (Kearney, 1991). England and the English are now the fundamental problem because they, more than the other constituent nations of the UK, have to deal with changing identities (Nairn, 2000, 2001). As Keith Robbins argues, the Irish, Scottish and Welsh, or the 'peripheral peoples of the state', 'have long experience of schizophrenetic identity, with all its joys and difficulties' (Robbins, 1990, 14–15).

Academic literature on Scotland since the 1990s has pointed to the contradiction between the definition of the UK State as a 'unitary' one and its multi-cultural/multi-national nature (McCrone, 1997). Authors such as David McCrone and Lindsay Patterson have argued that Scotland maintained a distinctive 'civil society' from 1707 through separate legal, educational and clerical systems which kept alive a sense of Scottish identity (McCrone, 1992; Patterson, 1994). Moreover, the research which has been conducted on national identity has explicitly tested the extent to which the Scots, Welsh and English have multiple identities by asking questions such as, 'Do you feel more Scottish than British?' It is significant that we have no such data on Ulster Unionists, despite the articulation of identity in similar ways. The Scottish literature is also significant in the light that it sheds on the development of the relationship between Scottish identity and British identity. This research has argued that the Scots had a pragmatic and contractual conception of the Empire and Britain (Walker, 1995; Harvie, 2004). David Miller's influential 1978 book, *Queen's Rebels*, also described Ulster Protestants' relationship with Britain in this way and this is widely recognised within Scotland. For example, Neal Ascherson observed:

> It [Protestant Ulster] has insisted . . . on its 'Britishness'. This is an old-fashioned use of the term . . . The last Britons are to be found in

County Antrim or County Down. But the words they use to proclaim their Britishness are often Scots. (Ascherson, 2002, 256)

Ascherson does not give full credit to the range of opinion within Ulster Protestants but his observations are nonetheless significant. Unionism's 'identity problem', and from this discussion it is not at all clear that there is one, cannot be analysed in an insular fashion, without reference to 'the unresolved nature of Britishness itself' (McBride, 1996, 1). These ideas have begun to filter into discussions of contemporary Unionism (Aughey, 1989; Walker, 1995) but have been more prominent in discussions of late nineteenth- and early twentieth-century Unionism (Hennessey, 1993; McBride, 1996).

Indeed, while Ireland is usually explicitly excluded from discussions on the development of Britain because of the existence of a large number of people who did not identify with the project (O'Leary and Arthur, 1990), this has been to the detriment of a proper understanding of the position of the Ulster Protestant. As Keith Robbins argues: 'The yearning for an Ireland (and particularly a Northern Ireland) with "Brits out" does as much injustice to the complexities of individual identity as simple unqualified assertion that "Ulster is British"' (Robbins, 1990, 15). Those Unionists who have been nudging the ideology in the direction of a more nuanced understanding of their own identity, which will be considered in Chapter 1, have been trying to remove such an assertion from the Unionist lexicon. Therefore, on one hand, this intellectual and political context has opened space where Unionism has been able to reflect on its own identity and how it relates to the state in which that identity is invested. On the other hand, its ability to fully explore these implications has been curtailed because it has not had the security so that identity can be fully appreciated.

Since the 1980s most analyses of the Northern Ireland conflict have treated ethnic and national identity as the main division in Northern Ireland, and proposed solutions of the conflict have involved various mechanisms of reconciling or balancing these identities. The Belfast Agreement of Good Friday 1998 reflected these intellectual trends and stated clearly that it was necessary to recognise political identities as part of a resolution to the conflict. The difficulty in defining Unionism and Unionist identity complicates the idea of an easy symmetry between Unionism and Nationalism and therefore has made the search for peace more difficult. Therefore, understanding Unionist identity, how it has changed and how it responds to change is an important part of understanding the origins and nature of the peace process. Moreover, the Agreement and key documents relating to it such as the Downing Street Declaration (DSD) all tackle these questions of definition as they all propose some answer to the 'constitutional question'. We shall see throughout this book that a recurring theme of Unionist dissatisfaction with various political initiatives lies in the definitions of Unionists, the Irish Nation and the various recognitions of national identity. These identity and ideational issues also form the background to other aspects of the peace process, such as changing relationships with Irish Nationalism and the political and legislative changes resulting from the Agreement.

If definitions form the backdrop to the discussion, the question of Unionist division has more immediate importance for how we examine the politics of Unionism and it should therefore be a crucial question for the analysis of the peace process. How has the peace process affected the dynamics of Unionist division? And, conversely, how has Unionist division affected the dynamics of the peace process? The central argument of this book is that the peace process has affected Unionist divisions to a greater extent than vice versa. In particular, the peace process, through the Agreement, has defined how Unionists relate to one another (see Chapter 4) and has fundamentally altered the dynamics of party competition (Chapter 5). These two factors have allowed significant party political realignments to occur. This picture is substantially different to the research that had been conducted prior to 1998, which emphasised social and cultural factors to Unionist party competition.

Unionists are aware of their divisions and this is evident in the desire for Unionist unity. This desire is a recognition of the deep divisions within the Unionist community; divisions of a 'political, cultural, class, regional and denominational nature' (English and Walker, 1996, ix). The fact that these divisions exist is unsurprising because Northern Ireland is undoubtedly a divided society and, in political science literature, resembles an unranked ethnic group system (Horowitz, 1985, 21–4), where each of the two communities in Northern Ireland is, essentially, a distinct societal structure, although there is a level of integration between the two communities (Ruane and Todd, 1992). Unionism obviously conforms to this model in that its divisions are largely the product of an internally differentiated community but the difficulties that organised Unionism has found in negotiating and accommodating these divisions are derived, in large part, from the fact that its political circumstances have forced it to try and suppress the natural diversity inherent within the Unionist community.

Unionism has, at least in organisational terms, been a reluctant participant in creating a society that is divided into two competing nationalisms. In the formative stages of the Home Rule crises in the late nineteenth century, Unionist political organisations had to be forged out of pre-existing political structures rather than around a nationalist project. Political Unionism was an umbrella organisation, the Ulster Unionist Council (UUC), and was created by another umbrella organisation, the Orange Order, explicitly to represent the various groupings in Unionist society. The priorities of Unionists in the late twentieth century have been to ameliorate differences which are essentially political in character. The fracturing of the organisational monolith of the Unionist Party occurred in the late 1960s and early 1970s as the Unionist government was unable to adequately meet the demands of the civil rights protests and the Unionist hardliners (Mulholland, 2000). The Unionist Party was able to maintain control of a growing number of ginger groups within the party when it was in power. Once Stormont was prorogued the party fractured and by the time of the Ulster Workers' Council strike there were five political parties appealing to a Unionist constituency (the Alliance Party of Northern Ireland (APNI), the Democratic Unionist Party (DUP), the Unionist Party of Northern Ireland (UPNI), the Ulster Unionist Party (UUP) and the Vanguard Unionist Party (VUP)). It was from this time that the remaining UUP members became known as Official Unionists. It was not until after the Constitutional Convention in 1975 that Unionist party politics settled into two main parties – the UUP and the DUP, and the Alliance Party. The UUP, VUP and DUP had formed a coalition to contest those elections but when William Craig advocated a coalition with the Social Democratic and Labour Party (SDLP) Vanguard lost the support of the other parties and the electorate. Since the paramilitary ceasefires in the 1990s we have seen another proliferation of Unionist parties. However, while two of these parties, the Progressive Unionist Party (PUP) and the now defunct Ulster Democratic Party (UDP), were self-consciously catering for a working-class Protestant constituency, and McCartney and his United Kingdom Unionist Party (UKUP) claim to be the repository for a liberal Unionism, Unionism has not split into its ideological parts.

The academic debate has tended to focus on what these constituent parts of Unionism might be. Feargal Cochrane argues:

> Unionist ideology contains diverse interest groups with little in common other than a commitment to the link with Britain. While this position remains relatively cohesive during periods of constitutional crisis when they can articulate what they do not want...the

coherence of the ideology begins to disintegrate when unionists are forced to establish a consensus for political progress. (Cochrane, 1997, 35)

We should not be surprised that different social groupings and interest groups want different things and undoubtedly the divisions are an important dynamic of how Unionist politics functions. Cochrane argues that the differences in political culture between the two Unionist parties are reflected in their style of politics and their analysis of their political situations. However, outlining and delineating these divisions is insufficient because Unionists are acutely aware of their variation and there have been attempts to either eliminate or nullify internal division. For instance, the major division within the Stormont cabinet was the importance of prioritising measures to maintain Unionist cohesion (Bew, Gibbon and Patterson, 1996), and anthropological research on the Orange Order has argued that this was the main function of the Order and was achieved through layers of representation (Bryan, 1998, 2000a, b).

Nevertheless, the majority of research on Unionism has been concerned with delineating the complex ideological web of Unionism. The seminal work in this regard is Jennifer Todd's 'Two Traditions in Unionist Political Culture', which, while published in 1987, is still the dominant model for political researchers. Todd identified two ideological traditions in Unionism based on different primary imagined communities and different conceptions of political life. Ulster Loyalism's imagined community is Ulster, its connection with Britain is conditional, and religion and politics are inextricably linked; the Ulster British tradition's imagined community is Great Britain and it professes liberal political values (Todd, 1987). This duality not only seems more comprehensive than other accounts aimed at distilling an 'essence' of Unionism (Coulter, 1994) but also seems to simplify a more fluid Unionist political discourse and reduces essentially political disputes to cultural structures (Doyle, 1994). Unionist political ideology is more integrated, or perhaps has become more integrated, than Todd's model allows and a political dynamic is discounted altogether under this dualist approach. Arthur Aughey, for example, has argued that Unionist political thought has centred around two ideas: the fact of the Union and its durability (Aughey, 1997; 2001a), and as Bew and Patterson note:

Although the history of Protestant politics and ideology is replete with divisions on democratic and class issues, on the national question . . . there is no significant intra-Unionist division – the liberals and the neanderthals make common cause. (Bew and Patterson, 1987a, 45)

This 'thick' interpretation of Unionism is ultimately more sophisticated than those interpretations which build on the ethnic conflict literature and which try to interpret party competition within Northern Ireland. Paul Mitchell has described the party system in Northern Ireland as 'an ethnic dual party system'; essentially two systems operating in tandem – one for Unionism and one for Nationalism (Mitchell, 1995) – and therefore it accords closely with Horowitz's unranked ethnic group system. Competition between the two Unionist parties is, for Mitchell, identifiably ethnic, perhaps more so than within Nationalism, as he argues there are real and ascertainable differences between the two Nationalist parties, such as electorates, politics and tactics (Mitchell, 1995, 782). Thus, the changing fortunes of the DUP from the early 1980s, when its fortunes declined after it captured 50 per cent of the Unionist vote, are explained in political and not social or economic terms:

The DUP has ultimately suffered from the ineffectiveness of its rejectionist stance. While the belligerency and theatricality of Paisley's opposition to Irish Nationalism has sustained his personal popularity, his party has fallen further behind the UUP. The DUP's tactics in trying to 'defend the Union' have been seen to be inept, unsuccessful and even counter-productive. (Mitchell, 1995, 785)

Indeed, the limited literature on voting behaviour in Northern Ireland would tend to endorse a rational choice model. Knox, McIlheney and Osborne found: 'The social and economic profile of the UUP and DUP voter, although not merging was at the very least converging.' Thus, it was suggested, 'the unionist electorate's expectations of these parties is *not* the extent to which they are staunch defenders of the Union, since it is assumed that both are, but their success in building a constitutional framework for Northern Ireland' (Knox, McIlheney and Osborne, 1995, 93–4, emphasis in original). This is supported by research by Ian McAllister who found that 'party has a consistently important influence in predicting Protestant political beliefs and preferences' (McAllister, 1983a, 281).

There are therefore two debates in the academic literature on Unionist divisions but little engagement between them. One addresses the social and cultural divisions within Unionism in general and the other focuses on the nature of party competition. The problem with both these debates is that the first neglects the importance of electoral competition while the second neglects the importance of cultural divisions. There are further problems with the literature on Unionist political parties in that, generally speaking, it is outdated.[1] This book goes some way to rectifying this problem by treating the political parties and their organisation seriously and examines in depth how the political parties function, how they perceive themselves and how they have developed. This is a key part of the overall book, which examines the politics of Ulster Unionism with reference to a political dynamic; in other words, how political debates, political behaviour and party competition are affected or determined by political circumstances rather than by ideological and cultural structures. This is not to deny the importance of, for example, differences in perceptions of national identity. Rather it argues that these are insufficient to explain the dynamics of Unionist politics because of the nature of the political circumstances of Northern Ireland since the AIA.

The structure of the book

Most of these debates and discussions have been overtaken by events since 1998, as political change has raised a series of other questions. However, they remain pertinent in explaining the shape and substance of Unionist politics post-Good Friday Agreement. The most important discussion is the relationship between Unionists and the process of change which occurred since the mid-1980s. There have been many studies since 1998 that have outlined Unionist dissatisfaction with political developments but the framework for the period prior to 1998 remains undeveloped. The 1998 Agreement significantly changed Northern Irish politics but in many ways the main questions remained the same: Would Ireland be united? Could Nationalists and Republicans find an agreed space with Unionism in Northern Ireland? Each chapter of this book addresses key questions about the relationship between Unionism and this process of political change. Chapter 1 discusses developments in Unionist ideas from the AIA. These developments have been seen as crucial in changing the Unionist interpretation of the direction of politics in Northern Ireland and therefore providing a rationale for participation in the negotiations of 1996–8 and the conclusion of the 1998 Agreement. Chapter 2 examines the Unionist interpretation of the AIA, which was an important staging post for many in Northern Ireland. The AIA is important as it brought about a reassessment among Unionists of Northern Ireland's relationship with the Republic of Ireland, sparked a major internal debate about various political options for Northern Ireland and prompted a reconsideration of Unionist's relationship with the British Government. While these processes were occurring, Unionist politicians at local government level were slowly finding a working relationship with Nationalists. This is examined in Chapter 3 through an analysis which is sensitive to class, religion and the manner in which political parties have been integrated into Protestant social organisations. Thus Chapter 3 also argues that local politics provides important insights into Unionist party politics. Chapter 4 then analyses the Unionist interpretation of the peace process, as it is commonly understood, and argues that this needs to be problematised in order to appreciate the different processes at work and how each affects the others. Moreover, it is also argued that there is a common Unionist analysis of these processes, which has been disguised by the subsequent divisions over the 1998 Agreement. These divisions form the backdrop to Chapter 5, which examines the political issues that have been most contentious for Unionists. More importantly, however, Chapter 5 examines the party political changes in Unionism and the changes from a fragmented party system in 1996 and 1998 to one which has solidified, at least temporarily, around two parties and has seen the UUP replaced by the DUP as the largest Unionist party.

1
The Development of Unionist Ideas

Political ideas have been a central place for debate in Ireland except that, unlike in the rest of Europe, these debates have been over the nature and extent of the 'nation' and the boundaries of the 'national community'. In many ways these debates are not exceptional but they do open a window into analysing how the differing political groups perceive and explain their national identity and their relationship with their respective state. They explicitly allow us a window into how groups self-define. There are many different research strategies which could be followed in order to explore these issues but, in order to keep the focus on the 'formal' political sphere, the interaction between public intellectuals is the subject of investigation here.

Of course, political ideas can change and in Northern Ireland it is implicit in many discussions that widespread social and political change will occur when the ideas which hold Nationalism and Unionism in place change. It is widely acknowledged that new thinking within Irish Nationalism and Irish Republicanism was crucial in bringing about political change insofar as it redefined the goals of Northern Irish Nationalism and prompted a strategic rethink among Republicans. However, what about Unionists? Was there new thinking within Unionism and how did this affect the peace process or more general political change in Northern Ireland?

McGarry and O'Leary illustrate how many commentators conceive of Ulster Unionist political thinking:

> Unionist writings have been less ably developed than those of Irish Nationalists. This judgement does not reflect cultural bias on our part, just the fact that Ulster Unionists, by and large, have been defenders of the status quo – at least until 1985 – and articulate defences of the

status quo are usually less often required than articulate cases for change. (1995, 96)

However, by contrasting Unionist and Nationalist writings some important points are missed concerning the political situations of the two groups. The role of intellectuals in nationalist movements has been crucial in constructing and articulating the nature and the demands of the group but as Monseratt Guiberneau argues, the crucial moment is before a nationalist movement becomes a mass movement. At this stage, intellectuals will articulate moral, political and economic reasons for self-determination but the role of intellectuals changes as it moves beyond an elite base (1999, 100). If the claims for self-determination are successful, then intellectuals can become significant as nation-builders (Alter, 1994, 12–15) and this process is evident in the development of Ulster Unionism from 1886, when it was an elite movement (Bew, 2001), to 1914, when it had become a movement rooted in the Protestant population in Ulster, to post-1921, when the new entity of Northern Ireland had a form of regional autonomy. Unionists were not looking for self-determination but their arguments were based on an economic, religious and cultural case and were similar to those of nationalist movements (Bew, 1994, 27–53; Todd, 1993). Analysts have noted that Unionists only tend to offer their arguments in times of crisis (Todd, 1993; McGarry and O'Leary, 1995) but it may be that this is not particularly unusual, as the state of affairs becomes assumed. What is more unusual is the regression back to the stage where intellectuals have to rearticulate the arguments for group distinctiveness, as occurred with Ulster Unionists in the late 1980s and 1990s.

In 1991 Liam O'Dowd argued that intellectuals had not played equivalent roles in Unionism and Nationalism for 'deep-rooted political and structural reasons' and this 'inhibited the construction of a common political discourse which might inform political accommodation' (O'Dowd, 1991). He argued that there were structural constraints within Unionism, which explained the lack of political intellectuals. Some of those constraints operated within the Protestant education system, which focused on science and technical subjects and thus discouraged professionals from engaging in politics but, perhaps more importantly, the mass appeal and nature of popular loyalism prevented any of those who were disposed towards active politics from achieving prominence. O'Dowd noted how the intelligentsia had 'opted out' of politics and left the leadership of Unionism to other professions, notably the land-owning and industrial classes. The clergy also played a different role in

Unionism; they were specific political lobbyists and less keen than their Catholic counterparts 'to inform political life with a coherent social philosophy' (O'Dowd, 1991, 158–9). However, it can be equally argued that intellectuals did not *have* to play a role within Unionism because Unionism had progressed through the stage where intellectuals were essential to its development. The civil rights movement involved a rearticulation of Nationalist demands and grievances and a galvanising of nationalism, which almost demanded a response from Unionism in these terms but which did not arrive until after the AIA. This therefore makes the literature developed after the AIA particularly important. This chapter will analyse four aspects of this post-AIA literature. First, who is involved in writing this literature? Secondly, what is this literature saying? Thirdly, what have been the critiques of this literature and what does this tell us about the nature of political change within Unionism? Finally, what impacts has this had on party political Unionism?

Who?

One of the most significant developments in Unionist politics in the 1990s was how a distinctive cadre of Unionist intellectuals emerged to develop and articulate Unionism. The integration–devolution debate in the 1980s (discussed in Chapter 2) was important in mobilising this element of Unionism and, following from that, the literary critic John Wilson Foster, resident in Canada but native to Northern Ireland, was foremost in raising the battle cry. Foster asked: Is the Union safe? He found his answer in those who believed in the cause:

> *The central task of the pro-Union intellectual is to appreciate the Union not simply as history but as a culture, a value-system, an idea (with its own force-field)* – to articulate the inchoate perceptions of the unionist populace, who have been tongue-tied, and so disempowered, for years. For the intellectual, the Union is open-ended: it is not a closed system meant to exclude anyone. It requires the integrity of local structures and powers, but it is also a causeway to the larger founding culture and, if that causeway is sturdy and broad enough (and two-way), it can welcome the causeway to the other founding culture. (Foster, 1995, 70–1, emphasis in original)

Foster pointed to the many negative stereotypes of Unionism as factors that hinder the progress of such developments in Irish intellectual life but he stresses its importance because 'an unrealistic nationalism has in recent decades flourished in the vacuum caused by the silence of intellectual unionism' (Foster, 1996, 93) and advocated a new strain in Irish intellectual life. He identified two strains that dominate Irish intellectual discourse, both of which assumed the inevitability of the political unity of the island: the Anglo-Irish strain and the partisan Nationalist strain. The Anglo-Irish strain sponsored the AIA and the DSD and, while sponsoring a plural nation, it was nonetheless a politically unified island (Foster, 1996, 81–3). The second strain is composed of those who would like to bring about a united Ireland and these intellectuals are therefore actively partisan. Therefore, if the intellectual project was to be undertaken by those intellectuals who had 'opted out' of Unionism, the actual project was to be a sophisticated formulation of Unionism within Irish intellectual discourse:

> A case can be made for the historical union of Great Britain and Northern Ireland and for its maintenance into the foreseeable future that is easily the intellectual equal of the case for a united Ireland constitutionally sundered from Great Britain, a case that is not merely a sophisticated socio-political rationale but also a deeply embedded socio-cultural rationale. (Foster, 1996, 91)

However, Foster's basic point, that Unionism has been marginalised and excluded by decision makers and that this position is partly of their own making, has been influential in Unionist circles in the 1990s. Roche and Birnie explicitly state this in the introduction to their book *An Economics Lesson for Irish Nationalists and Republicans*:

> The unionists of all parties and none also need to do some serious thinking. For example, why is it that the rest of the world is largely ignorant of the very good economic grounds in favour of the Union? Why is unionism often dismissed as an unpleasant form of tribalistic atavism? Why do many of Northern Ireland's middle and professional classes regard active adherence to unionism as a form of intellectual suicide? Of course, unionism need not be either sectarian or tribal and intellectual suicide is certainly not required. If this booklet has helped to demonstrate this then the authors will be well pleased. (Roche and Birnie, 1995, 13)

The most noticeable feature of these ideological reformers is their socio-economic composition. O'Dowd noted the dearth of intellectuals in Unionism but a cursory glance at the background of this group surely calls for reconsideration. Among them were Arthur Aughey, Patrick Roche, Graham Gudgin, Esmond Birnie, Dermot Nesbitt, David Trimble, Peter Weir, Steven King, Gordon Lucy, Ruth Dudley Edwards, Paul Bew, Henry Patterson and Conor Cruise O'Brien. In addition, there were a higher number of young graduates who were prominent in writing for Unionist publications and working for Unionist politicians. Trimble himself has gone a long way to dispelling assumptions about the lack of intellectual depth in Unionism; it would be difficult to name another political leader on the island of Ireland who has cited Karl Popper and Edmund Burke in his speeches (Trimble, 2001, 39–63). The significance of the Popper reference should not be undersold, as the speech was unscripted. Indeed, one journalist has cited an unnamed commentator who has called Trimble the 'intellectuals' intellectual' (De Bréadún, 2001, 189). Their relative importance is hard to quantify but a number have produced influential and complementary pamphlets and articles. For example, Gudgin and Birnie and Roche have written extensively on the economics of the Union, while Roche has also written important articles on Irish Nationalism which complements some of Arthur Aughey's work. The influence of others, such as Trimble and Nesbitt, lies in their position within the party but taken collectively this is an extremely important group of people. However, there is a dilemma to be confronted when considering the work of many of these authors and that is: to what extent do we make the distinction between academic and activist or partisan writings when we analyse their work?[1] Most are serious academics, although many have also openly declared their Unionism in their articles. However, this should not mean that they are 'pigeon holed' and then discounted. Many of the arguments which have been made are informed by developments within Irish and British scholarship.

What were they saying?

There was a significant amount of will to ensure that these authors had the medium for their writings. The Young Unionists and particularly their journal, *The Ulster Review*, were especially prominent in printing such articles and pamphlets. They were primarily concerned with providing a coherent and rational defence of the Union in order to counter what they saw as the dominant orthodoxy on Northern Ireland, which in their opinion had been informed by Irish Nationalism's analysis (Cadogan Group, 1992). There were three major themes for the discussions. There was a critique of Irish Nationalism, there was an articulation of Britishness and there were economic arguments.

Critique of Irish Nationalism

The critique of Irish Nationalism has two distinct elements. There is an attack on how Nationalism treats and analyses Unionism and there is a more general attack on Nationalism's assumptions and analysis on Northern Ireland and Irish national identity. These 'new' Unionists, as they have been termed, identified a

> Pervasive notion of general cultural superiority [which] fulfils a vital psychological and political function in Irish Nationalism. Its day must come because what opposes it in Northern Ireland, though it may have the temporary support of the alien, external power of Britain, is ultimately inferior and insubstantial. (Aughey, 1995a, 7)

Aughey argues that those[2] who maintain the philosophy that there can only be one authentic Irish nation make 'insulting and misconceived' analysis of Unionist culture; 'they can see no difference between what might be distinctively Irish...and what might be representative of contemporary cultural life in Ireland'. They reduce Unionism to its parochial distinctiveness; Orange marches, flute bands and so on are represented as the totality of Unionist culture because this allows them to show Unionism as distinctively Irish (because they fail to show the diversity of cultural life resembling Britain) but yet in a cultural identity crisis (Aughey, 1995a, 12–14). Unionists should respond in a positive way and not by playing the same game by disparaging the distinctive practices of Nationalism.

> Unionism is not a totalising way of life. As a political identity it has room for any manner of cultural expressions. Challenging the stereo-type allows the Unionist to assert a devastating argument which disorders the senses of cultural nationalism: that one can be Irish without being a separatist. To cultivate seriously the political idea of the 'greater number,' a phrase which is now part of the lexicon of Unionism, seems to imply such a disposition. (Aughey, 1995a, 15)

If the sphere of influence of the Nationalist analysis of Northern Ireland was restricted solely to Nationalists there would perhaps be very little to concern Unionists but these Unionists argue that Irish Nationalism influences much more than just the domestic political sphere. The Cadogan Group explicitly stated that their formation and publications were predicated on the 'widespread and largely unchallenged Nationalist or neo-Nationalist consensus' among commentators and that informed government policy (Cadogan Group, 1992). Roche (1994), Aughey, Foster and English (English, 1995) argue that the 'intellectual coherence and practical feasibility' of Irish Nationalism, on which these analyses are based, is not as obvious as it first seems. Like Aughey, Roche identifies 'one nationalism' as the problematic concept for Irish Nationalists because neither the subjectivist (the nation defining itself) nor the objectivist (an external definition of the nation) approach to nationhood sustain the idea that Ireland is one nation (Roche, 1996, 23–5) and therefore he terms Irish nationalism a 'self-refuting ideology' because it contradicts itself on its own criteria (Roche, 1994).

> Nationalists have been reduced to currently using a form of geographical determinism to produce a national identity which would embrace all the inhabitants of the island. The idea is that the geographical location of birth determines national identity. This absurd notion indicates the bankruptcy of Irish nationalism. (Roche and Birnie, 1996)

These Unionists are essentially arguing that an Irish national identity that relies on territory is unfeasible because it cannot adequately incorporate Unionists within that definition. This in itself is not a new argument – for example, Marcus Heslinga argued in 1968 that the divisions on the island were between people (Helsinga, 1979) – nor is the argument unique to Unionists; Fintan O'Toole is equally as critical of the construction of identity based on an island context, arguing that Irish identities are as much a product of the diaspora in America and elsewhere as they are from Ireland's island perspective (O'Toole, 1998).

This is compounded by arguments arising from an analysis of the nature of Irish nationality. For example, John Wilson Foster argues that the historical construction of Irishness went through several phases and definitions but all except the United Irishmen's definition excluded Ulster Protestants:

> As nationalist ideology developed from the early nineteenth century, there was an answering self-exclusion by Northern Protestants from nationalist Irishness, a self-exclusion that was nevertheless largely irrelevant to that ideological development... Partition in 1921 was not some devilish sundering of the island imposed from without, but an almost natural consequence (however regrettable or unacceptable

to some) of the culmination on the nationalist side of events long-preparing.(Foster, 1991)

Although some Unionists have maintained the historical tradition of a critique of political life in the south as inhospitable to Protestants (McCartney, 2001), the argument changed to a critique of the construction of the Irish nation. Unionists argued that for someone to be part of the Irish nation it was necessary to be Catholic and Gaelic (O'Brien, 1994) and therefore 'if there is ever to be peace on this island, one prerequisite is the redefinition of Irishness' (Foster, 1991, 260) because:

> nationalism, however you look at it, is opposed to unionism and Protestant self-determination. And I believe that Protestants seek self-determination, wanting union with Britain (which is primarily separation from the South, in actuality) because the alternative has been defined in a way that excludes them yet desires them, and therefore threatens them. (Foster, 1991, 260)

Therefore the combination of 'one nationalism' and the conception of Irishness as Catholic determines Nationalism's views on Unionism and partition, as Conor Cruise O'Brien succinctly notes: 'Nationalists are in the habit of referring to the "artificial partition" of the island. In principle, there is nothing artificial about the partition: it is a result of history, traditions and demography' (O'Brien, 1994, 152). Nationalists fail to recognise and understand Unionist national identity. Moreover, there is the added element of a qualitative distinction between Unionist and Nationalist political identities. Aughey, in the most extreme example, argues that Unionism is solely concerned with the citizen's relationship with the state and has little to do with cultural identities (Aughey, 1989), although he has recently moved to a position where he now argues that the distinction between Unionism and Nationalism is one between a first- and a second-order nationalism (Aughey, 2001b, 64–6).

What is significant here is the fundamental challenge to the Irish Nationalist analysis of Unionism, which has assumed Unionists were merely another part of the Irish nation. By arguing that the construction of Irishness as Gaelic and Catholic has excluded them and that, moreover, the geographical presumption of that identity is flawed, Unionists have been defining themselves out of Irish identity. This is not to say that there is no 'Irishness' within Unionism but that the Unionist conception of that identity is fundamentally different from Irish Nationalists' conception.

The articulation of Britishness

This analysis of Irishness was coupled with an increasing discussion on the nature of Britishness and it is in this respect that Arthur Aughey has been crucial to the development of Unionist thinking. He should be seen as one of the most influential Unionist writers and his writings on the UK state have been absorbed by many Unionist politicians and incorporated into their rhetoric and arguments. Aughey sought to demonstrate that Unionism could, and indeed should, be open to all by arguing that substantive identities can coexist within the UK, which itself is a larger and umbrella identification. Aughey was perhaps the first to formulate a Unionist treatise that attempted to reconcile the Unionist identity with the British state and argues, 'it [Unionism] is an identity that associates itself with the affairs of a multi-national state, expansive and outward-looking in a way that self absorbed Irish nationalism could never be' (Aughey, 1989, 14). Aughey attempted to move the debate on Unionism away from issues of cultural identities because, he argued, this was inappropriate and misleading in a discussion on Unionists' Britishness:

> the character of unionism has little to do with the assumptions of nationalism ... The identity of unionism has little to do with the idea of the nation and everything to do with the idea of the state ... The relationship has nothing to do with weddings, divorce or alimony but with the principles of the modern state itself. The relationship is not a civil one, nor is it based on arbitrary or private considerations. (Aughey, 1989, 17–18)

He attempted to abstract Unionism from its cultural connotations because, as the academic debate over the issue testifies, there is much confusion over how to classify Unionism precisely because of its relationship with the political institutions of the UK (Brown, 1991, 74–8). Moreover, Aughey is not out of step with academia in Great Britain over the thinking about British identity (for example Parekh, 2002).

In theory, Aughey's Unionism allows Irish Nationalists to be accommodated within the UK but in practice the 'pluralism' that has seeped into the Unionist rhetoric does not necessarily fulfil this function. For example, David Burnside described his Unionism:

> Core traditional values, the crown, the monarchy, sort of principles of the Orange Order, the crown, the Protestant religion but not exclusively, not excluding Catholics. There are sections of Unionism

probably you might call the Free Presbyterian–DUP Unionism that don't really want Catholics in the same room to be blunt about it. I've no problems having a Catholic at any Unionist meeting, any platform... They would have, that's the difference. I think you can have your traditional core values but you can still be reasonably inclusive... You can't have Nationalists within a Unionist organisation. [but] in Northern Ireland, in a form of local administration, you've got to have Nationalists there. (Interview with David Burnside, 13 September 2002)

Instead, Unionists, and particularly the UUP, have been concerned to appear more open to Catholics. They believe that a significant number of the Catholic population have some connection with the UK and could be persuaded to support the Union (see later) (Breen, 1996).

There have been developments within the wider Unionist population to provide Unionists with a richer appreciation of their history and culture. The most visible organisations are those working in the areas promoting Ulster–Scots connections and those promoting Ulster–British culture. In this latter category perhaps the only organisation involved is the Ulster Society, which was established in June 1985 'with the aim of promoting and preserving the distinctive culture and heritage of the Ulster-British in all their rich and varied forms, embracing language, drama, poetry, music, folk customs, symbolism and history',[3] because:

It has been demonstrated that the passive approach to culture and history has not been beneficial to our country's interest. As a result, many feel that a concentrated effort to deny the validity of Ulster-British heritage is on-going. Therefore, it is the Ulster Society's aim to set the record straight by promoting the long and proud tradition of the Ulster-British people. (www.ulstersociety.org/about.html accessed 5 May 2005)

Therefore, the Society provides one avenue for analysing how the 'Ulster-British' people see themselves and their culture. When asked what Ulster-British culture actually was, Gordon Lucy, a leading member of the Society, mischievously replied: 'Well Herbert Morrison once observed about socialism... "socialism is what a Labour government does"... so Ulster-British culture is what Ulster-British people do' (Interview with Gordon Lucy, 23 August 2002). Lucy continued to argue that he saw 'Ulster-British' culture as a subset of a wider British culture, not necessarily at odds with Aughey's Unionism, which was supposedly devoid of such cultural vestiges. Initially, its main work was through lectures, workshops and exhibitions but the society has since expanded its scope and publishes a journal, *New Ulster*, and has a large back catalogue on topics such as the Ulster Unionist Convention, reflections on Remembrance Sundays, the Twelfth of July and Britishness, the Battle of the Somme and Ulster connections with America; all of which are intended for popular consumption. Lucy also sees the work of the Ulster-Scots Agency as essentially complementary to a better understanding of the past and the future of the 'Ulster-British' people. However, the Ulster Society has lost out to its wealthier counterpart in the funding battle, as the Ulster-Scots Agency got special recognition in the Belfast Agreement (Interview with Gordon Lucy, 23 August 2002).

Despite these organisations there is a different quality to Unionist discourse when we compare it to previous examples of Unionist ideology. This is particularly evident if we consider the Unionist use of history (Farrington, 2003a). After the foundation of Northern Ireland there were a considerable number of polemical historians writing to legitimise the state and the Unionist position (Jackson, 1996, 126; McIntosh, 1999) but these histories perhaps fulfilled more important ideological functions. McIntosh has described how the histories written during the first half of the Stormont era set the Unionist experience into what she calls Unionists' 'seamless fabric of history', where their contemporary experience was set into their 'historically based self-image' of sacrifice and loyalty to the British Empire and state, betrayal by the same and juxtaposed with Catholic disloyalty and their attempts to destroy the Protestant community in Ireland (McIntosh, 1999, 36–68). Todd identified these ideological themes in her 'Ulster-Loyalists' and argued that this created a political ideology closed to political change (Todd, 1987, 20–1). Undoubtedly modern day anti-Agreement Unionists would see much to identify with these themes but the interesting change in the ideological writings of modern day Unionism has been a complete dissociation with the past. McGarry and O'Leary have seen an element of 'the politics of denial' in how these Unionists neglect to discuss the Stormont period (1995, 106–11) but the important function that is performed by changing the focus of the discussion of the British connection away from past sacrifices is that it provides Unionism with an abstract political theory that is less anachronistic than its previous justifications for the Union. Paradoxically, and while Aughey denies that this is the case, the modern day case for the Union becomes more contractual than the substance of the loyalties created by the Unionist sense of sacrifice for Britain.

The economic case for the Union

There has also been an increased emphasis on the economic case for the Union. Whyte argued that while Nationalism represented a serious challenge, the economic arguments for the Union were the strongest, if most underplayed, in Unionist discourse. In the 1990s a more vigorous defence of the economics of the Union from Unionist intellectuals, particularly Birnie and Roche and Graham Gudgin, accompanied the rearticulation of Unionism outlined above. Birnie and Roche have been the most prolific writers in this field, with a number of books, articles and pamphlets addressing various areas of the economic debate. These two authors should be considered as important members of a developing Unionist intelligentsia and important contributors to the debates. Birnie described his motivations:

> I think underlying it all was I felt certain cases were going by default, they weren't being made. Therefore I had a strong inclination to make them myself... what I felt strongly, as much as an economist as a person who happened to be a political Unionist, was that a lot of this was just based on bad intellectual arguments... even that as an academic exercise, quite apart from a political one, though politics mattered in it, that needed to be confronted and corrected. That would be one reason, another was I felt that not enough attention had been given to the socio-economic aspect of Sinn Féin ideology. Understandably most people and especially most Unionists have concentrated on the violence and militant Republicanism but that has sort of disguised the fact that underlying that, or behind it, was pretty much it seemed to me through looking at Adams' own writings in the 1980s, basically Marxist – Leninist interpretation of what was wrong with the way that Ireland had developed or not developed, as he termed it, economically and I thought that should be exposed again partly for intellectual reasons, partly for political. (Interview with Esmond Birnie, 4 October 2002)

This was perhaps important because of the thinking and analysis of the Framework Documents, with its extensive consideration of North–South links. Unionism had an argument against the political logic of self-determination and unification but not an economic argument against 'cross-borderism'. Birnie and Roche argue:

> The leaders of the business community in Northern Ireland have attempted to give pragmatic credibility to the all-Ireland institutions

of the Framework Document. The CBI/IOD/Chamber of Commerce argument is that all-Ireland bodies are required for the development of Ireland as a 'single island economy.' The problem here is that no substantive economic case has ever been made in support of the 'single economy' focus which is in fact deeply embedded in an introverted mentality remarkably akin to Irish Republican 'economics'. (Roche and Birnie, 1997)

The economic arguments of Republicans are based on the assumption that partition has caused the problems of the Irish economy and this also 'informs the whole "single island economy" project which has been employed to give credibility to the all-Ireland institutions which are central to the Framework Document' (Roche and Birnie, 1997). Graham Gudgin has argued that the popularity of a 'single island economy' allows the facts to become submerged. In particular, Northern Ireland's status as an integrated part of the UK economy has been overlooked; Gudgin argued that Northern Ireland has closely followed UK trends, whether these have been advantageous or not. Moreover, Northern Ireland is financially dependent on the UK exchequer because of the large inflow of public funds, not all of which are a consequence of the security situation, but a combination of, among other reasons, high unemployment and high birth rates: 'Whatever the causes, the high cost of running Northern Ireland locks the Province into the UK' (Gudgin, 1996). They have also revised the traditional assumptions that cross-border trade has been low and adversely affected by the political cold war between the two entities. Gudgin argues that cross-border trade is actually quite high and greater than Scottish–English trade, and higher, proportionately per head of population, than Northern Irish trade with the rest of Great Britain (Gudgin, 1996). Even in those areas that are cited as important for co-operation, tourism and industrial development, Birnie and Roche argue that friction will develop because there will be conflict of interests between North and South. Moreover, the idea that an all-Ireland tourism authority would be beneficial is suspect because of the 'possibly mistaken application to the tourism industry of ideas of economies of scale' (Birnie and Roche, 1995). Birnie and Roche suggested a Council of the British Isles on the basis that the economy of the Republic of Ireland is connected in so many ways to the UK that it would make better sense to combine Strands Two and Three of the talks process (those that relate to North–South and East–West relations): 'Where there are genuinely common social and economic interests there would be good grounds to manage these at the level of the RoI [*sic*] and UK as a whole' (Birnie and Roche, 1995).

The economic case seems rather pessimistic, resting on the arguments that Northern Ireland needs such a high level of subsidy that unification with the Republic of Ireland is unfeasible because they would be unable to maintain the required level. Gudgin argues that the 'reality is that living standards in Northern Ireland depend greatly on the huge financial subvention from taxpayers in Great Britain and hence on the Province's continued membership of the United Kingdom' (Gudgin, 1995, 75). Northern Ireland, as a poorer region of part of a larger, more prosperous state, receives a level of public services dependent on local need but which are assessed by national standards (Gudgin, 1995, 80).

> Even with a diminished subvention there is no prospect of the Republic of Ireland taking over any of the burden of financing public services in Northern Ireland...At present the UK subvention...is equivalent to the entire revenue from income tax in the Republic. (Gudgin, 1995, 84)

The positive case lies in the economic performance of the Republic of Ireland. According to these authors there was a 25 per cent to 30 per cent disparity in living standards between North and South (Gudgin, 1995, 86; Birnie and Roche, 1997) and the prospects for reducing this gap are minimal when the amount of European funds decreases and the precarious dependence on multinational companies for the Republic's economic growth are taken into consideration (Birnie and Roche, 1997).

Unionist ideology is therefore more complex and more sophisticated than its critics allow. A new cadre of intellectuals have injected new ideas and energy into developing a political ideology that is capable of responding to the twin political challenges of Irish Nationalism and changing British identity. If these ideas have not been able to achieve dominance within the wider Unionist community, this is because of the continued existence of a multi-faceted conflict. It is within this context that the developments of political discourse should be analysed and commentators should have a greater appreciation of the dialectical impact of one ideology upon the other. They should also be concerned to analyse Unionism within the proper terms of reference. This study has shown that the formula within Article 4c of the DSD is inadequate to address the 'totality of relations' because there is an insufficient British dimension for both Unionists and Nationalists. The complex web of interaction between Unionists and Nationalists (North and South),

Britain (identity and culture) and the British government is key to understanding political developments within Northern Ireland, and a greater sensitivity to Unionist interpretations of the nature of those relationships will illuminate many of the problems that 'progress' seems to discover. However, the interest within Unionism for these discussions about identity has diminished since 1998. Since the Agreement, almost all of Unionist energies have been channelled into discussing (and fighting over) the Belfast Agreement. In saying this, the diminishing intensity of the discussion has been complemented by a widespread absorption of the ideas, which are now commonplace and accepted.

The critiques

This group of intellectuals and this articulation of Unionism have been unimaginatively termed 'new Unionism'. It has sold itself as 'Pro-active, inclusive, open, pluralist, dynamic, progressive, outward-looking, articulate, intelligent, coherent, professional, confident: New Unionism.'[4] The implication here is that 'old Unionism' was reactive, exclusive, closed, regressive, introverted, inarticulate, incoherent, amateur and had self-esteem problems and while this may be true, closer inspection by its critics (and supporters!) have not identified much clear daylight between 'old' and 'new' Unionism. David McNarry remarked: 'It's old Unionism, that's a nonsense, it's traditional Unionism. Trimble is a hardline Ulster Unionist leader' (Interview with David McNarry, 27 September 2002). Duncan Shipley-Dalton argued:

> There hasn't been a project as such, alright it's been described as New Unionism and people like me get pigeon holed as New Unionists [but] I'm not sure how new it is really, it's not a particularly new idea. The newness of it I suppose was that the people who espoused those ideas became more important and more powerful within party groupings and were able to actually express them more fully because previously it was the traditionalists who ran the party. (Interview with Duncan Shipley-Dalton, 27 September 2002)

Aughey's thesis in particular has attracted much criticism, especially his link between Unionists and Britain (Coulter, 1994; Cochrane, 1997, 75–82), although some critics have praised it as intellectual progress because, they argue, it is the development of a type of civic nationalism (McGarry and O'Leary, 1995, 128; Schultz, 1997). There have been two main criticisms. In the first, 'New Unionism' is critiqued from an empirical perspective. It is found deficient because it does not match the evidence as to how Unionists conceive and express their identity. The second critique is normative. Here, 'new Unionism' is deficient because it does not provide the theoretical tools that it needs to justify its end goal of the maintenance of the Union, while simultaneously dealing with the arguments and normative demands of Nationalists.

Norman Porter finds Aughey's argument deficient because it finds no place for substantive identities, making his citizenship purely legal or procedural and therefore creating problems for the link between the state and the citizen because the state cannot survive solely on such an identification (Porter, 1996, 156–64). Cochrane has gone further and argued:

> In reality, many unionists exhibit a concern with identity/culture rather than merely an abstract desire for citizenship and liberal-democratic principles...unionism is not based solely upon rationalism, or on political, social and economic self-interest. At its most funda-mental, it is based on a sense of belonging...there is a complex web of historical, emotional and psychological bonds (though these are largely unreciprocated) which underpin the dynamics of unionist political behaviour (Cochrane, 1997, 78).

This is undoubtedly a drawback if we attempt to use Aughey's thesis as a tool to explain the dynamics of Unionism. However, if we consider that the pillars on which Britishness was built in the eighteenth and nineteenth centuries are diminishing in significance for the majority of the rest of the citizens of the UK (Colley, 1992, 395), then Ulster Unionism has to adjust to these changing circumstances. Ulster Unionists may have substantive identities to tie themselves to the UK but this does not necessarily equate with a shared national consciousness across the UK. In a sense Unionists were addressing two distinct audiences as they began to reconsider the constitutional bonds between the four constituents of the UK: Irish Nationalists and the people of the UK.

Ruane and Todd see the reconstruction of Unionist ideology reaching the same conclusion as traditional Unionism but they stress its plurality and are less sceptical of the motivations of these Unionists than other critics (Ruane and Todd, 1996, 105). The problem is not Unionism *per se* but the 'overlapping and mutually reinforcing nature of the dimensions of the conflict [which] makes difficult ideological reconstruction on less conflictual lines' (Ruane and Todd, 1996, 107). The conflict conditions the nature of ideological reconstruction and therefore the participants perceive 'open-ended self-critical ideological exploration' as very dangerous because it could endanger important positions and, further-more, limits the boundaries within which they work: a British and cultural Protestant framework (Ruane and Todd, 1996, 108). Ruane and Todd provide an important context to the discussion of Unionist ideology because, unlike the other critics that will be discussed here, they situate Unionism within the political context that shapes its development. Others, in their discussions of Unionism's 'blindness' to Nationalism, neglect the importance and the impact on Unionism of Nationalists' 'blindness' to British Ireland. The best example of one this tendency was O'Dowd, who argued for the necessity of the development of a new Unionist discourse by public intellectuals but was unimpressed when he returned to the subject 8 years later:

> In many ways, the rhetoric of the 'new unionism' sought to put old wine in new bottles. Its apparent embracing of the universalistic politics of equal citizenship is little more than an attempt to dress up traditional loyalist slogans of 'No Surrender' and 'Not an Inch' in a new, more modern and more marketable rhetoric. This rhetoric asserts the inviolability of British citizenship and British sovereignty in Northern Ireland. No reciprocal recognition is to be given to Irish citizens in Northern Ireland or to nationalists. Irish nationalism is presented as politically and morally bankrupt and in the case of Republicanism fundamentally violent and undemocratic. (O'Dowd, 1998a, 118–19)

O'Dowd argues that 'new Unionism' exudes a sense of superiority but this is misplaced because this Unionism neglects the important role that a strong variant of British nationalism, including ethno-national and class hierarchies, plays in their ideology. Thus British nationalism is an impediment to a solution because it involves inviolability of sover-eignty but somewhat confusingly O'Dowd concedes that the relation-ship between British nationalism and Ulster Unionism is complex and ambiguous, providing simultaneously not only advantages in structural power but also a sense of insecurity (O'Dowd, 1998a, b). Colin Coulter argues that the discourse Unionists have developed around the positive case for the Union and the negative case for unification with the South of Ireland has been challenged by the social and political changes in the south during the 1990s. This, he contends, shows that Unionist claims that their aversion to the twenty-six counties is based on 'sober and reasonable reflection' is 'distinctly threadbare'. He argues: 'Those who seek to promote the Unionist cause frequently employ a discourse that emphasises the rational and universal in order to advance interests that are thoroughly unreasonable and particular' (Coulter, 2000, 223). The admission among Unionist intellectuals that such changes would be ultimately insufficient to alter Unionist opinion on a united Ireland demonstrates clearly, for Coulter, that this literature is about identifying the Unionist 'other' and that these Unionist intellectuals are really the bearers of a version of British nationalism (Todd, 1989; Coulter, 2000, 221).

The critique here is fairly straightforward: New Unionism is no different to Old Loyalism and therefore the development of a civic nationalism has been unsuccessful. Undoubtedly Aughey's thesis in *Under Siege* is overstated and should be seen as a distinct product of the intellectual environment in Northern Ireland in the 1980s, which will be discussed in the next chapter. However, those who see this as the development of a civic form of nationalism do not do full justice to the complexity of the dynamics at work, as the distinction between 'civic' and 'ethnic' nationalisms is not clear-cut (Brown, 1999). In saying this, it was argued in the Introduction that British identity was different to Irish identity in terms of the relationship with the state and the co-existence with territorial and ethnic identities. The articulation of 'New Unionism' has been a combination of a number of factors. First, there was undoubtedly an attempt to move Unionism away from a purely ethnic mode but this was not necessarily a major departure, as Graham Walker has shown that this was also attempted in the 1960s and before (Walker, 2004b). Secondly, it also represented an attempt to provide a reconciliation between the experience of British identity in Northern Ireland and the manner in which it was analysed. In this sense it was less important whether it was civic or not and more important that it started a debate about Unionist identity and how it related to Britain. Norman Porter is one of the few who has made this link between Unionist arguments about citizenship and Unionist national identity. Porter argues that 'liberal Unionists' like Aughey neglect the role of substantive cultural identities in citizenship (Porter, 1996, 156–64) but it is perhaps from the over analysis of these cultural identities that 'liberal Unionists' are trying to distance themselves. The Unionist intelligentsia under investigation are responding to a perceived change in the nature of the substantive identities that bind the UK together.

Normative political theorists have a similar critique of 'new Unionism'. Here, the critique centres on the implications of these arguments for a resolution of the conflict. Shane O'Neill has argued that a solution to the Northern Ireland question is to be found in discourse ethics, which provide a normative set of procedural rules for mediating the conflict (O'Neill, 2000). The key to this approach is that each side should be able to bring anything for discussion and that these should be engaged with and supported by a rational and open argument. The difficulty with this approach, according to O'Neill, is Unionism. The first problem is Unionism's position of strength. 'The Irish border is itself a structure of inequality in the dispute about the constitutional status of Northern Ireland' (O'Neill, 1994, 374). Therefore, even the compromise of equal British citizenship which is offered by 'liberal Unionists' is illegitimate. This hides a deeper problem, which, for O'Neill, may well be key. The reason why even 'liberal Unionists' are unable to engage with Nationalism in a constructive and, by O'Neill's implication, rational fashion is because of 'their blindness to Nationalist reiterative rights', where reiterative rights are those that relate to Irish Nationalists' morality, creativity and particularism. In order for this process to get underway, Unionists have to start a process of critical reinterpretation and, in particular, shed the 'surviving vestiges of imperialistic attitudes' and overcome their sense of superiority over Irish Nationalists (O'Neill, 1994, 372–5). In a further article, O'Neill elaborates on his normative procedures for a solution and, expanding on John Rawls' 'overlapping consensus', suggests that the inclusion of political self-expression of national identity should be a 'primary good'. Moreover, to facilitate the overlapping consensus, affirmations of national identity should be expressed in a non-exclusivist manner (O'Neill, 1996).

O'Neill has attracted a greater response than O'Dowd, perhaps because his is a more sophisticated projection of the consequences of a similar analysis of Unionist ideology. Nevertheless, there is still a relatively unsophisticated understanding of Unionism at the heart of both of these critiques and neither fully engages with their subject matter. They are over-reliant on stereotypes of Unionism, which have been consistently challenged by modern scholarship. As Richard English argues:

> It is unfortunate to witness the persistence, within representations of unionism, of the image of triumphalist supremacism: for scholars have powerfully demonstrated that feelings of vulnerability and even inferiority play a larger role in modern unionist thinking than do any senses of superiority or supremacism. (English, 1996, 227–8)

Moreover, both O'Neill and O'Dowd make the further error of reducing Unionism to one aspect of a multifaceted ideology and identity. Perhaps the most insightful analyst of Unionism, Jennifer Todd, did identify such a strand within Unionists' Britishness, defined against the 'Others', which are the Irish (Todd, 1989, 13) but this was one part of a more complicated relationship with British identity and British institutions (Todd, 1989). Moreover, Richard English makes the observation of O'Neill's work that:

> It is a matter of assumption rather than demonstration...that unionist intransigence in opposing constitutional change is more central to the conflict than is Irish nationalist intransigence in demanding that such change be made, and made in a nationalist direction. (English, 1996, 229–30)

Aughey's counterargument is that the assumption behind O'Neill's work is that Unionists have no rational arguments and this disguises the lack of effort that Nationalists have expended in trying to persuade Unionists of the merits of a United Ireland (Aughey, 1999, 130). Moreover, O'Neill is wrong on his fundamental premise that power is a contingent aspect of the political and ignores the public support for the Union (Aughey, 1999, 130). Therefore, by Aughey's reckoning, O'Dowd and O'Neill both fall into the trap that has been set by nationalism's success in setting the agenda for the two governments and, by extension, the peace process. By inverting Nationalist arguments and by paying attention to Unionist arguments we can see that nationalism is at least equally at fault for a 'zero-sum' ideological battle and that this creates defensive mentalities among Unionists. Richard English agrees and argues that to portray Unionism and Nationalism as symmetrical ignores some very basic facts about Northern Ireland – in particular, the majority in favour of the Union, the military, political and economic support needed to sustain Northern Ireland which can only be provided by the British state and the Republic's position on unification (English, 1995, 138).

If O'Neill's and O'Dowd's arguments are blighted by a superficial understanding of Unionism, then it is perhaps appropriate that the sharpest critic of 'new' or 'liberal' Unionism is one who comes from the Unionist community (Porter, 1996).[5] Norman Porter has attracted more attention than any other Unionist or Nationalist theorist; attention that has usually been positive from outside the Unionist community.[6] First, like Whyte, O'Dowd and O'Neill, Porter sees the minority Nationalist community as the biggest challenge to what he terms 'liberal Unionism' but this is because he argues that the idea of equal citizenship does not enable Unionists to argue effectively against Nationalists' demand for parity of esteem (Porter, 1996, 156). These Unionists fail to show how their brand of Unionism is sufficiently grounded in negative liberty to demonstrate that Unionism is a necessary condition of a liberal society in Northern Ireland, therefore removing a central pillar of the case that Unionism is based on more progressive and modern political ideas than nationalism (Porter, 1996, 146–55). Secondly, Porter argues that 'liberal Unionists' have a political philosophy that is unable or unwilling to recognise the legitimacy of other non-Unionist interpretations, with particular reference to their thesis on sovereignty, which is based on a legal-positivist reading of the position and allows no space for alternative sovereignty claims (Porter, 1996, 143–6). Porter's conclusion then is similar to those critics above:

> Liberal Unionism is as closed to political movement in Northern Ireland, on terms other than its own, as is cultural unionism...It is only when unionism is released from its cultural and liberal straight-jackets that proper dialogue with non-unionists will be possible. It is only then that concessions to certain nationalist arguments will be seen as something other than selling out the Union and capitulating to nationalist discourse. (Porter, 1996, 167–8)

Porter's critique is a serious one because, unlike O'Dowd or O'Neill, he engages with the substantive arguments instead of attributing to those who make the arguments a desire to dominate. Nevertheless, the theme is the same throughout: Nationalism is the problem. Unionist ideology, for these authors, is too closed and exclusive for Unionism to remain a tenable political ideology because of the existence of a large, disgruntled minority, which Unionism cannot accommodate.

Nearly all of these critiques were written prior to the Belfast Agreement of Good Friday 1998 when the outcome of the talks process was uncertain. However, nearly all cast doubt on whether this 'new' thinking provided Unionism with the intellectual tools to conclude a deal with Nationalists as equal partners in Northern Ireland. We know now that an agreement occurred on this basis in 1998 and that the objections to this deal have not included the principle of power-sharing (see Chapter 5). So, how did this change come about? The party political effects are discussed in the next section and it will be shown that, while the intellectual reasoning of these critiques may be sound, the effects of the ideas was quite different to what was expected by these authors.

Party political effects

This intellectual discourse has informed debates within Unionism, and Unionists have realised that they have a part to play in altering the perceptions of Unionism. They have been centred exclusively within the UUP but have received very little attention in any studies of contemporary Unionism. They have embarked on a mission to radically alter the structure and organisation of the party in order for it to articulate the Unionist case more effectively and thus improve the domestic and international image of Unionism. The process has been haphazard at best but there are two discernible stages and several discernible arenas in which it has taken place. The first stage occurred in the 1980s when some Unionists 'looked south' and worked to promote the Unionist case in southern Ireland. This was a brave step, considering the hostility to southern Ireland in some Unionist circles and the treatment reserved for Unionists who ventured in that direction. This campaign was neither organised nor sanctioned by the party hierarchy. Initially it consisted of individuals with personal connections attending conferences, meetings or writing newspaper articles. Chris McGimpsey, one of those involved in this process, noted, 'A lot of these links tended to start off through social contact' (Interview with Chris McGimpsey, 6 June 2002). Others who were also involved included some Fermanagh Unionists such as Ken Maginnis and Raymond Ferguson, whose contacts were through rugby or university. David McKittrick called McGimpsey 'a sort of unofficial ambassador from Unionism to the Irish Republic', working in tandem with Ken Maginnis to give Unionism a human face in the south and, moreover, achieving some success (*Independent*, 31 March 1994). McGimpsey returned to Ireland from studying abroad in 1979 and went to a meeting of The Irish Association for Cultural, Economic and Social Relations in Bangor and met influential people whom he claimed had not encountered a Unionist argument before (Interview with Chris McGimpsey, 6 June 2002). This was an important motivating factor for McGimpsey, who describes a trip to Cork:

> I have to say it was a one man band; a one man operation... I remember going down to Cork one time...to do a TV show and one bloke put his hand up and said 'you're the first Unionist I've ever clapped eyes on' and I thought to myself that really that just summed up the entire malaise of Unionism. (Interview with Chris McGimpsey, 6 June 2002)

His contacts grew and he began to get invited to party conferences. In 1984 he had written a submission to the New Ireland Forum and then, with his brother Michael McGimpsey, had travelled to Dublin to give evidence. He had spoken in favour of a formal submission at the UUP conference in 1983 but encountered, in his words, 'a lynch mob'. Perhaps surprisingly the *Irish Press*, de Valera's old paper, frequently asked him to write for them. Raymond Ferguson described similar motivations: a mixture of frustration with the Unionist leadership, personal contacts and personal initiative.

> Well a lot of it was my own personal initiative. I didn't get any sanction from Unionist headquarters; at the same time I didn't get any prohibition from it and indeed some people said they were interested to see what the mood was. I've always taken the view that the influence of the Republic of Ireland on politics within Northern Ireland is one that the Unionists really can't ignore . . . and I always had the view that we should be a lot more proactive in influencing the thinking of politicians and people in the south and at least getting them to understand our position. Now during the Jim Molyneaux years there was very little done in that respect and indeed even before Jim Molyneaux there was an attitude in Unionism that they should mind their own business and we should mind ours but that's unrealistic and it proved to be unrealistic throughout the Troubles starting with the civil rights campaign . . . I did a lot more during the Molyneaux era because I thought Molyneaux was very lacking to the detriment of Unionism generally in selling the Unionist case every-where and particularly down the south . . . and I think in many ways it gained a lot of sympathy down south and I think that that's still apparent in for instance the *Irish Independent* and *Sunday Independent* thinking and they're quite sympathetic to the Unionist case. (Interview with Raymond Ferguson, 9 October 2002.)

Chris McGimpsey's efforts became more publicly visible in 1990 when he took advantage of his Irish citizenship rights to challenge the AIA in the Irish Supreme Court. Initially his lawyers felt that there was not a case but after the Crotty decision on the Single European Act, they reassessed and it was at that stage, about 18 months after McGimpsey had started, that Ken Maginnis got involved. There were severe financial problems before Maginnis raised enough money to fund the case, as the Unionist Party turned down three requests for funds, while Maginnis raised about £80,000 in 6 months (Interview with Chris McGimpsey,

6 June 2002). McGimpsey thinks that the case had a positive influence on the UUP by setting an example:

> I think there was an element of people starting to say 'a bit of lateral thinking sometimes works,' we were able to go down without compromising our Unionist principles or our Britishness and there was no comeback to that. And I think in a way it gave official Unionism the confidence to be a bit more adventurous. (Interview with Chris McGimpsey, 6 June 2002)

However, it was 2 years later that Molyneaux sanctioned McGimpsey to go to the Progressive Democrats' Conference as an official representative of the party, a move McGimpsey argues should have happened 20 years earlier (Interview with Chris McGimpsey, 6 June 2002). Summing up his efforts in the south throughout the 1980s and 1990s, McGimpsey said:

> For years Unionism was able to avoid the Irish Republic...it was clear that Thatcher and the British government were not prepared to do that...so it was self-evident to me that more and more of the battle for Ulster would be won and fought and lost in London and Dublin. I was even starting to think in those terms prior to the Anglo-Irish Agreement...Seemed to me that the 80s would be the decade where everything would be won and lost in the south. So I think where it was important, I don't want to blow my own trumpet a bit, is that twigging that so early I got in first. (Interview with Chris McGimpsey, 6 June 2002)

McGimpsey, Ferguson and Maginnis seem far sighted and important when one realises that it was the mid-1990s before which other senior party members began to talk in a similar language. For example, in 1995, John Taylor was writing with a sense of urgency that there was an international momentum to bring the island of Ireland closer together and that Unionists should be taking more advantage of the opportunities to put their case and build alliances abroad and have less reliance on Conservative governments. Significantly, however, he did not mention the Republic of Ireland as a place where Unionists should concentrate their efforts (Taylor, 1995).

There were other groups lobbying for modernisation within the party, with particular regard to organisation and information. The structure of the UUP is complex and archaic and is still the same structure that was developed to respond to the needs of the Home Rule crises at the beginning of the twentieth century. Authority and power does not flow in any one direction, as there is no one site of policy and decision-making. Technically the Ulster Unionist *Party* only exists in the elected chambers. The body that actually comprises the 'party' is the UUC, which is composed of nearly 900 delegates from constituency associations and affiliated bodies. The affiliated bodies are the Young Unionists, the Women's Unionists, Queen's University of Belfast (QUB) association, the Orange Order and the Women's Orange Order. The Apprentice Boys and the Black Preceptory were also members until restructuring under Brian Faulkner in the 1970s (Harbinson, 1973; UUP, 1989). Initially, this structure was designed to enable Unionists to coordinate a united campaign against Home Rule and was founded after overtures from the Grand Orange Lodge of Ireland. Executive and policy decisions were made by the Cabinet during the Stormont era, with pressure and ideas from the grass roots through, for example, the conference. The body that is now responsible for policy is technically the Executive but it usually rubber-stamps decisions of the leadership. The Executive is selected from the Council; a mathematical quota system determines the numbers from each of the constituency associations and the affiliated bodies that sit on the Executive. The quota is based on the perceived voting strength of Unionists in constituencies and not the strength of the party in that area. Therefore, West Belfast has a smaller representation than East Belfast (Interview with Martin Smyth, 21 August 2002). In 1990 the Ulster Unionist Conference passed a motion, proposed by Jeffrey Donaldson and seconded by Banbridge councillor Drew Nelson, to review the rules and constitution of the UUC (Hume, 1996, 40–1) and this started a debate within the party over the nature and extent of such a reform. There were several themes in the debate but those pushing most for change were concerned to create a party that could be legitimately termed 'modern' and this involved a review of the affiliated bodies, a review of the constitution and a more professional approach to politics from the leadership.

The group that was pressing most for this sort of change was the Young Unionists who began to argue for modernisation in the mid-1990s. It used the pages of its magazine, *The Ulster Review*, to publish articles arguing for changes by its members and other prominent party officials. The journal was, surprisingly, the only publication produced by party members and was clearly targeted at the senior party (Hume, 1996, 25). Their arguments ranged from simple organisational change to a more complex change in attitudes. They addressed the Orange link, the position and treatment of Roman Catholics within the party and Unionism more generally and adopted wholesale the political philosophy of the 'New Unionists'. In particular, there was a focus on the nature of the media image of Unionists and how they could influence that image. In the 1990s these debates focused on how to present the Unionist case through the media. Unionists have made a distinction between media management, which Burnside defined as 'spin' (Interview with David Burnside, 13 September 2002) and media presentation (Harris, 1995). Prior to Trimble's election Martin Smyth was Director of Information but there are two different interpretations of the role of Public Relations officers. The Young Unionists wanted a professional media-orientated approach and were encouraged by the creation of a Public Relations Officer. However, they appeared to have little faith in the ability of the party to use that person correctly. Richard Holmes felt it important to stress the necessity that the successful applicant should have a successful Public Relations background and, moreover, that the party should act on their advice. Ideally he felt that the party should employ a Public Relations firm, a point with which David McDowell agreed (McDowell, 1995/6). The greater media awareness would lead to substantial change in the type of image that Unionism would portray. They were frustrated with the manner that Unionism had previously been articulated:

> There must be no displays of bigotry or ignorance, nor references to God; religious references are nonsensical in a party of the union with a secular, pluralist state and are blasphemous and offensive. It is not for us to say how the Almighty votes ... We must also avoid constant negativity about the Irish Republic. Dublin has made an effort to show that it is aware of how its failings have caused trouble between us ... Ostracism of a land which nationalists regard as their spiritual home does not help to win them over. (McDowell, 1995/6)

Therefore, a greater attention to media presentation would enable the 'New Unionist' project to become the dominant image of Unionism. The target audience seems to be wider British, Irish and international opinion. On the other hand, there are members that are sceptical of the utility of such advisers. Martin Smyth's concern, when he held the position of Director of Information, was to disseminate information (Interview with Martin Smyth, 21 August 2002) rather than the cultivation of a media image. Smyth feels the traditional methods of political canvassing are more effective than extensive use of the media because newspapers and television do not guarantee access to every elector:

> I have a suspicion that some in our leadership at the moment who think that they can win elections through the media...it's what people know on the ground and it's getting to the people on the ground that matters...The average person reads the part of the paper that they're interested in and it's usually the back page...So, it's getting to the people and that's where I believe quite frankly Sinn Féin have won the battle over the SDLP and I think at times the DUP have won the battle over us. (Interview with Martin Smyth, 21 August 2002)

Nevertheless, under Trimble's leadership there has been a dramatic increase in the use of Public Relations advisers and consultants, outside advisers and professionals on political issues. Burnside said:

> Jim Molyneaux, very fine man, very fine leader of the Unionist Party but Jim was not really a media communicator. Jim was an old fashioned, excellent MP and excellent leader of the party. Trimble brought a sort of new more professional approach to media nationally and internationally, which I think helped and you've got to do that when you're getting all the propaganda churned out by Republicanism. So that was one of Trimble's pluses. (Interview with David Burnside, 13 September 2002)

David Burnside has played an important part in this process. A Public Relations expert by profession, he was the brains behind the now defunct Unionist Information Office (UIO) in Great Britain. The UIO and its publication, *The Unionist*, were 'established to promote the cause of the Union; to argue the benefits, cultural, social, political and economic, of maintaining and strengthening the unity of the Kingdom' (Burnside and Watson, 1996). The glossy magazine they produced contained articles from people beyond the immediate Ulster Unionist family and included Simon Heffner, Mo Mowlam, Harry Barnes, Bruce Anderson, John Lloyd, Gary Kent and Viscount Cranbourne, writing about a variety of topics related to the peace process, the Union and Ulster Unionism. *The Unionist* also attempted to portray the 'caring' side of Unionism and the photographs and illustrations adorning the magazine occasionally verged on the ridiculous – clouds shaped as doves; pictures of kittens; puppies and kittens kissing in a park; families walking along a beach, among others. Burnside also contributed to the debates within the party, as he termed it 'professionalising'. He emphasised the importance of a positive image for Unionism:

Unionists must not retreat into the woods. We must produce a customer friendly image for Unionism – uncompromising but fair – and offering constitutional democratic leadership in Northern Ireland, increasing and strengthening the links that we have with friends of the Union in Great Britain. (Burnside, 1995)

In 1996, he was positive about the future:

Since David Trimble was elected as leader, the public image of unionism has improved. We are now beginning to be seen as exhibiting a new unionism committed to our fundamental principles but much more prepared to propagate our cause and our policies to a wide range of audiences... The mood has changed in Northern Ireland. Unionism is regaining its confidence as a political force not just relying on saying no. (Burnside, 1996)

He recommended several important changes. The party needed to widen its network of friends in Great Britain in influential media positions and it should open new administrative offices in London and Washington. The London office, connected to the UIO, was short-lived and concerned with media relations but the Washington office has been more successful, although it is limited in scope because the staff is only part-time and the office itself is the only one of its kind in the United States (Interview with Martin Smyth, 21 August 2002). The two Unionist parties made a co-ordinated effort in the 1980s to travel to America and meet politicians and policy formers and put the Unionist case, usually once every quarter (Interview with Martin Smyth, 21 August 2002) but there were two 'campaigns', one in 1982 by McCusker, Taylor and Robinson and one in 1994 when the number of visits and deputations increased (Donaldson, 1995, 21–2). Since that time the Unionist parties have made a more determined and sustained effort in America to the extent that Trimble could claim to have met the then President, Bill Clinton, more times than any world leader. The purpose has also widened from a concern merely to influence policy to an effort to engage pro-Union Americans in an effort to promote the Unionist case to the wider American population. The most prominent American involved is an ex-Londonderry man, Tony Cully-Foster, who helped finance the Washington bureau (Wilson, 2000).

The majority of those Unionists who were advocating substantial change to the party structure were also those who were trying to create a pluralist and tolerant party and one which Roman Catholics would find attractive and welcoming but they had to persuade the rest of their colleagues of the necessity of, at times, emotional changes and also, at times, of the necessity of the project in general. There is a pessimistic streak running through much of this debate. The growth in the electoral and demographic strength of the Nationalist bloc has created a sense of impending doom within Unionism and this debate was a belated recognition that Unionism's appeal should lie beyond its traditional constituency. John Taylor may have argued that 'Unionism should be attractive to Roman Catholic and Protestant alike because, if Unionism were to fail, the whole of our community would suffer' (Taylor, 1995) but most of the debate was premised on the assumption that there were a large number of Catholic voters who identified with the British state, who had benefited from the Union and who would be materially disadvantaged by unification. The party should therefore make a determined effort to attract these people to vote UUP and, moreover, join the party. These Unionists felt there were two main elements to achieve this goal. One was the ideology of the party; the necessity to divorce Unionism and Protestantism, about which Foster, Aughey and others were particularly concerned. The other aspect was the structure and ethos of the party. Therefore the link with the Orange Order came under increasing pressure and the opportunities for Catholics within the party were scrutinised. Alan McFarland, UUP MLA for North Down, paraphrases the debate as he saw it:

> Our slogan for the year ['our duty to the greater number'] was reflected in the leader's address to the AGM. The speech set out the need for the Party to make itself more welcoming and user-friendly towards unionists who are Roman Catholics by religion. The question touches on one of the key issues which the party will have to address in the coming year. Is unionism only synonymous with Protestantism? Should the Loyal Orange Institution retain its special place in the Party?
>
> Some suggest that the maintenance of the Union should not be directly connected with religious and cultural affiliations. Long term demographic trends purport to show that Roman Catholics may eventually outnumber Protestants in Northern Ireland. Such a statistic

ignores the possibility that a substantial number of these will be pro-Union. This argument states that the exclusion of this potential support, which could be created if the Party was pluralist, may risk the future of the Union. Others, however, argue that tinkering with tradition for some unquantifiable gain would risk splitting the Party. Either way, these issues need to be fully debated, and quickly, so the Party's ethos is clear. (McFarland, 1995/6)

There were attempts to end the link just after Trimble became leader. Trimble made it clear that he wanted to end the institutional link and a motion on the issue was debated but defeated at the party conference in 1995 (Cochrane, 1997, 343–4). Drew Nelson argued at that conference that the UUP was a child of the Order but had grown up and needed to sever the link to create a 'modern political party' (Cochrane, 1997, 344). Likewise, the journalist and academic, Dennis Kennedy argued that Unionism had to meet the challenge of the 'pan-Nationalist front' and help the British government resist the pressure from this quarter:

> To start with the UUP must get rid of its own Article 3 – that section of the Rules of the Ulster Unionist Council which gives the Orange Order representation on the Council and establishes the formal link between the Order and the Party. The Order is a Protestant organisation, anti-Catholic, as it has every right to be. But the Unionist Party is a political organisation seeking to preserve the Union. By retaining the Orange link, it is telling Catholics in Northern Ireland that the Union is not for them. (*Belfast Telegraph*, 13 October 1994)

David McDowell argued that the Orange link should be likened to Labour's link with the Trade Unions:

> It must be understood that the Orange is to unionism what the unions were to Labour – an essential organic connection years ago, but a liability today, its significance changed in a modern society . . . The link with the Order must go for unionism's self-perception as a genuinely pluralist, modern party to be justified. Catholics may not rush to join us but they may be less inclined to view us with contempt. (McDowell, 1995/6)

There were many who were wary of such a fundamental change to the party; it was, after all, the Grand Orange Lodge of Ireland that was responsible for the creation of the UUC but part of the reluctance to change may be because the links with the Order are much deeper than an affiliation to the UUC. The delegates that the Order sent to the UUC have to be UUP branch members (Interview with Robert Saulters, 21 August 2002) but there are more than those 120 delegates that are members. Moreover, the informal links between the two organisations are quite extensive. For example, many UUP associations hold their meetings in Orange halls, for which there is frequently no charge (Interview with Martin Smyth, 21 August 2002; Interview with Robert Saulters, 21 August 2002; Hume, 1996, 31–2). The opponents of ending the link also feel that the supposed benefits (many new Catholic members) would fail to materialise and the only effect would be to alienate a large number of UUP supporters, which should be the party's first priority in any case (Interview with Martin Smyth, 21 August 2002).

The link with the Orange Order became the battlefield for reform of the UUC and many members felt it was the most important issue facing the party and its potential support but the debate that this masked was the general relationship between the affiliated bodies, the UUC and the party leadership. During the review of the party organisation, Jeffrey Donaldson assessed the role of the individual member. What inhibited a closer link between the party and the member was the federal structure of the party. In order to improve communication and efficiency he argued that the party should create a centralised register of party members and the only route to membership should be through the local branch but, in deference to the sensitivities of the constituency associations, maintained that they would maintain a degree of autonomy in, for example, candidate selection. The end of the link with the Orange Order would be a consequence of these reforms but he pleaded for the debate to move beyond this contentious issue (Donaldson, 1996). Donaldson's pleas were to no avail and the debate never even really reached a conclusion on the Orange link. Indeed, when the link was ended, it was the Orange Order that took the initiative (*Irish Times*, 14 March 2005) and the failure of Trimble to effectively reform the party structures was widely seen as his biggest failure in the immediate aftermath of his resignation.[7] The UUP remains a highly decentralised body and is easily described, by more than one member, as seventeen or eighteen separate political parties (Hume, 1996, 40; Interview with Chris McGimpsey, 6 June 2002). The majority of the membership value this autonomy and seem unperturbed by the political anomalies that it can create; for example, the discrepancy between local council areas where UUP councillors will co-operate with a SF Chairman or Mayor in one area but refuse to even take the Deputy Lord Mayor position in another, most notably Belfast. Roy Garland, who spoke at the Forum for Peace and Reconciliation and shared platforms with Gerry Adams, Martin McGuinness and others, remarked: 'In a sense I shouldn't have been able to get away with things I've done when it wasn't party policy' but then observed that he probably would be uncomfortable with tighter control by the leadership (Interview with Roy Garland, 18 November 2002).

Conclusion

There have been two main effects of these ideas. First, there have been significant developments in promoting Unionism as a coherent and intelligible political idea. The ideological reformers have, in many respects, led the way and most of those discussed in this section have been heavily influenced by the writings of the former. Indeed, the media project would not be possible without the groundwork that Aughey, Foster and others prepared. The success of each is difficult to ascertain. It is becoming clear that the ideological reformers have achieved dominance within the UUP at least and there is evidence that the DUP and the PUP were also adopting some of these characteristics (Farrington, 2001). They are also influencing academic studies of Unionism. However, the real test for many of these authors is not their popularity within their own ideological bloc but their influence on wider perceptions of Unionism. This is definitely changing but an answer to that question is beyond the scope of this book (although see Parkinson, 1998). The importance for Unionists is that they thought that a campaign was necessary and coherently thought about how to conduct it. The DUP has not the same tradition of debate within its party and there is less awareness of a need to address a wider audience than its own constituency within Northern Ireland. However, the primary source material does not currently exist to enable us to reconstruct debates within the DUP (if there were any) after the fact. Nevertheless, the DUP would not usually express derogatory opinions on such debates except where the Republic of Ireland was concerned. In the 1990s it was involved in developing a Unionist presence in the United States (*New Protestant Telegraph*, May 1994; February 1995), although not to the same extent as the UUP and it was only really those Unionists such as McGimpsey, Maginnis and Ferguson to whom the DUP objected. For example, the *New Protestant Telegraph* started a new section in September 1993 entitled 'City Hall News', which was basically an opportunity to tell stories of how UUP councillors had links, contacts and conversations with Nationalists. When the then UUP councillor Sandy Blair became chair of the Community Services Committee and announced that he, not unreasonably, planned to visit community centres, some of which would be in West Belfast, the paper stated: 'Mr Blair is yet another convert to the liberal Unionist group in the City Hall, no doubt influenced by the gurus of that cult, Chris McGimpsey and Ken Maginnis' (*New Protestant Telegraph*, September 1993). Thus the extent to which these debates are party political debates is minimal. Indeed, the extent to which national identity is a live political issue is questionable. Notions of a secular ideology and a pluralist national identity are not contested ideas within Unionism. These coexist with more exclusivist and ethnic notions of ideology and national identity, frequently within individuals, and makes analysing the political responses of Unionists on this basis complicated.

The second effect is perhaps more important and was not even explicitly intended by these reformers and lies less in the wider international perceptions of Unionism and more within the Unionist community in Northern Ireland. This relates to the willingness to engage with Nationalists. Liam O'Dowd had argued:

> In the case of unionism...intellectuals have failed to forge an enduring link between a popular political culture and any major political ideology such as liberal democracy, socialism or nationalism... popular loyalism is not easily transmutable into a mere collection of abstract ideas because it has proved too successful as a vehicle of popular *power*. (O'Dowd, 1991, 165, italics in original)

The intellectuals discussed did manage to attach abstract ideas to Unionism but, as we have seen, this did not change the substance of Unionism. Therefore, instead of looking towards ideational change as an explanation of a willingness to negotiate with Nationalists, we should look at the effects on Unionism. We saw the vigour with which elements of the UUP picked up on these ideas and internalised them into political debates and party strategy and so we might look to the examples from community relations work to provide a framework for analysing these developments. The long-term goal of community relations work is to promote engagement between opposing communities but this is combined with recognition that some communities are not ready for this type of engagement. Some of the key elements of single identity work are confidence and capacity building (Community Relations Council, n.d.). These ideational developments can be seen as performing these types of functions within Unionism and, indeed, Trimble's rationale for participating in the 1996–8 talks was that Unionism needed to transcend its siege mentality (see Chapter 4). The ideological debate within Unionism functioned like single-identity work, giving Unionists the confidence to engage with Nationalists rather than intellectually convincing them to engage. Thus, the project of building a rational Unionist argument was the first stage in a project which culminated in Unionism concluding the Good Friday Agreement. However, the two political parties related to this debate differently and the DUP developed an analysis at a later stage that provides an alternative avenue to political engagement, which will be discussed in Chapter 5.

2
The Challenge of the Anglo-Irish Agreement and the Unionist Response

If new political ideas were important in providing an impetus for political change within Unionism in the 1990s, how did these changes interact with political developments at an inter-governmental level? The AIA provided arguably the greatest challenge to Unionists since the Third Home Rule crisis. Their analysis and response is key to understanding the evolution of Unionism to the Belfast Agreement of Good Friday 1998. It has been seen as an important dynamic on the Northern Ireland peace process. At an inter-governmental level, at which it was undertaken, it has formalised British–Irish relations and promoted friendly co-operation between the two states. Paul Arthur has argued that the signing of the Agreement represented the two governments entering 'the debate as a prestigious third party with the support of much of the international community' (Arthur, 1999a, 252). However, while much work has been done on the importance of the AIA at this intergovernmental level, an assessment of its political consequences on the actors in Northern Ireland is lacking. More important, perhaps, has been the trend to use the chronology of the peace process in Northern Ireland for analyses of changes within the ideological blocs of Northern Ireland's political parties. The changes in the political context in the 1990s are arguably the most important factor on the peace process and a convincing case can be made for the paramilitary ceasefires acting as a catalyst for the whole process. The intention here is not to confirm or dispel these competing, or even complementary, theories on the origins of the peace process, as it will be argued that Unionists had little involvement in this process, but to show how the genesis of the process affected Unionism and how this has had long-term implications on the peace process.

The AIA defined how the political conflict was to be managed. O'Leary and McGarry find its significance in the fact that 'it formalised inter-state co-operation in conflict management' (O'Leary and McGarry, 1996, 226). One group of authorities has observed that the negotiators of the Agreement were those officials and civil servants who were most interested in shifting the locus of the management of the conflict to an Anglo-Irish one (Bew, Patterson and Teague, 1997, 60). The Agreement recognised that the Irish government had a legitimate interest in Northern Ireland and it should be party to a solution. Throughout the 'peace process' the Irish government developed its role so that it was perceived as a facilitator to a solution and not part of the problem. The Agreement began this process by attempting to change the role of the two governments by establishing a symmetrical balance of power between the two communities in Northern Ireland politics (English, 1999, 102) by promoting the equality of the aspirations of the two communities, framed in bureaucratic rationalist language (Aughey, 2001a; see Hadden and Boyle, 1989, 16). Therefore, the Agreement was supposedly premised on the symmetry of aspirations. Aughey argues 'it was that symmetry, so finely rationalistic, which guaranteed the widespread support for the Agreement in Britain and Irish public life, as well as in Europe and the United States' (Aughey, 2001a, 304). However, the Agreement went further than simply to assert this symmetry. It attempted to create it by giving the Irish government a unique role in relation to their 'client' community. Article 5c of the AIA states:

> If it should prove impossible to achieve and sustain devolution on a basis which secures widespread acceptance in Northern Ireland, the Conference shall be a framework within which the Irish Government may, *where the interests of the minority community are significantly or especially affected*, put forward views on proposals for major legislation and major policy issues, which are within the purview of the Northern Ireland Departments and which remain the responsibility of the Secretary of State for Northern Ireland. (Hadden and Boyle, 1989, 30 my italics)

Furthermore, Article 4c states:

> Both Governments recognise that devolution can be achieved only with the co-operation of constitutional representatives within Northern Ireland of both traditions there. The Conference shall be a framework within which the Irish Government may put forward

views and proposals on the modalities of bringing about devolution in Northern Ireland, *in so far as they relate to the interests of the minority community*. (Hadden and Boyle, 1989, 28 my italics)

The Agreement envisaged no reciprocal role for the British government on behalf of the Unionists, nor would Unionists have welcomed such a role by the British because, for them, the AIA was proof that the British could not be trusted to protect their interests. They were particularly concerned with Article 2b, which stated that 'in the interests of peace and stability, *determined efforts shall be made* through the Conference to resolve any differences' (Hadden and Boyle, 1989, 22 my italics). This alteration to the balance between Unionists and Nationalists was done in an asymmetrical fashion. Unionists were neither party to nor consulted about the new arrangements[1] and this exacerbated the problems that the new approach would have created for Unionism regardless of consultation because it meant fundamental changes to their position within Northern Ireland.

Moreover, as O'Leary and McGarry have argued, 'it [AIA] signified that whilst the unionist guarantee remained...unionists would have no veto, tacit or explicit, on policy formulation within Northern Ireland' (O'Leary and McGarry, 1996, 226). It was thus the case that the AIA represented a significant defeat for Unionism, and one over which they had no control or input. John McGarry has argued elsewhere: 'The agreement represents a significant victory for that [Social Democratic and Labour Party (SDLP)] party. It fully accepts the SDLP position' (McGarry, 1988, 241). Thus the Agreement allowed Hume to argue that it 'implicitly declared Britain to be neutral or agnostic on the question of a united Ireland' (Hume, 1993, 228). The asymmetry is again demonstrated by the intellectual origins of the Agreement, which were rooted in the New Ireland Forum Report, whose analysis of Unionism has been described as 'singularly banal and traditional' (Bew and Patterson, 1987a, 44), and the logic of the new inter-governmentalism was joint-authority (Bew, Patterson and Teague, 1997, 66). Given such intellectual origins and the lack of any input by Unionists, the new symmetry envisaged by the Agreement was clearly not reflected by it. Indeed, it can be argued that the Agreement's effect was to empower the Nationalist argument at the expense of Unionists and thus, as Arthur argues, Unionists 'were isolated, victims of the new asymmetry' (Arthur, 1999a, 253) and therefore 'the challenge which faced unionists after November 1985 was...one of strategic political recovery' (Aughey, 2001a, 311).

The Unionist campaign against the Agreement has been the subject of a recent study, which has stressed the diversity within the campaign (Cochrane, 1997) but what is infrequently acknowledged is that the Agreement created enormous cohesion with regard to its common interpreted meaning. The subsequent divisions and political debates that characterised Unionist politics in the late 1980s have to be explained with reference to the nature of the political challenges presented to Unionism. The political arguments that were utilised by Unionists are ascertainable and coherent on a broad level when set in the context of those contemporary events. Social and cultural differences within such a disparate and broad ideology will make analysis difficult but political differences can be explained by a thorough analysis of the political challenges of the period.

There are three levels of analysis to demonstrate the contemporary dynamics operating on Unionist ideas. First, consideration will be given to the political effects of the AIA. It will be argued that the Agreement imposed on Unionists a fundamental change in the power relationships between the two communities and that this created many of the commonly discussed aspects of their campaign against the Accord. The basis of their argument was that they had not been consulted about, nor had they consented to, the new political arrangements that affected them. Such an understanding is essential in providing the backdrop to the other two levels. The second level concerns the debate within the Unionist community over the desirability of integration. This debate is frequently misunderstood as indicative of a confused and fragmented ideology but there is no coincidence between the fact that the argument for integration was popular in grass-roots Unionism and the political context created by the Agreement. Thirdly, the Agreement created a consensus on the need for a new Unionist understanding of North–South relations while simultaneously disadvantaging the devolutionists. Overall, the accusations of incoherence in Unionist thought were a product of the reflective process of analysis within that community caused by contemporary political changes.

The Unionist withdrawal of consent

There is a broad consensus on the messages that Unionists were supposed to take from the AIA. Cochrane has argued that

> The Agreement was concluded because the British came to identify a greater common interest with the Dublin government than with the Ulster Unionist community. The signing of the Hillsborough Accord

was thus a formal recognition of the cultural alienation of Great Britain from Northern Ireland in general and the unionist community in particular. (Cochrane, 1994, 383)

Elsewhere he has argued:

> The Agreement shocked many unionists because they finally realised that they were an unwanted child... the realisation dawned on many unionists in November 1985 that they remained part of the United Kingdom on sufferance, a residue of Britain's imperial past and a diplomatic loose-end yet to be tied up. (Cochrane, 1997, 31)

The Agreement was a unilateral change to the Union by one of the partners and this brought the nature of the connection between Ulster Unionists and the British State into sharp focus. Unionists first had to come to terms with these changes and how they affected their political philosophy and then formulate a response that could change the structure of the relationships that were now implicitly weighted against them. Thus the campaign against the Agreement was about demonstrating the lack of Unionist consent to the changes that the Accord introduced and this was the meaning that was attached to many of the activities and strategies utilised by Unionists in opposing it. Bernard Crick argues that the situation was more complicated than Unionist proclamations made it seem. He argues that their withdrawal of consent was a withdrawal of active, or explicit, consent and not tacit consent because there was no civil war or revolution, or threat of such events. Active consent was only necessary for constitutional changes emanating from the Agreement – for example joint authority, power sharing or a federal Ireland – but not necessary for Direct Rule, albeit with a consultative element for the Irish government (Crick, 1988). The following exposition will outline Unionists' 'withdrawal of consent' and demonstrate that it came very close to a withdrawal of tacit consent. It will be clear that if this did not happen it had very little to do with the politicians.

The Unionist reaction to the Agreement was initially marked by bewilderment and disillusionment which reflected the important changes that the Agreement made to the political landscape of Northern Ireland. All the other parties to the conflict had made these changes but there was no input from Unionists. Unionist interpretations of the Accord and their campaign were based around the assumption that the Agreement had altered the terms of the Union, without their consent. A joint

UUP/DUP press release on the day the Agreement was signed in Hillsborough stated: 'In essence, this accord represents the end of the Union as we have know it [*sic*] and the beginning of joint London/Dublin authority – an ill-disguised Trojan Horse' (*News Letter*, 16 November 1985). In the opinion of Unionists it altered the Union for several reasons. First, it allowed a foreign government a say in Northern Ireland thereby explicitly governing Northern Ireland differently. Secondly, this was done without the consent of the majority of the people in Northern Ireland. Thirdly, there was to be differential treatment for the two communities, as evident in the asymmetry described above.

On the same day in November 1985 that Ian Paisley called British Prime Minister Margaret Thatcher the 'Jezebel of Northern Ireland', Frank Millar, chief executive of the UUP, made a more sophisticated, although probably less effective, political point:

> If Britain found it difficult to govern Northern Ireland without the consent of the minority, I believe the British government will find it impossible to govern it without the consent of the majority. Britain has broken the contract with which she governed Northern Ireland. (*The Times*, 19 November 1985)

Thus, the rally at the City Hall on 23 November 1985, the Day of Protest Action on 3 March 1986 and, most importantly, the by-elections of 23 January 1986 were all billed and analysed by Unionists as demonstrations of the lack of Unionist consent. The by-elections were particularly important in this respect because, for Unionists, they neatly demonstrated Thatcher's hypocrisy. At a rally in Ballymoney two days before the elections, Molyneaux argued:

> It is simply inconceivable that Her Majesty's Government should propose to disregard the freely expressed will of the people...The Prime Minister for years has chided her opponents in the trade union movement to put their trust in the ballot. Her government has shown earnest of its commitment to the constitutional process by its proposal to fund trades union ballots. Yet here we are told the result of Ulster's ballot will also be disregarded...the future of democracy itself is therefore on the line. (*News Letter*, 22 January 1986)

Reactions to the Day of Action were more muted considering the violent scenes that dominated every provincial and national newspaper but DUP headquarters still managed to argue that consent was the key issue. They stated 'we've proved our point. Without the consent of Ulster Unionists joint authority can't be successfully implemented' (*News Letter*, 4 March 1986). A rhetorical flourish on the same theme came from John Taylor: 'President Marcos, the much despised President of the Philippines, has more moral authority and a greater democratic base than the NIO ministers at Stormont' (*Irish Times*, 19 February 1986).

Unionists began to turn to civil disobedience to demonstrate their withdrawal of consent after the failure of these three Unionist initiatives to affect British policy. The timing could not have been better as the striking of the local rate was due in mid-February. Seventeen Unionist-controlled councils were following an adjournment policy and due to miss the deadline while Belfast City Council (BCC) was engaged in a High Court battle as to the legality of its adjournment policy. The government blinked first and imposed rates on the adjourning councils, including Belfast. The council strategy was supplemented by a wider call by Unionist parties to withhold rates and taxes. A UUP Assemblyman and lawyer, Jeremy Burchill, had been withholding his taxes since January but the first prominent advocates of this strategy were two UUP MPs – Ken Maginnis and Harold McCusker (*Belfast Telegraph*, 17 February 1986). The first martyr for the cause was Rev. Ivan Foster, DUP Assemblyman for Fermanagh and South Tyrone, who was jailed in April 1986 after refusing to pay a fine (*The Times*, 22 April 1986). However, it was not until 23 April that the policy was formally announced at the Assembly (*Irish Times*, 24 April 1986). Unionists envisaged the rates strike dovetailing with other demonstrations of withdrawal of consent which had been ongoing since November but had now run into difficulties.

In his analysis of these events Feargal Cochrane overstates the importance of divisions between the two Unionist parties (Cochrane, 1997, 184–213). Unionist councillors sustained a much greater level of unity than has been appreciated especially when it is taken into account that they had to cope with much more local pressure from outside the Unionist family than either the Assembly members or the MPs. It is clear from BCC's resumption of business that the five 'rebel' councillors were among the very few who opposed the strategy; it was to be another 5 months before another Unionist council would vote to resume business. Moreover, the five who rebelled had all put on record their unease at the strategy long before the High Court's suspended fine. John Carson in particular had irked the DUP on more than one occasion in the past (before and after the AIA) over his role and engagements as Lord Mayor. That individual attitudes were more important than party disputes is given credence by statements made by Frank

Millar after the BCC resumption. He made it clear that each of the 'rebel' councillors knew that they would not be liable to pay the fine if the council adjourned once more. The cost was to be met by the two Unionist parties (*Belfast Telegraph*, 7 May 1986).

Inter-party division was less important for the events in BCC than division within the UUP, and the actions of the constituency organisations towards the rebellious five are indicative of this. Dorothy Dunlop was severely censored and threatened with expulsion for her role by the Knock and Ballyhackamore branch of East Belfast Unionist Association, while John Carson and Alfie Redpath, although jeered and heckled on their way to a North Belfast constituency meeting, faced no action. The attitude of the North Belfast Association is particularly interesting because, in contrast to other areas, its members were foremost in expressing dissension with the adjournment and boycott strategies. Cecil Walker, the UUP MP for the area, had been calling for an end to the Westminster boycott for some time and the constituency was the first to declare openly for integration when it launched a ginger group, the Ulster Unionist UK Group, in June 1986 (*Irish Times*, 27 June 1986), while the first meeting of the Campaign for Equal Citizenship (CEC) had only taken place a month earlier on 14 May 1986 (Bew and Gillespie, 1999, 200). When North Down resumed business in August it followed the pattern established by BCC. Court action by the APNI had brought pressure on the councillors and, while this had been bypassed by some measures in the council, the Mayor, Hazel Bradford, had also expressed her dissatisfaction with the varying standards seemingly applicable to the hierarchy of political representation. North Down, it should also be noted, was Robert McCartney's constituency.

The other aspect of the campaign that demonstrated a withdrawal of consent was much less effective. The campaign within the Area boards was more problematic than in the councils because Unionists were not in a majority and were therefore reduced to walkouts and disruption. The methods did vary but only rarely was a meeting adjourned. Moreover, there was more chance of dissension because the boards were dealing with issues such as education, which had the potential to directly hurt the communities that the councillors were representing. Thus, many that were unhappy with the council protest were also unhappy with the board protest. The best example is William Corry who sat on both BCC and the Belfast Education and Library Board, as he voted for a return to business on the former and continued chairing meeting of the latter, despite the vocal protests of other Unionists (*Belfast Telegraph*, 28 January 1986). The difficulties of the local government protest were not so much a matter of principle but the fact that the principle was not universally applied (see Dunlop quoted in Cochrane, 1997, 191–2). This was probably not a result of double standards and it can be more plausibly argued that Unionists found the Northern Ireland Assembly a useful forum for opposition to the AIA.

The analysis and actions of Unionists led to accusations, such as that made by *The Guardian* that 'the logic of the Unionist position since the AIA is an independent Ulster' (*Guardian*, 25 November 1985). It was able to state this because Unionist resistance began to resemble the militant resistance of 1912–14, which its detractors were keen to describe as hypocrisy – resisting the British Parliament in order to remain British. *The Equal Citizen*, which was produced by Boyd Black and was later to become the publication of the CEC, compared the Unionist situation to a Catch-22:

> This one goes as follows: you call yourselves unionists and say you want to remain within the United Kingdom, therefore you must accept the will of the United Kingdom Parliament, which wants to manoeuvre you out of the United Kingdom. To be a thorough going unionist you must acquiesce in the breaking of the Union – Catch 22. (*The Equal Citizen*, No. 2, 7 December 1985)

In order to address this conundrum, Unionists differentiated between an Act of Parliament as the law of the land and the AIA as a resolution of Parliament passed by a transient government. They felt the latter had less moral authority and therefore justified Unionist resistance (*News Letter*, 15 January 1986). However, some Unionists did not see the need to make this distinction. They were able to point to the contradictions inherent in their opponents' arguments. This argument calmed fears over the frequent questions and allegation that Unionists were really angling for a Unilateral Declaration of Independence (UDI), which surfaced frequently in the initial stages of the campaign. Paisley and Molyneaux had to fend off questions of this nature at nearly every press conference. They were not helped in this regard by the protestations of some senior deputies. Frank Millar was treading a very fine line between two very similar concepts when he stated in the Assembly:

> We do not seek an independent Northern Ireland. Negotiated independence would be something very different from UDI. If the government did try and remove us from the Union, at that moment it would forego any right to determine the future of this Province. (*News Letter*, 6 December 1985)

Paisley found that people like Gregory Campbell were not averse to even more extreme statements, and Peter Robinson's remark that Ulster was on the 'window ledge of the Union' (*News Letter*, 18 November 1985) is a manifestation of this sentiment. Nevertheless, the two leaders confronted the issue head-on and this reveals the base analysis of the nature of the challenge of the AIA. Paisley argued: 'When we win this battle and Mrs Thatcher has to withdraw, we are not going back to where we were before. We will have to renegotiate our position so that we will never again be put in this situation' (*News Letter*, 6 December 1985). Unsurprisingly, Paisley advocated a strong devolved government as the solution. However, Molyneaux, who was well known for his integrationist leanings, analysed the problem the same way: 'We can't be left in a position of vulnerability... We must renegotiate our position within the United Kingdom and we must have an undertaking that never again will the government embark on a similar process' (*News Letter*, 6 December 1985).

Unionists were essentially arguing over the role, function and control of the state. For a community used to wielding power, or at least having a controlling say, the AIA was a profoundly disturbing development. One of the first proposals articulated by Unionists after the AIA was by the Charter Group and part of its analysis reveals this argument. The Group consisted of three members of the UUP who were strongly in favour of devolution: Harry West, former leader of the UUP, Austin Ardill, former deputy leader of Vanguard and prominent anti-Faulkner Unionist, and David McNarry. They state, in the section 'Dealing with the Anglo-Irish Agreement':

> If a new Northern Ireland is to be stable it is vital that the complex network of relationships between the Government of the United Kingdom, the Government of the Republic of Ireland, the British Ulster Tradition and the Irish Tradition in Northern Ireland is stable... The Anglo-Irish Agreement was entered into by the two Sovereign Governments because of a lack of stability in this network of relationships. It has substantially changed those relationships and further destabilised them. One of the four parties to those relationships, the British Ulster Tradition, was excluded from consultation about and from the formation of the Agreement. (Northern Ireland Charter Group, 1986)

While it is doubtful whether consultation would have reconciled Unionists to the AIA, the identification of four parties involved and the exclusion of one of them was to be highly significant in Unionist analysis because it struck at the core of the conflict. As Richard English states 'this has been the essence of the Northern Irish conflict – the question of power – and it is one which focuses on possession of the state' (English, 1999, 99). With the AIA, Unionists perceived that possession of the state had changed hands and that they had not been involved in the transfer.

Moreover, while possession of the state had changed hands, its role had also altered. Integrationists became particularly preoccupied with the role of the state, promoting it as a pluralist arbiter between competing factions within its territory (Aughey, 1995b, 19). However, this is clearly not how Unionists saw the situation after the AIA. In December 1985, Martin Smyth stated that the Agreement amounted to 'institutionalised separate development'; 'This plan quite clearly envisages that Catholic and Protestant political development will proceed along totally different lines' (*Belfast Telegraph*, 14 December 1985). Frank Millar also expressed dissatisfaction at the role of the state after the AIA:

> This is not democracy. This is not justice...As a Unionist I seek nothing for myself which I will not gladly share with all my fellow citizens. But I am equally adamant I shall have none with privilege over me. The Anglo-Irish Agreement gives privilege and advantage to a minority. (*Belfast Telegraph*, 15 January 1986)

Furthermore, there was a definite sense that Unionists were losing the argument and, because the argument concerned the state, their whole existence was threatened. As Harold McCusker said:

> Thatcher and King's acceptance that the Government of the Irish Republic has a legitimate right to share in the government of our country concedes the analysis, the conclusions and the demands contained in the report of the New Ireland Forum. (*News Letter*, 8 January 1986)

In Unionist rhetoric there were frequent references to breaking the contract with the governed or the ties of loyalty. This indicates that this was an important factor in explaining Unionist opposition. It also explains some of the questionable rhetoric that was employed during the Unionist campaign. Cochrane argues that cultural differences between the DUP and the UUP explain a perceived difference in attitudes towards violence. This analysis ignores the rhetoric of the UUP and the motivations of the DUP. Indeed, one of the remarkable aspects of the campaign is the thinly veiled threats of violence made by the softly spoken and unassuming Molyneaux and other prominent members of the UUP. For example, twice in one week following the signing of the Agreement, John Taylor spoke of the inevitability of violence if the government insisted on pursuing the AIA (*The Guardian*, 25 November 1985; *News Letter*, 30 November 1985). Another example that combines these contractarian attitudes to violence in such a manner is the following extract from a speech made by Ken Maginnis at a rally organised by Larne Orange District No. 1:

> It may come to the day when Unionists will have to step outside man's law if man's law is unjust. That I accept. When that day comes you will be told and your elected leaders will not be behind – they will be in front leading you. But there is another law which any man should not want to break in their opposition to the Anglo-Irish Agreement and that is God's law. I would ask every unionist to remember the difference between man's law which can be unjust and God's law which can never be anything but just. The only justification we ever have for violence is that which is used in defence of our own lives or the lives of our fellow citizens. (*News Letter*, 3 February 1986)

The condemnation of violence is ambiguously qualified, a theme recurrent in UUP threats which, with the DUP, began to resemble a good cop, bad cop routine. For example, after the violence, disruption and intimidation on the Day of Action, Molyneaux distanced himself from any more action similar to that of the 3 March but qualified his position with the remark:

> If the Government continues to turn a blind eye [to constitutional opposition] I fear that our control over some elements in the community will be inevitably weakened and nothing we will do or say will placate them. (*News Letter*, 4 March 1986)

The 'bad cop' role was filled by the more extreme elements in Unionism. During the summer of 1986, Peter Robinson began to make Paisley look like a moderate as he organised shows of force, most spectacularly on the 11th night when he marched 4000 people into Hillsborough (*Irish Times*, 12 July 1986). However, it was the Ulster Clubs that were most unambiguous in their threat of violence. Under the ingenious headline 'Gandhi "Out"' (alluding to Mrs Thatcher's infamous press conference), the *News Letter* reported the following speech made by Alan Wright, founder of the Ulster Clubs.

> Ulster people are not Gandhi – it is not in our nature. Apart from that we simply don't have the time Gandhi had... As long as John Hume and Garret FitzGerald are in control of Northern Ireland we don't have the time or the tolerance for passive resistance. It has been shown that the Government pays no attention whatever to passive resistance. It must not be under-estimated how many people would respond to a call for firm action, though I don't necessarily mean violence. (*News Letter*, 27 June 1986)

Quite what he means if it is not violence is unclear because he was clearly expressing dissatisfaction with the joint Unionist policy of civil disobedience. Despite this exposition of Unionist ambiguity towards the use of violence, Arthur Aughey is still right to insist that Unionists did not utilise violence in the campaign and that there was little possibility of violence (Aughey, 1989, 72–7) because Unionists were using the tactic, as in 1912, of constitutional intimidation.[2] What it does represent is a crisis of confidence in the institutions of the state to safeguard Unionist interests, or perhaps to even acknowledge them. This is important because if the AIA was to be truly symmetrical then the implication was that this was to be the role of the British State. This crisis of confidence and Unionist contractarian attitudes is further illustrated by the astonishing attacks on the Royal Ulster Constabulary (RUC) by Unionist politicians in March 1986. That month saw a large number of physical attacks by loyalists on the homes of members of the RUC (Owen, 1994, 71–82) and a political attack on the institution alleging Dublin interference and political control over the police in order to thwart the Unionist campaign against the AIA. Parkinson rightly points to the media's focus on the violence rather than the cause of the grievance (Parkinson, 2001, 281) as Unionists had also been alleging political interference over the personal views of members of the civil service, who were opposed to the Agreement, since its signing (*News Letter*, 1 March 1986). The two issues came to a head over the Day of Action when Unionists claimed civil servants who took part in the protest were being threatened with losing their jobs and the RUC had been given a political role in policing the day. On 7 March, Paisley and Molyneaux placed the following open letter in the *News Letter*:

We realise the pressures on you but we cannot sit back and allow you to be misled by false assurances that the Anglo-Irish Agreement does not interfere with the integrity of the RUC or involve a foreign power in directing your affairs...The Dublin Government now have an equal say in 'setting in hand' the work of the Chief Constable. This radically alters the role of RUC officers, who were employed and took an oath to 'truly serve' our Sovereign. Now you are being asked to serve a second master – the Government of an Irish Republic which spawned the Provisional IRA and which still harbours the murderers of so many of your gallant colleagues – and all this within a framework of a code of conduct to be dictated by Dublin. (*News Letter*, 7 March 1986)

Molyneaux later tried to distance himself from this but it nevertheless is a graphical illustration of the issues that we have been discussing. Unionists were attempting to redress the imbalances of the AIA.

The integration debate

The Agreement not only heralded mass Unionist protest but also sparked intense debate within the UUP as to preferred Unionist political options. The debate became known as the integration–devolution debate. Broadly speaking, devolution refers to a form of government with substantial responsibility for Northern Ireland based in Belfast and integration refers to changing the structures of government (and also party politics) to bring Northern Ireland into line with mainland Great Britain. Many argued that it went to the heart of Unionism and is one of the few occasions in this period that Unionism looked to history for ideological legitimacy. David McNarry argued:

I think that as the integrationist argument was teased out you could sense the number of people who then began to think about the history of our party, began to think about the traditions and began to think, as I had argued all along, that this place [Stormont] was closed down by our enemies and the greatest victory that we can deliver is to have these doors opened again, took a long time but more or less. (Interview with David McNarry, 27 September 2002)

In contrast McCartney has argued:

I've always been a good believer in and admirer of Edward Carson and his constitutional policy for Ulster was a very simple and clear one which unfortunately the Ulster Unionist Party abandoned and was one of the reasons why I parted company with them in 1987. (Interview with Robert McCartney, 19 September 2002)

Aughey certainly proposed the idea that integration was central to Unionist ideology (Aughey, 1989). Academic debate has also centred on the ideological importance of the debate and Todd argued that devolution was a key political preference of those 'Ulster Loyalists' while integration was a preference of those who could be described as 'Ulster British' (Todd, 1987). This seems to simplify the complex ideological web and the interplay between the two concepts. For example, Jeffrey Donaldson, who was an advocate of integration while he was involved in the Young Unionists, said:

> I would say that in terms of my current position we went into negotiations and our objective was to replace the Anglo-Irish Agreement with a new agreement that would be more acceptable to Unionism and if we could achieve that new agreement then the context for devolution would be altered and might be more favourable for Unionism and so I've always held the view that integration and devolution were not mutually exclusive...I've never been against devolution in principle, my difficulty post the Anglo-Irish Agreement was that the context within which devolution would take place was wholly unacceptable. (Interview with Jeffrey Donaldson, 11 November 2002)

In a devolved UK the two concepts seem even less distinct, as even McCartney has acknowledged:

> Political integration means integrating on an equal basis into the United Kingdom on the same democratic understanding as is applied in the rest of the United Kingdom. If proper devolution is the norm in the United Kingdom politically then integration into the United Kingdom means devolution on the same terms as it is democratically applied throughout the United Kingdom...when you talk about integration you mean the same standards, the same principles, the same accountability, the same protection under the rule of law is as afforded to citizens on the mainland should be afforded to citizens on the mainland. (Interview with Robert McCartney, 19 September 2002)

Nevertheless, the debate itself is important for analysing Unionism in a post-AIA environment and particularly for subsequent political discourse.

O'Leary and McGarry have observed that 'Oddly the best of this [Unionist] literature depends on arguments initially advanced by orange and red Marxists, but it modernises the unionist case before the bar of British and international opinion' (McGarry and O'Leary, 1995, 96). The Orange Marxists that O'Leary and McGarry are referring to are the British and Irish Communist Organisation (BICO), which published a range of pamphlets after the AIA reflecting on Northern Ireland's position within the UK and advocating electoral integration. The BICO were just one of a plethora of organisations involved in developing integrationist thinking. The integration movement has to be broadly defined to accommodate all the varying interests and interpretations, but a thorough understanding of the divisions within it is key to grasping its effects on Unionism. Initially a key distinction should be made between those integrationists within the formal Unionist party structure and those outside it. Indeed, the absence of a political party was the major grievance for those outside Unionism. Integrationism existed before 1985 but was confined to the Stalinist left (Coulter, 2001) and the parliamentary Conservative Party (Cunningham, 1995) and its supporters in the UUP, particularly Molyneaux and Enoch Powell, former Conservative minister and UUP MP for South Down. This latter group was active in opposing devolutionists' proposals in Westminster such as Prior's rolling devolution (O'Leary, Elliott and Wilford, 1988, 71–9) or the AIA. They had an ill-defined strategy, ill-defined goals and restricted their proselytising to the House of Commons until after the AIA. The integrationists on the other side of the ideological spectrum had a clearer project. They explicitly advocated electoral integration, a position that was resisted by those in the Conservative Party who referred to a cryptic paragraph in their 1979 manifesto on regional administration.[3] The proposals for electoral integration originated with the BICO and their Athol Street publishers. They were significantly more active and more identifiable as a pressure group than the parliamentarian integrationists. The next phase in the development of the integration movement occurred in 1978 with the formation of the Campaign for Labour Representation (CLR). This leftish group lobbied the Labour Party to organise in Northern Ireland and their dissatisfaction with the political options available to them in Northern Ireland was obviously a key motivation. However, these groups and individuals were ineffectual in gaining elite endorsement or popular support before the AIA.

The Agreement changed the political environment so that there was a greater receptivity of their arguments by the Unionist populace and the immediate post-Agreement period saw the heyday of integrationism. The disparate movement of Stalinists, socialists, parliamentary Conservatives, academics, Unionists and the occasional Nationalist came under the banner of the Campaign for Equal Citizenship (CEC). The CEC pursued a vigorous campaign extending beyond the traditional constituencies and methods of each of these groups and entered into mass politics. However, each group fulfilled a different role and this is important in explaining the movement's disintegration. The BICO provided much of the intellectual basis and the reading literature for the CEC (See *The Equal Citizen*) but the public meetings, a hallmark of the campaign, were addressed by the heavyweight political figures of the British Conservative Party, such as Ian Gow or John Biggs-Davison, or Unionist politicians such as Robert McCartney. The movement's popularity (or success) was reflected in opinion polls indicating a high level of public support for the idea (O'Leary and McGarry, 1996, 255–6). Its major achievement was in 1989 when the Conservative Party affiliated a number of local branches (Coulter, 2001). Ultimately, the CEC could not hold its component parts together and its problems with internal factionalism were compounded as the Tories joined the new local associations rather than retain their CEC membership (Coulter, 2001). The infighting that had characterised the left's contribution to the organisation continued past its demise. This was publicly demonstrated by the formation of and argument between two South Belfast Constituency Labour Parties, one centred around Athol Street publishing and the other around the old CLR, in the early 1990s. McCartney observed:

It disintegrated I think because you know the Athol Street people. I knew very little about them; I took them at face value, it may even be described as politically naïve. I thought what they were about was the Union but in fact, like all Stalinist groups, they're cannibals; they begin to eat themselves after a while and that's exactly what they did...the result is that although very clever able people intellectually and politically intelligent people, they were absolutely self destructive. Doubtless they would claim that had I been elected [in 1987] that they were the authors of it but I got elected in 1995 and 1997 without Athol Street or anybody else and eventually they went off as they always do...as soon as anything grew successful to the point where it was going to require them to do something rather than sit back and have intellectual discussions about the viability of some theory, they started to destroy it because it was going to pose for them the reality of actually having to practice politics as opposed to writing the *Worker's Weekly*. It's sad because I thought and still do that people like Brendan Clifford and others had a hell of a lot to contribute. (Interview with Robert McCartney, 19 September 2002)

The debate on electoral integration was started and pursued by actors outside Unionism. It is useful to see these integrationists as the intellectual heirs of constructive Unionism, which Andrew Gailey has shown extends past its traditionally associated period of the late nineteenth and early twentieth century and can be found in Jack Sayers, editor of the Belfast Telegraph in the 1960s (Gailey, 2001). Sayers was never a formal part of the UUP but had a considerable influence, and a similar situation pertains to the driving force behind the CEC. This was provided by two academics, Peter Brooke and Clifford Smyth. The non-party and non-Unionist character aspects of the CEC are important to consider because, in the context of Unionist politics, the CEC was a remarkable agenda-setter, despite being an outside body and inimical to the interests of the party.

The emergence and popularity of the movement was entirely without prediction, although there have been some attempts to explain its prominence. Colin Coulter has argued that the popularity of the integration movement is connected to the experience of the Protestant middle classes of Direct Rule. The major contradiction of Direct Rule has been that:

> the execution of public policy over the past two decades has simultaneously nurtured the political alienation of middle-class unionists from the British state and established their increasingly rewarding instrumental dependence upon the metropolis. (Coulter, 1996, 177)

The AIA, by this analysis, shook the Protestant middle classes from their abstentionist acquiescence in Molyneaux's 'minimalism' to actively seek electoral integration which:

> promised not merely to prosecute the instrumental interests of the Protestant middle-classes but to do so in a manner which avoided the political impotence which had debilitated minimalist integrationism. (Coulter, 1996, 183)

This class-based analysis casts some light on a neglected aspect of Unionist politics in the late 1980s. However, it neglects the wider impact of the integrationist movement. Coulter's analysis focuses on those who had previously opted out of politics (Coulter, 1996, 178) but the debate within the UUP occurred among seasoned veterans and was more than simply the re-engagement of the Protestant middle classes. Therefore, it is necessary to scrutinise the debate within the party.

It is important to make the distinction between electoral integrationists and these Unionist integrationists. The distinction has been noted before. Aughey and Coulter have both endorsed Bew and Patterson's classification of the integrationists in the UUP such as Molyneaux and Powell as 'minimalists' (Bew and Patterson, 1987b). Minimalists advocated changing the administration of Northern Ireland so that it was in line with the rest of the UK. Common demands included an end to Orders In Council and a Select Committee on Northern Ireland. It did not exclude devolution of some description, mainly for issues of party management, but this was administrative and not legislative or executive devolution. This position found expression in the 1984 policy document *The Way Forward* (Allen *et al.*, 1984; Aughey, 1989, 138–46). However, there were members of the party who found this 'minimalism' insufficient and they became active in advocating this after the AIA but the philosophical roots of the ideas are indicative of political positions. Brendan Clifford (the main polemicist in Athol Street and BICO) based his influential pamphlet 'Parliamentary Sovereignty' on a reading of Bagehot while McCartney grounded his integration in Edward Carson. Clifford's was an explicitly secular political philosophy but McCartney's was a secular variant of Ulster Unionism. In his speech to the controversial 1986 UUP party conference he said:

> I am asking you [conference] to endorse no new policy. I am not even presenting an old policy in different words. I am asking you to raise again the standard of your forefathers. I am asking you to restore their policy of equal rights and equal citizenship as the declared, the defined and the united policy of this party. (McCartney, 2001, 68)

When McCartney was asked about the origins of the CEC he replied:

> If I am a Carsonite Unionist believing in the principles of equal citizenship as set out 40 years before the Athol Street mob were heard of in 1912 and right through, if that's the basis of my Unionism, it's equal citizenship. If we're going to talk about who is the author of

equal citizenship it's not Bob McCartney, Peter Brooke nor our other friend Clifford Smyth, it's Carson. So it was just a matter of people having the same idea and at some point they were going to be thrown together and it would coalesce but the idea of equal citizenship is, indeed the term equal citizen, is a central paragraph in Carson's speech so . . . I don't think it matters if I was in on day two or day one or anybody else because that's talking not about the idea but the coalition. (Interview with Robert McCartney, 19 September 2002)

There are two main quotations cited by McCartney. The first is:

Our demand is a very simple one. We ask for no privileges, but we are determined that no one shall have privileges over us. We ask for no special rights, but we claim the same rights from the same government as every other part of the United Kingdom. We ask for nothing more, we will take nothing less. (Quoted in McCartney, 2001, 67)

The second is from Carson's speech in May 1920 in the House of Commons:

It has been said over and over again, 'you want to oppress the Catholic minority; you want a Protestant ascendancy over there.' We have never asked to govern any Catholic. We are satisfied that all of them, Protestant and Catholic, should be governed from this Parliament and we have always said that this Parliament was aloof entirely from these racial distinctions and religious distinctions which was the strongest foundation for the government of Ulster. (As quoted in McCartney, 2001, 55)

For Unionist integrationists, electoral integration (the explicit project of the integrationists outside the party) was a small part of a much larger project created by the AIA. The Ulster Unionist UK Group, a ginger group of the UUP launched in June 1986 (*Belfast Telegraph*, 26 June 1986), demonstrated this. Their policy document, 'No Longer a Place Apart,' contained five aims and objectives:

1. The abolition of Orders in Council system. In Great Britain legislation ought normally to apply to Northern Ireland automatically. Where it does not it should go through the same parliamentary process as legislation for other regions of the United Kingdom.

2. The establishment of a Grand Committee of MPs to oversee Northern Ireland affairs.
3. Any change in the constitutional position of Northern Ireland being subject to the same procedure as that for England, Scotland or Wales.
4. The establishment of a system of local government on a par with that which operates in the rest of the United Kingdom, with administrative functions democratically accountable to the local community.
5. The extension of the right for people in Northern Ireland to join and vote for the mainland political parties which may form the Government of the United Kingdom. (UK Group, 1986, 1)

This combination of minimalist integration, Unionist anti-AIA thinking and electoral integration was not unique to this group. The document displays the overwhelming Unionist desire emanating from the AIA to be consulted on new political arrangements. Integration happened to provide a useful tool to further articulate this proposition. The UK Group included electoral integration in its document almost as an afterthought and devoted very little to its consideration or its implications. It demonstrated no desire to follow the logic of its position and call for the dissolution of the UUP upon the organisation of mainland parties. Instead it focused, almost exclusively, on the need for consent for constitutional change. This corruption of the electoral integrationist case by Unionists to provide ideological substance to their arguments against the AIA was a particularly high-profile affair. The integrationists who were pushing the UUP in their direction resembled an advancing army destroying anything that appeared to stand in its way. Constituency organisation after constituency organisation discussed and then declared for the idea (see for example East Antrim in Hume, 1996, 89–93). The Young Unionists (*News Letter*, 19 May 1986) and the Queen's University Association (*Belfast Telegraph*, 2 July 1986) formally advocated the policy, and Glengall Street faced a major challenge to its leadership. In many ways UUP party structure allowed the integrationists to make such advances. In May 1986, before the establishment of the CEC, the UUP policy committee was debating the issues (*News Letter*, 7 May 1986; *Belfast Telegraph*, 31 May 1986). The eighteen-strong committee received submissions from prominent party members on the issue (*News Letter*, 14 October 1986) and there were a number of heated debates.

Robert McCartney, Peter Smith, William Ross and Martin Smyth all made submissions to this committee. McCartney argued that devolution played into the hands of the enemies of Unionism because it treated Northern Ireland differently and was an unobtainable goal because it would have to exist within the framework of the AIA with power sharing and an Irish dimension. At this point he did not argue for the establishment of mainland political parties (the goal of the CEC) but, in line with his co-authorship of 'The Way Forward', points to administrative devolution as a possibility (McCartney, 1986). Smith argued that Unionists should spend their energies pushing for the adoption of the Convention Report of 1975 written by the United Ulster Unionist Coalition (UUUC)[4], which had been rejected by the government because it lacked minority approval. He rejected administrative devolution as insufficient to secure the Unionist position within the UK but did argue that they should be prepared to negotiate and regard his proposals as a 'top line' rather than a 'bottom line'. Nevertheless, he quoted the Convention Report in regard to power sharing: 'that no country ought to be forced to have in its Cabinet any person whose political philosophy has revealed his opposition to the very existence of that State' (Smith, 1986). William Ross argued that the UUP should pursue Airey Neave's proposals for administrative devolution because it was originally the Conservative Party policy and therefore had feasibility. Moreover, it could not be boycotted because it lacked real power and there was no possibility of Unionists losing out because if it fell apart they would simply be back to the status quo of 1986 (Ross, 1986). The final submission by Martin Smyth argued that 'Unionists should be in the vanguard to promote a federal Kingdom' along the lines of the United States or Germany as a means of fusing the integration and devolution arguments. Federalism was the best way to acknowledge regional distinctiveness while maintaining the cohesiveness of the UK (Smyth, M., 1986).

These debates, while public knowledge, were fairly well contained. More damaging and a bigger publicity success for the integrationists was the decision by the UUP Executive Committee to allow a debate on integration at the 1986 party conference. There were two motions tabled on 'Constitutional Issues', one from the Ulster Young Unionist Council (UYUC) and one from the North Down Unionist Association. The UYUC proposed:

> This Conference believes that the only way to destroy the Anglo-Irish Agreement and to remove the undemocratic system under which Ulster is presently governed is to develop and promote a policy of equal citizenship, thus giving the people of Ulster the opportunity to play a full role in the political life of the United Kingdom. (UUP, 1986)

North Down Association proposed a similar motion:

> This Conference believes that the way forward for this Party and the cause of the Union is not to be found in the re-establishment of a separate and devolved legislative parliament for Northern Ireland which will only serve as a badge of difference from our fellow British citizens, but by the full integration of Northern Ireland into the political institutions which apply to the rest of the United Kingdom and to thereby secure for the people of Northern Ireland the same rights and privileges which are presently enjoyed by British citizens in every other part of the United Kingdom, and that this Party will, like Edward Carson, seek nothing more and accept nothing less. (UUP, 1986)

The Executive decided not to debate two other motions on the subject. Mid-Ulster Association proposed to support devolution but added that it objected to the mass resignation of councillors and East Belfast Association's motion proposed working towards the UK Group's five aims (UUP, 1986).

Sanctioning this debate was a disastrous decision for the UUP leadership. On the morning of the conference, party chairman Jack Allen and Molyneaux decided to hold the conference behind closed doors (except for Molyneaux's speech) to avoid having the debate in public, much to the consternation of the journalists outside (*Belfast Telegraph*, 8 November 1986). Inside the Europa Hotel, the leadership of Molyneaux and Powell was busy passing an amendment postponing the debate until after the AIA had been destroyed (*News Letter*, 8 November 1986). Many people interpreted the North Down motion, which was McCartney's, as a threat to the leadership (See David McNarry in *News Letter*, 8 November 1986 and Jim Cusack in the *Irish Times*, 10 November 1986) but the move was a public relations disaster for the UUP and ample evidence that they were unable to control their internal dissidents. The devolutionist lobby remained muted throughout and did not assist the leadership, partly because relations with the leadership were strained, as McNarry explained:

> I never disguised the fact that we were challenging the leadership because it would be a nonsense to say otherwise. I wasn't going to do then what I hear people saying now 'we're totally in support of the leadership it's the policies we want to change.' I just could never take that on and therefore it was quite clear that you had to take that

accusation... I was challenging the policies of the leadership... I was also very, very conscious of the fact that both Harry and Austin and Harry in particular having been a former leader, it's just a bad show if a former leader gets involved in criticising his successor and that just never arose. There was never going to be a comeback for Harry West on the back of devolution nor was I ever going to be you know myself projected into the sense that I was going to challenge for the leadership... You know our party eventually finds people out; it found out Bob McCartney... Well we were sent to Coventry, we were totally almost ostracised, sent to Coventry. I wasn't allowed to speak; it was very, very obvious that I was prevented from speaking at conferences and Unionist Council meetings... and that basically was because I think we were hitting home with great truths and effectiveness. (Interview with David McNarry, 27 September 2002)

None of Charter Group attended the conference on the basis that it was not the conference that made policy (*Belfast Telegraph*, 6 November 1986) and therefore allowed the integrationists a free hand. It would be May 1987 before the UUP took action against McCartney, when they expelled him, but this was over the issue of the electoral pact with the DUP (*Belfast Telegraph*, 20 May 1987).[5] Later in the week, the UUP Disciplinary Committee expelled the entire North Down Association over the issue (*News Letter*, 27 May 1987). McCartney's parting shot was to call the UUP, DUP and SDLP 'single issue pressure groups' and 'pygmy parties' (*Irish Times*, 21 May 1987). However, McCartney's expulsion was only one of a number of high-profile departures from Unionist party politics in the spring of 1987 over the electoral pact issue. The other notable absentee was to be the DUP's James Allister (*Belfast Telegraph*, 22 May 1987).[6]

The devolutionists were not passive. The Charter Group, the most active organised body articulating devolution, published proposals in March 1986 (Northern Ireland Charter Group, 1986) and a number of revision documents later in the year (*Belfast Telegraph*, 29 October 1986; *Belfast Telegraph*, 19 January 1987). McNarry assessed the impact of the Charter Group:

I think the valuable thing we did was that we actually held the devolution argument within the party; that we were able to collate an alternative to direct rule we were able to say that here is something that is workable... what we were able to do was basically to be there, a thorn in the flesh of the integrationists... We were working on the basis that integration only showed the lazy side of Unionism in that Unionism didn't need to work too hard in integration, it just needed to bluff the people and tell then 'well we'll still fight your corner and we'll still shout but we actually can't do anything about it.' (Interview with David McNarry, 27 September 2002)

However, the devolutionists were victims of a number of different types of disadvantages. The structural disadvantages related to the AIA context will be discussed later but there were other important factors. First, they had no designs on the leadership of the party. Ardill and West were both 69 and at the end of their political careers, and McNarry had no position within the party hierarchy. While these debates were being conducted, the Charter Group remained outside the policy committee. Unlike the CEC, their search for influence did not extend to garner a mass public following. Instead they were keen to promote their ideas in whatever circles of power that they could. There was contested SDLP involvement in the drafting of the Charter Group's proposals but the Group also met civil servant Ken Bloomfield in April 1986 and Secretary of State Tom King in June (*News Letter*, 3 June 1986) in order to argue their case without Molyneaux or Paisley's knowledge and despite the fact that there was a boycott of government ministers. They were also the first to propose and then send a petition to the Queen about the AIA in May 1986 (*News Letter*, 26 May 1986). The parties arranged another petition but not until January 1987.

The interaction between the two camps tended to be less than cordial. McCartney, never one to mince his words, claimed that devolutionists belonged to the 'political flat-earth movement' (*Irish Times*, 17 May 1986). The Young Unionists were even more forthright when they 'unreservedly' condemned the actions of the Charter Group, even before they met King (*Belfast Telegraph*, 9 May 1986). This prompted a response from McNarry who said, 'at a time when Unionists are still reeling from the shock of the Anglo-Irish Agreement, the integration insurrection is an unnecessary distraction' (*Belfast Telegraph*, 9 May 1986). The bitterness spilled over the confines of the debate in August 1986 when a row erupted between McCartney and Frank Millar over UUP policy on the AIA and negotiations. Millar said a suspension of the AIA would be sufficient to occasion negotiations between Unionists and the government while McCartney argued that in the context of the discussion over devolution or integration, which had not existed when that policy had been adopted, negotiations would be inappropriate: 'I am not against negotiations in the right circumstances but these people including Frank Millar who are talking about windows of opportunity should spell out what they propose to negotiate about' (*Belfast Telegraph*, 22 August 1986). Millar was supported by five members of the policy committee, on which McCartney also sat; Jack Allen, Ken Maginnis, Jim Nicholson, Peter Smith and Raymond Ferguson, who were all devolutionists.

The devolutionist case was characterised by a number of other factors. First, there was a clear geographical divide. North Belfast, East Antrim, North Down and East Londonderry Ulster Unionist Associations were all pro-integration whereas Associations west of the Bann were more likely to be devolutionist like Mid-Ulster, Fermanagh, and Newry and Armagh. Second, there was no strong devolutionist organisation. The Charter Group was active but lacked influence, as we have seen. A number of prominent Unionists were involved with the Campaign for a Devolved Parliament (CDP) but it had a low profile. The devolutionist influence came from individuals in prominent positions such as Nicholson or Maginnis, although they were clearly not as influential with Molyneaux as Powell. This balance of forces between integrationists and devolutionists was never resolved. The integration debate died but not because the leadership took an active role in killing it, and at the end of the day it was those with influence in the party structures who were able to push their solutions and not those with external power bases.

The remarkable characteristic of the debate was its insularity. It was conducted almost without reference to actors outside Unionism. Devolutionists were more likely to refer to the opinions of non-Unionists but this was more to make their point against the integrationists than any conscious engagement with their arguments or the implications of the SDLP in their preferred solution. Frank Millar was one of the few who seemed remotely affected by the feasibility of the arguments. Speaking in Armagh he said:

> I confess I have long been emotionally and intellectually an integrationist. But I must also tell you that when Peter Robinson and I led an Assembly delegation to meet the Prime Minister, Mrs Thatcher told us in unequivocal terms that integration simply is not on. (*News Letter*, 15 March 1986)

The debate should therefore be seen in the context of the post-AIA political environment. The electoral integrationist ideas were corrupted by Unionists to create a coherent and intellectually sound rationale for their political campaign against the Agreement. Unionists who espoused integration did so with reference to Carson and the 1912 Covenant, and not Brendan Clifford and the BICO. Moreover, that dovetailed with a general dissatisfaction within the UUP over Molyneaux's leadership and the pact with the DUP. The integration debate did, however, bring Unionism to a debate on their relationship with the British State. Colin Coulter has argued that Unionist mistrust of the ambitions and actions of the British State ultimately proved to be the undoing of the 'equal citizenship' project (Coulter, 2001, 44) and that the humiliation of the Northern Ireland Conservatives is the clearest example of this (Coulter, 2001, 45). In the context of the late 1980s and the AIA, this is perhaps unsurprising but the debate brought new and articulate defences of the Union to the fore. Arthur Aughey's polemic *Under Siege* was as sophisticated a defence of the Union as anything before it, and its analysis (and by implication, the integrationists') has had a profound effect on subsequent Unionist political discourse (as we saw in Chapter 1).

Devolution and North–South relations

It is possible to argue that the Belfast Agreement of Good Friday 1998 is essentially a political deal between the two main political parties – the UUP and the SDLP. The institutions proposed and established by the Belfast Agreement broadly reflect the political thinking of these two parties over the course of the Troubles, and more particularly since the AIA (Horowitz, 2002). The paramilitaries have been peripheral to this process but essential to the context (see also De Bréadún, 2001, 65). Therefore, if we are to discuss the Belfast Agreement in these terms, we have to understand the political pressures and formative environment on the two parties. It has been argued that the AIA has been crucial to this process. There is an influential argument that the AIA was an attempt at coercive consociation but this misrepresents how the Agreement shaped the political context. It will therefore be argued that the AIA cannot be seen as succeeding with a project of coercive consociation and that its effect was to act as a brake on the prospects for 'agreed devolution'. This will be shown by analysing the effects, implications and fossilisation of the Agreement on Northern Ireland's political parties and in particular on Unionism. It will be shown that we have to widen the scope of interpretation to ascertain the effects of the Agreement and that the failure of the Brooke and Mayhew talks were the result of the AIA context. Moreover, the Belfast Agreement of Good Friday 1998 was only facilitated by a move away from the structural bias implicit in the

Agreement towards the two competing blocs as the two governments widened the number of parties involved in the process.

Brendan O'Leary has argued that the AIA should be seen as an experiment in what he terms 'coercive consociation'. In 1987 he argued that Article 4 of the Agreement should be situated in the context of British policy initiatives in Northern Ireland since the 1970s, which had promoted power sharing arrangements. Other scholars (O'Duffy, 1993) have supported this view but the important point is that the Agreement was an attempt to coerce key factions of the Unionist bloc to accept power sharing as the lesser of several evils, the biggest being an extensive role for Dublin, and thus create a faction autonomous enough to negotiate a settlement with the SDLP. In 1987 O'Leary stressed that this interpretation could not be understood as a rational policy-making scenario but that this was its importance and meaning nonetheless (O'Leary, 1987, 19–21). In his 1996 work with John McGarry, he rectified the internal contradiction of an apparently coherent policy strategy which lacks rational calculations by the actors making it. In this it was asserted that:

> The Anglo-Irish Agreement was signed as part of a jointly designed British and Irish Machiavellian master-plan to coerce Unionists into accepting a power sharing devolved government together with an Irish dimension, knowing that the intergovernmental conference could survive whatever strategy the unionists would use to undermine it. (O'Leary and McGarry, 1996, 238)

The AIA was thus designed to bolster the SDLP and to fragment Unionism and therefore create power sharing, as the Unionist faction willing to negotiate would opt for the 'agreed devolution' of the SDLP's preferred hue (O'Leary and McGarry, 1996, 234).

Machiavellian plots, by their very nature, are hard to disprove and there is evidence that the idea of dividing Unionism to achieve power sharing was the thinking of the SDLP and others. Moreover, Bew, Gibbon and Patterson may be dismissing this aspect too readily when they argue that a coercive consociation plot was not in the minds of the British and when they quote one senior negotiator that the Agreement simply 'paid lip-service to devolution' (Bew, Gibbon and Patterson, 1996, 213–7) as another, David Goodall, has argued recently that at least part of the Agreement was 'intended as an inducement to the unionists to move to power sharing' (Goodall, 1998, 54; 2002, 122). In the absence of archival evidence it seems difficult to make a conclusion one way or another. It seems more probable that the Agreement may have unintentionally cemented the pre-existing synonymity between devolution and power sharing in governmental circles. It did this by explicitly passing the decision in the form of devolution to the Nationalist community in Northern Ireland. However, it is doubtful if the two governments were primarily motivated to sign the Agreement because of a desire for an internal settlement; in many ways the AIA was about expanding the boundaries of a settlement. Moreover, O'Leary and McGarry neglect that the institutions for devolution had already been established in 1982 by the then Secretary of State, James Prior. These had been disappointing as a means to a settlement but not because of Unionist reticence on devolution, although they had proved to be unimaginative in accommodating the minority (Cochrane, 1997, 128). The Assembly was unable to grow into its envisaged role because of a boycott by the SDLP. Farren explains SDLP hostility as deriving: 'From continuing unionist opposition to power sharing and to any institutionalised relations with the South, as well as from bitter memories of previous failures' (Farren, 2000, 50). Indeed, by the time of the signing of the AIA in November 1985, the Assembly had already made steps towards devolution as the Devolution Committee, designed to propose a development of the institutions and chaired by Sir Frederick Catherwood, had already met and reported. Moreover, the two Unionist parties were advocating constitutional solutions based on their submissions to this committee and both the UUP submission, *The Way Forward*, and the DUP submission, *The Future Assured*, proposed devolution, to a greater or lesser degree. As Farren noted, power sharing was opposed by both Unionist parties at this stage but the coercive consociation argument simply demonstrates the structural bias of the Agreement enshrined in Article 4c because, by this thesis, any 'agreed devolution' was envisaged as a settlement on SDLP terms. Bew and Patterson term this Hume's 'crude manipulative logic' (Bew and Patterson, 1987a, 46) and argued 'as the reasoning behind the Agreement about Protestant politics was fundamentally flawed, the chances of devolution are slim' (Bew and Patterson, 1987a, 48).

The real internal significance of the signing of the AIA lies in what was to become known as Strand 2. O'Leary and McGarry actually note that 'the decisive actor in the making of the Agreement was the SDLP and its leader John Hume' (O'Leary and McGarry, 1996, 238), but, somewhat bewildered, later state that 'contrary to what most British architects of the AIA imagined, the SDLP appeared to lose interest in 'agreed devolution' after Hillsborough' (O'Leary and McGarry, 1996, 259).

My contention is not that the SDLP were uninterested in some kind of internal arrangement but that this was not their primary interest in 1985. It was, after all, only 2 years since the New Ireland Forum Report and its three options did not allow for a purely internal solution (New Ireland Forum, 1984). Hume's attitude toward 'agreed devolution' can be seen from the Brooke talks of 1991. Bloomfield argues that suspicion of Hume's commitment to a Strand One solution is unfounded but:

> His commitment to a Strand 1 result was, of course, tempered by the need to balance it with strengthened North–South institutions in Strand 2. Once it was clear that Strand 2 was not going to make headway, his enthusiasm for Strand 1 progress was bound to wane. (Bloomfield, 1998, 167)

Significantly, in Sean Farren's account of the SDLP's contribution to the peace process he argues that the AIA, premised on the SDLP's analysis, was the mechanism through which British–Irish co-operation could be fostered which would give due recognition to Unionist and Nationalist rights and which would produce a settlement (Farren, 2000, 50–1).

However, the AIA had a greater impact in contributing to a reassessment of North–South relations by Unionists. The Agreement initially weakened the devolutionists and gave impetus to the integrationist movement within (and without) the UUP. Its popularity was partly due to the vigour of its advocates and the freshness of its arguments and also because the AIA had tarnished devolution for Unionists. Integrationists persuasively argued that devolution would have to be in the context and terms offered by the Agreement, which Unionists saw as a mechanism to remove them from the Union. These issues were played out in a well-publicised debate in Carrickfergus in front of UUP members of the East Antrim Constituency Association. The two advocates were the best-known personalities on either side of the integration–devolution debate – Robert McCartney, who at this time was still a member of the UUP, and David McNarry. During the debate McCartney argued that 'negotiations, allegedly outside the Agreement, would amount to endorsing the Agreement's essential terms under a different name' (*News Letter*, 12 September 1986; Hume, 1996, 89–93). However, after losing the vote by 55:5, McNarry observed in the newspapers that 'I was quite surprised to find that the real argument, when it came down to the bit, was really about bigoted scare mongering on devolution [over power sharing and an Irish dimension]' (*Belfast Telegraph*, 12 September 1986). Furthermore, the removal of the Agreement was seen as a greater and more immediate danger by most Unionists and so they were unwilling to actively campaign for such a settlement until it was defeated. Taylor echoes many Unionist statements when he argued that 'until this constitutional trap which has been imposed by the Government on Northern Ireland has been replaced, there can be no agreement to a devolved institution at Stormont' (*Belfast Telegraph*, 4 January 1988). A motion proposed, and passed overwhelmingly, by East Londonderry Constituency Unionist Association at the UUP conference in 1987 stated:

> This conference of the Ulster Unionist Party would not accept a system of Devolved Government for Northern Ireland whose decisions were subject to a veto by any minority within it or which was created within and overshadowed by the Anglo-Irish Agreement and Anglo-Irish Conference. (UUP, 1987)

Therefore, until the Joint Unionist Task Force went outside its remit and proposed talks and devolution, those arguing for such a solution were confined to small pressure groups on the fringes of the UUP or individuals making speeches or statements.

However, despite this constitutional debate, none of the arguments were new or significantly influenced by the Agreement. Its lasting legacy was to emerge in early 1988 as many newspapers were predicting the destruction of the accord over a number of diplomatic disagreements between the British and the Irish governments, which included the Birmingham Six,[7] The Gibraltar shootings,[8] the McAnespie case,[9] the Stalker–Sampson inquiry[10] and new Irish Taoiseach Charles Haughey's less than enthusiastic support for the Agreement.[11] In this climate Unionists began to make noises about North–South relations. In February John Taylor, in a radio interview, alluded to a Dublin–Unionist rapprochement when he argued that Dublin and Belfast had a better understanding of each other than London had of either (*Belfast Telegraph*, 20 February 1988). Two days later Harold McCusker gave an extraordinary interview on television and said:

> We have always wanted to co-operate for our mutual advantage, and have increasingly – maybe through force of circumstances – come to realise that the Dublin government believes it has a legitimate interest in Northern Ireland, in its role towards the minority community. We were told that that was being met through the Anglo-Irish Agreement. That was a heavy price for us to pay to meet that particular

commitment, and if Unionists can meet it by some other means, I think we should explore those means. (*News Letter*, 23 February 1988)

Moreover, it was not just Ulster Unionists that were proposing a new relationship with Dublin. Leading figures in the DUP were also active in this revisionism. Paisley was the first to speak publicly about proposals put to Tom King in January 1988 when he said in a speech in his own constituency in Ballymena:

The British government must be present at round table talks, and these would be for some sort of devolution. But there would be no room for the Eire government in an internal settlement. When this settlement has been hammered out, then we can come to grips with the Dublin government. But we would only be doing this as equals and not with the British government involved... You only talk to a head of government when you have something to say. We have nothing to say at this stage, but there may be when we have an internal settlement. (*News Letter*, 19 April 1988)

This accurately reflects the position on talks or negotiations held by most Unionists at this time and was reproduced at length by David Trimble at a conference held in Keele University on 'Consensus in Ireland' (Trimble, 1988). The formal compromise on an Irish dimension as a facet of the solution did not occur until the Mayhew talks in 1992 (Bew and Gillespie, 1999, 268) but the assertion that Northern Ireland should deal with the Republic on an equal basis and through an internal dimension of any settlement was to be the Unionist bottom-line negotiating position from 1988 until the 1998 talks. This is evident by the UUP reaction to the draft Mitchell document and its provision for a North/South Ministerial Council deriving its functions and authority from London and Dublin (Hennessey, 2000, 159–68). However, the purest expression of the Unionist position is seen in the negotiations with Dublin during the 1992 talks. Here the Unionists proposed an 'Inter-Irish Relations Committee of the Assembly operating within a wider Britannic framework' developed by Trimble (Hennessey, 2000, 64).

It is at the North–South level that the AIA was crucial in fostering a more sophisticated analysis of the Northern Ireland conflict by Unionists. The Agreement forced Unionists to see the solution as part of a wider, and more complex set of relations. They began to absorb 'Humespeak' and spoke of the 'totality of relations' but extending the definition beyond Hume's to include Great Britain. Unionists began to see a hitherto elusive security and stability in defining and conditioning these relationships. As Sammy Wilson, of the DUP, said when talking of the failure of the Brooke talks:

> We had a very great interest in Strand 2, because it was our view that if you could cement something at Strand 2, you stopped the drift that there had been since the Agreement, you drew a line in the sand and defined what co-operation between Northern Ireland and the Irish Republic means... [But] the agreement [on the talks formula] was that there had to be 'substantial' progress in Strand 1, and we would not have committed ourselves to a Strand 2 meeting without substantial progress. (As quoted in Bloomfield, 1998, 140–1)

This explains, in many ways, why the Unionist argument against the Belfast Agreement of Good Friday 1998 focused disproportionately on the non-constitutional aspects. Issues such as positions in government for ex-terrorists held real emotional and political problems for Unionists, whereas constitutional issues, as defined by Unionists, held the possibility of removing the Unionist sense of siege.

Therefore, by focusing on the AIA as 'coercive consocation' we neglect the most important impact that it had on Northern Ireland's parties. However, it is worth examining what effects the Agreement had on Unionist attitudes to Northern Ireland. The first and immediate effect was the exact opposite to what O'Leary and McGarry allege was the intent of the two governments. Unionism did not fragment but united and maintained that united front into the early 1990s. On four occasions within the first year and a half of the Agreement, Unionists demonstrated the size of their opposition. The two rallies at the City Hall in Belfast attracted crowds of 200,000 people each; the by-elections in 1986 brought a combined Unionist vote of 418,000 and the petition to the Queen in January 1987 collected 402,752 signatures. Unionists were, and remained, totally united in their opposition to the AIA (Cox, 1987). Secondly, the Agreement actually decreased the possibility of constitutional negotiations and a settlement. It has already been noted that the AIA created problems for devolutionists articulating their case but on a more general level it acted as a handbrake to talks. Unionists were adamant that constitutional negotiations would not take place within the framework offered by the agreement for a number of reasons, some of which are illustrated by the following quotation from Ian Paisley:

Unionists have always desired talks with the other constitutional parties in Northern Ireland and remain willing to enter such talks. They are not 'Johnny come Latelies' to the idea of talks, unlike the SDLP, the Roman Catholic Church and the British and Dublin governments, all of whom refused point-blank to talk to unionists before or during the process which led to the signing of the Anglo-Irish Agreement...Now the clamour is to talk while the gun of the agreement is pointed at the heads of unionists. (*News Letter*, 25 March 1988)

Even the low-key talks (but not, as Unionists were at pains to point out, negotiations) with Tom King which began on 14 September 1987 were conducted on the very narrow mandate that was contained in the joint UUP–DUP manifesto for the 1987 General Election which stated:

We will urgently seek to ascertain whether the new government is prepared to create the circumstances and conditions necessary to encourage successful negotiations, including the suspension of the working of the Agreement and of the Maryfield Secretariat. (UUP and DUP, 1987)

It is worth noting that the Unionist pact began to fracture in the early 1990s over the prospect of talks with Dublin and not, as O'Leary and McGarry argue should have happened, over talks with the SDLP.

Unionists have been retrospectively criticised by academics such as Feargal Cochrane for their supposedly self-defeating and regressive policies and strategies in this period (Cochrane, 1997). However, Unionists had good cause for an inflexible position. Cochrane has argued that the current phase in Anglo-Irish relations has been marked by an isolation of both communities and political elites in Northern Ireland and that:

The two sovereign governments are primarily concerned with maintaining good relations with *one another*, rather than working for the achievement of more fundamental political objectives such as Irish unity or the preservation of the Union (Cochrane, 1994, 381, italics in original).

The nature of this isolation of the communities has been challenged. Paul Dixon has argued that 'there is a fundamental *imbalance* rather than *symmetry* in the relationships between the British government and the

Unionists on one hand, and the Irish government and the Nationalists on the other' (Dixon, 1995, 497 italics in original) and this was most evident in the aftermath of the AIA.

In a situation where the framework of negotiations contains a bias against you, it would be foolish to enter into those negotiations without trying to change the framework. In a manner envisaged by O'Leary and McGarry, Unionists would have spent much of their negotiating energies compromising on trying to remove the Agreement while conceding ground on other issues that would otherwise have been of paramount importance. In fact, it could be argued that this did happen in 1998. The Brooke talks spent 2 years trying to negotiate a way around this problem and Unionists eventually secured a quasi-suspension before entering into dialogue. Indeed, Bloomfield argues that during this process 'the important concession had been wrung from both governments that the Agreement was, at least in principle, replaceable' (Bloomfield, 1998, 170). However, it is significant that these talks, ostensibly the pre-planned progression from the AIA according to O'Leary and McGarry, failed, at least in part, because of the AIA context. Through Unionist perceptions of its structural inequality, it was the Agreement that imposed an arbitrary and very short time limit on the negotiations that contributed to their failure. The change in government thinking and the movement from exclusion to inclusion of paramilitaries in the political process changed the political context from the sterile environment of the AIA, based on Nationalist assumptions which fostered Unionist unity, to a context where the original AIA was no longer the framework for negotiations. This was accompanied by changes in Unionist relations with the Republic of Ireland and the fracturing of the Unionist pact. This change gave Unionists who wanted the opportunity to participate in the definition of the four-way relationships to do so and to have a crucial role in shaping the institutions created to reflect these relationships.

Conclusion

The interconnections between political events and ideas are crucial to understanding the dynamics of Unionist politics. Events shape and constrain the actions of political leaders and parties but, simultaneously, the reflexive nature of political debate means that developments cannot be analysed in a void outside the responses of the subject community. The AIA demonstrates these issues. The inter-communal conflict was addressed by the altering of the balance of relationships between Unionism and Nationalism. This would have crucial effects on Unionist attitudes towards the 'peace process'. The roots of pro- and anti-Belfast Agreement Unionism are to be found in the period immediately following the AIA. The AIA created a disjuncture between political developments and Unionist interests. This was particularly evident with respect to the divergence between British Government policy and Unionist interests; we have seen how the British Government was rhetorically sponsoring Unionists but yet was pursuing a policy which Unionists perceived as inimical to their interests. It could be argued that this disjuncture occurred with the proroguing of Stormont but the AIA seems like a significant staging post in this relationship in that the British Government was clearly *defining* how it saw the relationships involved in the conflict and how they were to develop rather than merely responding to political crises. The AIA was more than simply the latest in a long line of British Government 'betrayals'.

The origins of anti-Belfast Agreement Unionism can be seen here. Anti-Agreement Unionism rests on disquiet with the nature of political developments and the AIA isolated the Unionist argument at the genesis of the process and this meant that Unionists never owned the process; they were merely carried by the Nationalist analysis. This is not to say that they did not make substantial gains or shape the resulting (Belfast) Agreement but the forces shaping the accommodation with Nationalism, starting with the AIA, contained a bias in favour of Nationalists. This bias was manifested by the asymmetrical structure of the AIA, the asymmetry of the options which it presented and the prioritisation of the SDLP argument. The protests against the AIA were partly an objection to this alteration but the concerns of Unionists were inadequately addressed and it is here that we find the roots of modern day anti-Agreement Unionism. Chapter 4 will elucidate the Unionist interpretation of the peace process in general but it is sufficient to note here how the sense of marginalisation that is part of the Unionist experience of the process of political change can be found in the ideas and policies of the AIA; by excluding Unionists from the AIA process (indeed not even informing them it was taking place), the Agreement merely created the conditions whereby a large section of Unionism saw anything that happened as inimical to their interests.

Conversely, the roots of pro-Agreement Unionism are to be found in other areas of re-analysis in the aftermath of the AIA, although there is no neat correlation between integration or devolution and support or opposition for the Belfast Agreement. It may seem paradoxical that McCartney can claim influence for the introduction of pluralism into

Unionist ideas given his subsequent opposition to the Belfast Agreement of Good Friday 1998 but Chapter 4 will show that the ideological leanings of Unionists are less important than an assessment of the benefits of the Agreement in explaining divisions after 1998. Instead, the integrationist reflection on the nature of the political system operating in Northern Ireland and the British State created a powerful rhetoric and argument that Unionists utilised. Integrationist thinking had a significant impact on Unionism and has provided Trimble with his 'Pluralist Parliament for a Pluralist People' (Trimble, 2001, 79) and also on the introduction of key ideas to Unionist discourses on national identity. In this way McCartney is correct when he says:

> I think where possibly my role in Unionist politics in Northern Ireland has not been so important in terms of party numbers or party size, I think it's real importance has been in the contribution of ideas... and I sometimes smile quietly to myself when I see phrases and statements issued by, among others, David Trimble when the name plate on them is as obvious as the UKUP [United Kingdom Unionist Party] on that door and I haven't been aware of anyone else, I may be wrong I don't want to sound ego centred, maybe because there are few people who are doing it and therefore those who are do do it are more evident, but I don't find any great writings or any great analysis addressing politically or philosophically the problems of Unionism. (Interview with Robert McCartney, 19 September 2002)

The integration debate is more significant than has been hitherto appreciated. It was more than mere intellectual abstraction because of two factors. First the CEC was active in proselytising its message, and second the debate was a real political issue in Unionist branch meetings across Northern Ireland and at Ulster Unionist conferences. The actual nature of this ideological development has been discussed in Chapter 1 but in terms of its practical effect on the UUP, it should be acknowledged as extensive. It is perhaps significant that the DUP did not engage in such a debate and also that DUP activists are less likely to speak in terms familiar to integrationists.

3
Unionism in Local Government

Chapters 1 and 2 have taken a holistic approach to Unionism and has looked for and identified common strands within Unionism relating to ideas and political and strategic analysis. When differences have taken on an institutional character, insofar as they have been reflected in political parties, these have been noted, such as the differences between the culture of debate in the UUP and the DUP. This chapter begins to explore these institutional differences in a more sustained manner. It does so by considering a neglected aspect in analyses of Unionist division and party politics by examining Unionism at a local level. The local level is where Unionist competition has been most intense and provides important indicators of how the local political parties operate and perceive themselves and each other, in particular when the key issues at local level intersect with the key issues on a provincial one. Local Government in Northern Ireland is not usually considered as an important area of study because of its lack of powers and lack of political status. However, this chapter will argue that the politics of local government is highly significant as to how we analyse political relations between the UUP and the DUP and between Unionists and Nationalists.

Four local government areas have been chosen and these will allow a comparative study to provide important conclusions on the nature of the two Unionist political parties, the nature of Unionist party politics and the nature of Unionist interaction with Nationalism. The four areas are Ballymena Borough Council (BBC), Derry City Council (DCC) (which is also coterminous with the Foyle Westminster constituency), Fermanagh District Council (FDC) and Craigavon Borough Council (CBC). In order to examine these different elements of Unionism it was necessary to select a cross-section of councils that would include urban/rural areas, Unionists-controlled/Nationalist-controlled and marginal councils and councils with differing Unionist majority parties. Therefore Ballymena is a Unionist-controlled council with minimal Nationalist representation which has a strong DUP presence (although the party in the majority changes over the course of the study). Derry City Council is an urban, SDLP-dominated council with the DUP as the strongest Unionist party. Fermanagh is a marginal rural council that has been UUP dominated and has had a very weak DUP presence but with fluctuating SF strength. Craigavon is a largely urban, Unionist majority council, with a strong Nationalist presence but has been controlled by the UUP. The research is a combination of extensive studies of local newspapers, which have been supplemented and supported by interviews with a selection of the major Unionist councillors in the respective areas and the minutes of the local council meetings.

Through these studies several key questions are addressed: How do Unionists act when they are in a minority? How do the party structures of the UUP and the DUP work at a local level? How does political party affect relationships with Nationalists? What are the political divisions within and between the Unionist parties?

Local Government politics

The political institutions in the local council chambers deserve consideration because they are not well known and yet are the institutions with which local politicians in Northern Ireland are most well acquainted. Local Government elections are held every 4 years and around 500 councillors are elected to 26 councils using the Single Transferable Vote electoral system. There are three types of council – district, borough and city – and they vary in size from the very small Moyle District Council with a population of 15,933 to BCC's 277,391.[1] The powers and functions of local government have been extremely limited since 1973. In 1969 the then Minister for Development, Brian Faulkner, appointed a body to review the practice of local government. The Macrory Report, as it became known, recommended two levels of executive responsibility: a regional level and a district level. Education, health, welfare and child care, planning, roads and traffic management, motor taxation, housing, water and major sewerage systems, tourism, electoral arrangements, criminal injuries compensation, gas, electricity, transport, major harbours and fire were to be regional responsibilities. Four area boards were recommended for education and health for the day-to-day management of these regional services. The number of councils was to be reduced from 73 to no more than 26 (Birrell and Murie, 1980). The Macrory Report was explicitly designed to operate in a context where there was a regional parliament and government at Stormont but when Stormont was prorogued Macrory's recommended system of local government was retained, which left little power in local hands.

The structure of local government is straightforward. Most decisions are made in committee and are then taken for ratification by the full council. Annually, the full council elects a Lord Mayor, Mayor or Chairman (depending on the status of the council) and his/her deputy selects the composition of each of the committees and representatives on outside bodies. Until recently all of these appointments have been made by majority vote. As has been noted, local councils have limited powers and the ceremonial positions have largely symbolic value and this makes it slightly difficult to talk of governmental systems in a meaningful sense. Yet, given the lack of local input into the majority of government decisions and the deficiency in democratic accountability, local government has to be considered as an important site of political activity. Between 1998 and 2003, 77 per cent of MLAs had experience of local government and many held prominent positions in the local community and political organisations.

The relationship between party politics and local government is not clear and this is not just in Northern Ireland (Copus, 2004). Local government is a curious half-way house between public administration and politics in Northern Ireland. The majority of issues for which local councils have responsibility or which concern local communities are not even issues which are party political, let alone products of the communal divide. Many of the councillors interviewed for these studies expressed the opinion that on local matters political affiliation was irrelevant. Joe Miller (DUP Londonderry) said:

> I mean poverty is totally unsectarian ... if a street light isn't working outside your mother's house or my mother's house, a street light doesn't know whether you're a Unionist or a Nationalist. Good roads, good rates, the development of our city, young people, jobs, something which we can all work together. 90% of council business is about the ordinary bread and butter issues. Certainly council divides right down the sectarian middle when we get to the border or the big issues ... That is a very, very small ... part of council work that we actually do. (Interview with Joe Miller, 16 September 2002)

Moreover, there are a number of councillors, particularly in the east of Northern Ireland, who believe that political parties should not be associated with local government. Jack Allen (UUP Antrim Borough Council), who was Northern Ireland's longest serving Mayor, proclaimed during a debate on the Framework Documents in Antrim council that it was:

> Very sad that the matter had been brought up at council. I am not a politician, I am a councillor to do what I can for the people of Antrim. No matter what we say it won't change the situation one iota. (*Ballymena Guardian*, 19 April 1995)

Within the council, party is a less than accurate predicator for voting behaviour on the majority of issues and the party whip system is used infrequently. This is particularly evident within communal blocs and in Unionist-dominated councils with little Nationalist representation, such as Ballymena. In Ballymena, even the annual elections to the ceremonial posts and committees seem less overtly party political. The majority of Mayoral appointments were made unanimously, although determined by political party, and frequently the UUP seconded the DUP's nomination. Almost all of the Mayoral appointments between 1985 and 1998 were unopposed. This is perhaps due to the particular candidate and a tradition of long-standing Mayors; the DUP's Alexander (Sandy) Spence was Mayor for 15 years from 1977 to 1993 and was subsequently given Freedom of the Borough after the UUP regained control of the council.

However, the introduction of party politics is one of the most important developments in local government since the beginning of the Troubles. Birrell and Hayes point out that prior to reorganisation in 1973 most council seats were uncontested, a pattern that was irrevocably changed in 1973 (Birrell and Hayes, 1999, 91), although that was due, at least in part to the important changes in the party system in Northern Ireland from the 1967 local government elections. Councils became organised on this new party politics and councillors are elected on a party ticket. Moreover, the proportional representation (PR) electoral system negated the need for any electoral pacts such as those in place for the Westminster elections and there was therefore open competition between all the parties.

Birrell and Hayes' survey research indicates that party is important for the initial decision to stand for election, as around 50 per cent of their respondents cited a request from a political party as the impetus for this decision (Birrell and Hayes, 1999, 106) and it is also important for a successful campaign, as the number of independents has declined to around 6 per cent of the returned candidates in 2001[2] from 14 per cent in 1973 (derived from Elliott and Flackes, 1999). There are also a number of overtly party political issues in the local council chamber, most notably the annual elections for the ceremonial positions of Mayor or Chairperson, their deputies and representation on council committees. Nevertheless, representing a political party is a notable and distant second place to a desire to represent the community in the reasons cited for becoming a councillor (Birrell and Hayes, 1999, 105). Therefore, while it is impossible to argue that party politics is irrelevant to local government, the actual role of the party is somewhat circumscribed.

Unionists political parties and local government

There are a number of key themes in relation to Unionist political parties which are evident in local government politics: the role of religious belief; class dimensions; the balance between civic responsibility and communal representation; the role of Protestant social structures; and the importance of contingent factors.

Religion

The most influential analysis of the DUP is that of Steve Bruce. Bruce argues that Paisleyism, and therefore the DUP, is intimately connected with evangelical Protestantism. First, evangelical Protestants were over-represented in the party, particularly in terms of elected representatives (Bruce, 1987). Secondly, evangelical Protestantism is a core part of the ethnic identity of Ulster Unionists (Bruce, 1994, 25). Thirdly, as the support for the DUP is in excess of the numbers of evangelical Protestants in the population, the broader population must recognise this brand of Protestantism as particularly useful. Bruce suggests that Protestants prefer their representatives to be members of this brand of Protestantism because it is recognised as more secure and less likely to compromise than other Protestant denominations (Bruce, 1989; 1994). Clifford Smyth extended this argument through his analysis of the DUP's methods of electioneering and organisation and called the party a 'politico-religious organisation' (Smyth, C, 1986) and Paisley the 'voice of Protestant Ulster' (Smyth, 1987). The DUP in Ballymena conform to the dominant stereotype of the party. It is dominated by activists who do not make the distinction between religion and politics and its conception of politics in Northern Ireland is zero-sum, therefore every issue takes on an importance that most would assume is not warranted. There is little evidence of pragmatism but there are a few interesting anomalies. The first is the problems that are coterminous with running an electorally successful party. This means there are more members and more elected representatives and therefore a greater number of viewpoints to take into consideration. In areas such as Fermanagh, where the party has remained small, cohesion has not been a significant problem. In Northern Ireland as a whole, the party has not had much time for dissenters or mavericks within its ranks, and their experience has usually resulted in retirement from politics. Ballymena provides evidence that this was the favoured method of discipline, as shown by the experience of Fred Coulter, who was pushed out of the DUP after he had difficulties with some DUP policies and practices (*Ballymena Guardian*, 20 December 1995), and also interesting evidence that the party is more restricted than its traditional strident dogmatism might suggest. The clash between religious values and political protest for some party members is an important tension that has not been fully appreciated and was shown by the retirement, in 1987, of John McAuley, the first DUP Mayor in Ballymena, because of the clash between his religious views and the protest campaign against the AIA (*Ballymena Guardian*, 5 March 1987). The difficulties that the DUP experienced in maintaining a united party were the result of these strains.

The borough also gives indications that the divisions between the two political parties are significantly more locality dependent than has previously been appreciated. The UUP in Ballymena is not the polar opposite of the DUP. It too consists of members who believe in strong links between religion and politics and this is shown in both the language used by their representatives and their position on key issues such as Sunday observance, where the DUP was not isolated in taking a fundamentalist religious policy. Even on overt political issues there were leading members of the UUP who took a quasi-DUP position. To dismiss this as political posturing or ethnic-outbidding would be a mistake because there were issues on which the UUP was not afraid to take a significantly different policy and nowhere was this more obvious than in relation to the Nationalists in the borough, an area where the 'dual ethnic party system model' would predict that the UUP would be most reluctant to offer concessions to Nationalists or show a 'liberal' attitude (Mitchell, 1995). In Ballymena, on 'Protestant' political or religious issues the UUP and the DUP were occupying narrow ground with few real differences between them but on 'borough' issues such as relations with Nationalists, the UUP cultivated real and ascertainable differences between the two parties.

Class

Londonderry Unionism is dominated by the DUP. This is partly accident, partly due to its efforts and partly due to the weakness of the UUP in the city. In the May 1985 local government elections both parties had five councillors but within a year the UUP had expelled their two most prominent and able councillors in a dispute over a boycott campaign against the changing of the name of the council. Without the services of Jim Guy and David Davis and with the most senior Unionist politician in the city, Jack Allen, too busy for local government, the UUP fell into a severe decline, which it was unable to halt effectively. The loss of Davis and Guy over the issue was more serious than the UUP would admit. Both were popular councillors. Guy held his Waterside seat as an independent until 2001 and Davis survived a serious electoral challenge by Jack Allen in 1989 only to lose his seat in 1993 because of the decline in Protestant numbers in the Fountain estate. The UUP also had a different candidate profile to the DUP. This is most visibly demonstrated by the 1989 elections. In 1989 the average age of the UUP candidates in the local government elections was 58 and a half years and the party did not have a candidate younger than Jack Allen who was 49. In contrast, the average age of the DUP candidates was 34 and a half years and it did not have a candidate over 39 years. The UUP was conscious of this problem and deliberately selected a number of younger candidates in 1993. That election saw the diminution of the UUP's representation to its lowest point, as only two candidates were returned: long-serving retired Second World War veteran John Adams and the young graduate Richard Dallas (*Londonderry Sentinel*, 8 April 1993). Dallas briefly altered the fortunes of the UUP when he topped the poll in the Waterside ward in 1997, ahead of Gregory Campbell, but the renaissance was brief.

Traditional theories of the DUP have identified two strands to the DUP: a rural religious party and an urban secular party (Moloney and Pollak, 1986, 299–300; Cochrane, 1997, 45–7). The development of the latter is credited to Peter Robinson, who built up a power base in East Belfast independent of Paisley (Moloney and Pollak, 1986, 293–4) and Clifford Smyth who established the QUB branch of the party, which was the entry point for many of the secular members of the party (Moloney and Pollak, 1986, 296–8). The evidence from Londonderry would support this thesis and also provides some important modifications. It is obvious that a political style similar to Ballymena was not going to be effective or popular in Londonderry and therefore there would appear to be a clear urban/rural division within the DUP. However, it is also obvious that Robinson was neither responsible for nor had any significant influence over the direction of the DUP in the city. It would suggest that the DUP was sensitive to changes in the political environment and also that there is more to the DUP than simply an evangelicalism that strikes a chord with Unionist voters (Bruce, 1994, 25). Indeed, in Londonderry, we see a party which would accord more closely with Desmond Boal's original vision for the DUP: 'right wing in the sense of being strong on the Constitution, but to the left on social policies' and would have a democratic infrastructure and would be responsive to grass-roots opinion (Smyth, 1987, 29–30). Paisley himself realised that his previous emphasis on religious issues would 'ghettoise' his new party and so the DUP represented a synthesis of Boal's secular radicalism and Paisley's religious fundamentalism (Smyth, 1987, 30). This study of Londonderry Unionism indicates that the appeal of the DUP to working-class Unionists is not that these Unionists like to be represented by evangelicals but that the DUP changes the nature of its appeal. It would be naïve to assume that this was mere populism on the DUP's part but there is clear evidence of a secular political party with a particular political agenda originating from the party's roots; it is one which is becoming more evident as the party positions itself for government in a Northern Ireland Assembly.

Civic responsibility vs. Communal representation

There is an underlying tension in the discourse of many of Northern Ireland's political parties. There is an appeal to the greater civic good and at least lip service paid to the idea that parties have a responsibility to the good governance of Northern Ireland. On the other hand, there is a more particular, and perhaps stronger, attachment to the idea of communal representation. However, this tension is not readily apparent from the behaviour of the MPs at Westminster. It was an issue on occasion in the Assembly, although that institution was not established for long enough to fully draw out the implications. Nevertheless, there was an expectation of Ministers that, in executing their duties, they would abandon the communal representation in favour of civic responsibility; among other things, the pledge of office required Ministers 'to serve all the people of Northern Ireland equally, and to act in accordance with the general obligations on government to promote equality and prevent discrimination' (HMSO, 1998, 10). Local government did, however, illustrate the tensions between the two positions. In particular the role of Chairman or Mayor as an institution provided a moderating influence upon politicians and an important rhetorical weapon for use in instances where an individual was seen to place communal interests first. This was most clearly the case when the SF Chairman of Fermanagh District Council could only express regret and sympathies rather than condemnation at the Remembrance Day bomb in Enniskillen in 1987. The SDLP and the UUP joined together to propose a motion of no confidence in the chair when the council reconvened after two weeks of adjournment. The SDLP leader on the Council stated:

> We feel that Fermanagh District Council did not have a Chairman as such when the tragedy occurred... When it came to the tragedy he saw fit to act as the leader or mouthpiece of his party, rather than represent all of the people when they were most crying out to be represented. (*Impartial Reporter*, 26 November 1987)

The UUP was more likely to prioritise civic responsibility over communal representation as a matter of course. This was clearly shown in Fermanagh. The UUP dominate Unionist politics in Fermanagh and here the party is well organised, efficiently run and able to attract professionals, who have opted out of local government politics elsewhere in Northern Ireland. Simultaneously it has maintained the position of the nobility and attracted the working-class people. The nature of society has allowed a conciliatory and pragmatic Unionism to flourish with relative impunity from attack from the DUP. Perhaps more important is how the UUP has maintained their self-image as the *Official* Unionist Party. The UUP has functioned as a broad church, accommodating many varying interests and opinions (Farrington, 2003b), and it has also kept a sense that it is a party of government linked to the idea of civic responsibility. Thus Sam Foster stressed that the UUP was 'responsible' and Bertie Kerr argued that the party was 'honest' and 'open', wanting to look after the general needs of the people of Northern Ireland (Interview with Bertie Kerr, 8 October 2002; Interview with Sam Foster, 27 September 2002).

The DUP, on the other hand, had greater difficulty with finding a balance. In Fermanagh and Craigavon there was very little pressure on their representatives to find such a balance, as they were not in a position to take up civic posts. The situation was different, however, in Ballymena and Derry. In Ballymena, Sandy Spence shouldered most of the burden of this tension. He saw the position of Mayor as an institution and not as a reward for electoral success and, by becoming synonymous with that institution, insulated some of his colleagues from those pressures. In Derry, however, this was not the case. The SDLP was clearly uneasy appointing DUP councillors to civic positions and there was an extensive internal debate before they finally offered William Hay the Deputy Mayor position in 1991 (*Londonderry Sentinel*, 18 July 1991). What is perhaps more significant is the shift in Hay's rhetoric from his somewhat belligerent acceptance speech to a defence of his record in January 1992:

> As Deputy Mayor of this city ... I have tried to represent both sections of the community because it is my duty to do so. Every week I deal with nationalist minded people and do so without hesitation ... I must state that I have never watered down my principles and, if elected to the position of Mayor, I would never consider doing so. There is a myth that a strong unionist could not represent the whole of this city. But I have always held strong unionist views and yet have given adequate representations to all sections of this city (*Londonderry Sentinel*, 9 January 1992; *Derry Journal*, 7 January 1992).

This was further bolstered by his acceptance speech on becoming Mayor:

> I will do all I can to represent this city to the best of my ability and, in doing so, represent all of the citizens of this city ... But I am a Unionist of a very strong tradition and make no apology for it ... I am conscious there is another tradition in this city and I hope in my year I will demonstrate that. This is a city at peace with itself and I want to encourage prosperity and investment for the benefit of all. (*Londonderry Sentinel*, 4 June 1992)

The manner in which the DUP and the UUP negotiate these concepts is key to understanding the dynamics of Unionist party competition and represents one of the most important, and neglected, differences between the two parties.

Contingency

Unlike Fermanagh, the UUP in Craigavon resembles a loose federation of independent fiefdoms. The management of the party thus centred on issues associated with locality. Until 1989 the local DUP leader was

David Calvert. He was a fiercely anti-Catholic Free Presbyterian and dominated the council. Overall the council was characterised by bitter sectarian arguments, which earned it the reputation as one of the most divided councils in Northern Ireland; more than one councillor decided against seeking re-election on the basis of frustration at this state of affairs.[3] Many of the established patterns on CBC were ended in 1989 when a long-running local issue had important effects on the political parties. In 1978, CBC had initially agreed to lease a piece of wasteland to St Peter's Social and Recreation Club for development as Gaelic sports pitches. The council then changed its mind and refused permission for the lease, a decision which the club contested in the courts. The club was finally granted a land lease 8 years after the initial application but the council vote was only passed after eight Unionists abstained to avoid challenging a judge's ruling. In November 1986 the club won a court case granting them damages of £125,000 and costs. The judgement was damning and stated that the decision not to lease the land 'was motivated by sectarian bias through the unjustified action of the majority of the council' (*Portadown Times*, 28 November 1986). In September 1987, the local government auditors announced they were to carry out an 'extraordinary audit' of the council's accounts, with the open possibility of surcharging councillors. Councillors could be surcharged and disqualified under Section 81 of the Local Government Act, 'by whose negligence or misconduct the loss of deficiency has been occurred' (*Portadown Times*, 11 September 1987).

The local government auditors surcharged seventeen councillors serving on the council between 1977 and 1985 the sum of £13,277 each. Despite the auditors' findings, the council still did not approve St Peter's application without more manoeuvrings, including trying to stipulate that the club build a high wall on one side of the ground (*Portadown Times*, 21 October 1988; *Portadown Times*, 7 October 1988). The councillors appealed against the surcharge but this only had mixed results. A further four councillors were exonerated and the surcharge was reduced to a total of £90,000 but this still meant that twelve councillors would be disqualified from holding council office. The group included six former Mayors and five of the six DUP councillors (*Portadown Times*, 3 March 1989; *Portadown Times*, 17 March 1989).

The disqualification had long-lasting ramifications. Fred Crowe described the saga: 'It was a grievance and a victory...and left the Unionists sore' (Interview with Fred Crowe, 19 November 2002). Many of the councillors disqualified only returned to local government after a long period and local representatives have cited it as a watershed which heralded much improved relations between Unionists and Nationalists in the council. Mervyn Carrick, for instance, argued:

> St Peters was probably, on reflection, a watershed . . . and there was a recognition particularly by the new councillors who came in to replace the surcharged councillors that we had to pick up the pieces. We had to start building again because of the poor image and the poor relations that were in the council at that time. But it's also got to be said that the St Peter's affair left open sores for a number of years and it was a slow healing process and it's a tribute to those nationalist councillors and to those Unionist councillors who worked in that environment through those years of the 90s in order to reassert and re-establish Craigavon as a leading local authority. (Interview with Mervyn Carrick, 21 October 2002)

Describing political relations in the council George Savage stated: 'Most certainly they've changed over the last number of years . . . I'm not disputing the fact that 12, 14 years ago the working relationship in Craigavon Borough Council just wasn't what everybody would have desired it to be.' When asked what the catalyst had been for change he replied: 'Personnel . . . Different personalities are now on the council' (Interview with George Savage, 18 November 2002). Mervyn Carrick concurred arguing that the new faces brought new ideas:

> I think there was a recognition that Craigavon could go on tearing itself apart on these constitutional issues and at the same time make no progress on economic and social welfare for the people. So, without any agreement being negotiated, those on the nationalist side and those on the unionist side just, if you like, 'wised up' and said 'OK if Craigavon is going to be one of the leading 26 councils in Northern Ireland we better begin to look at the bread and butter issues and give a bit of time to those and not be continually caught up with the constitutional issue, important as it is.' (Interview with Mervyn Carrick, 21 October 2002)

This affair demonstrates the crucial role that contingency and personality play within these relationships and illustrates that there are remaining traditional elements of the Northern Irish party system (McAllister, 1983b). The DUP and the UUP party structures were heavily reliant on prominent local personalities for electoral success. The DUP position in the council was disproportionately affected by the disqualifications following the St Peter's affair. It would have been unlikely that any of these councillors would have been ousted from their position of local leadership without the extraordinary events of the local government audit. Similarly, the same event removed the personalities from the DUP who were, arguably, the greatest hindrance to progress in the council and this was consolidated by a split in the local party over candidate selection (*Portadown Times*, 16 April 1993; 23 April 1993; 7 May 1993; 14 May 1993), which permanently excluded them from public life. These changes were perhaps the single most important factor in changing local government politics in Craigavon as they simultaneously removed obstacles to better relations and demonstrated to those replacing them that those relations could not stay as they were.

The role of Protestant social organisations

Political parties are organised locally and it is an examination of this organisation that gives important insights into Unionist politics. A qualitative analysis of comparable local government areas gives important data on party competition. In particular, it reveals that the relationship between political parties and Protestant and Unionist social organisations, particularly the Orange Order and the Apprentice Boys, is an important variable in explaining variations in the support of the UUP and the DUP. The Orange Order is widely considered an atavistic organisation and many would interpret it as existing purely for exercising Protestant supremacy over Catholics. Its role within the Protestant community has been seen as providing opportunities for reinforcing group definition, particularly through its parades (Bryan, 2000a). Nationalists have traditionally credited the Orange Order with strong malignant powers over the political system in Northern Ireland and obstructing movement towards justice and equality for Nationalists (Farrell, 1980). However, this interpretation of the Order does not allow a full appreciation of its role in Northern Irish politics and society. The most important role has traditionally been its strong links with the UUP, which helped create strong territorial diffusion of that party. It is a well-remarked observation that the connections between the UUP and the Orange Order go further than the 120 delegates (of the total 860) the Order sends to the UUC, the governing body of the UUP. Harbinson remarked in his 1973 study of the party: 'It is obvious that local Unionist associations show a preference for Orangemen as candidates; indeed it would be reasonable to assume from the evidence that most local associations insist on membership of the Orange Institution as a necessary qualification for selection as a candidate' (Harbinson, 1973, 79).

The overt political power of the Order was also remarked upon by William McCrea (DUP former MP and MLA):

> When I was a young person and even when I was standing in elections in 1973 it was a great thing if you had the official stamp of the hierarchy of the Orange Institution; that was very, very important to you if you were standing in elections. (Interview with William McCrea, 26 November 2002)

The endorsement or lack of endorsement of a particular candidate no longer has the importance that it once did; nevertheless the sheer number of Orange members that are elected politicians does raise questions. The reason may not be as conspiratorial as Nationalists suspect if we adjust our analysis of the nature of the organisation away from one which simply stresses its importance in defining and reinforcing group boundaries. Eric Kaufman has recently conceptualised the Orange Order as a fraternal organisation (Kaufmann, 2002). This would give the Order a range of other functions, including the creation and development of social capital and in providing linkages between the political party and the grass roots. What is of crucial importance is that the social capital generated by the Orange Order represents an electoral resource that the UUP has utilised in its favour. Unionist politicians, both inside and outside the Order, have recognised this role. Jim Wells, a DUP MLA and a member of the Orange Order and its sister organisations the Royal Black Preceptory and the Apprentice Boys of Derry, argued:

> I find being in the Orange, I've been an Orangeman for 27 years, is extremely useful in my own constituency because Orangeism is very strong within the Unionist community in South Down. I get invited to lots of functions and banner unfurlings and hall openings and it keeps me in direct contact with grass roots Unionism right across the spectrum. (Interview with Jim Wells, 7 November 2002)

As a social organisation with, at least until recently, a substantial membership base, it provided an effective network of contacts and opportunities to speak in public. It has a strong claim to the title of the largest community-based organisation in the Protestant community, and its halls, which are a common feature of most small villages in Northern Ireland, would regularly hold many community events. The significance of this is that these networks have been reserved for the UUP and the DUP, with a few exceptions, has not had the same unrestrained access to these networks. For example, at a basic level, most UUP branch meetings take place in Orange Halls whereas, with one exception (Ballymena), DUP meetings do not.

If the Orange Order provides a range of organisational and electoral resources for the UUP then this has structurally disadvantaged the DUP. However, it also provides explanations for some of the unexplained dynamics of Unionist party competition. The rural–urban split no longer seems acceptable when we examine those constituencies where the DUP have been strong in relation to these considerations. The evidence would suggest that the Orange Order has faced disproportionate decline in the east of Northern Ireland and particularly in Belfast (Kaufman, 2002). This is unsurprising and, indeed, we would not expect such an organisation to be as strong in urban areas as it would be in the smaller rural areas. Putnam's research on similar organisations in America argued that, while there are important exceptions, urban areas lack the strong social networks of less urbanised areas (Putnam, 2000). Moreover, social dislocation in urban areas has been the subject of greater blame for declining social capital, perhaps even more so than urbanisation in general (Fukuyama, 1999).

The two major urban areas in Northern Ireland exemplify these trends. The conflict in Northern Ireland has been marked by stark territorial differentiation and Belfast and Derry have been two of the most intense areas of conflict. The late 1960s saw large population movements as the conflict destroyed many communities in both cities. For our purposes, the dislocation of the Protestant community in West and East Belfast and the Cityside of Derry is significant. Many of those Protestants who were moved from inner city of East Belfast were transplanted to various areas in what became the Castlereagh Borough Council area, which is widely regarded as Peter Robinson's bailiwick. The widespread disruption of communities both through dislocation and the conflict more generally removed the barriers that prevented the DUP from making electoral breakthroughs elsewhere. In Londonderry the particular situation was different but when we account for social changes and differences then DUP strength becomes explicable there also. Londonderry Unionists have experienced demographic change on a more exaggerated level than Unionists in the rest of Northern Ireland. There has been a net decrease in the Protestant population of the city of between 5000 and 6000 people between 1971 and 1991; this is combined with a decline of almost 84 per cent on the Cityside alone. This means that Londonderry has lost over one-third of its Protestant population in 20 years, in a city with a population growth of 8 per cent (Templegrove Action Research Limited, 1995). Therefore, Derry has experienced social dislocation, at least in the Protestant community, on a level comparable to Belfast. However, in addition, the social structures for Protestants differ significantly from the rest of Northern Ireland. In Derry it is not the Orange Order which is the major community organisation. Instead it has its own organisation, which is similar in terms of the functions it provides, called the Apprentice Boys of Derry. The differences in the political relationship between the Orange Order and the Apprentice Boys are also significant. The Apprentice Boys had a link with the UUP, like the Orange Order, but it was severed by the UUP in 1972 (Harbinson, 1973). Since then it has not taken any party political stance and it has acted as an organisation for Protestant unity in the city. Therefore, unlike the Orange Order, it has not had the effect of structurally disadvantaging the DUP. Indeed, unlike the Orange Order in most other areas of Northern Ireland, the UUP do not form the leadership of the Apprentice Boys, and DUP councillors are integrated into the social structure of the organisation.

This, however, does not explain the DUP strength in North Antrim and particularly BBC. Here the pattern is significantly different from other rural areas, such as Fermanagh and South Tyrone. Ian Paisley, leader and co-founder of the DUP, holds the North Antrim seat but he won the Stormont seat for part of the area, Bannside, in 1970, despite lacking strong ties with the constituency. Paisley had some childhood ties to the area (Moloney and Pollak, 1986) but his initial political career began in working-class West Belfast. The notable features of the background of DUP councillors in Ballymena is, first, their evangelical Protestant background (Bruce, 1987) and, secondly, their involvement in the Orange Order. If we take this approach emphasising the integration into the social networks of an area rather than emphasising the appeal evangelicalism may or may not have to a wider Protestant population then we can also explain the inability of the DUP to expand its electoral base before 2001. The Orange Order is a more effective organisation of political mobilisation than the churches for Unionist politicians because, although both are essentially communal organisations, it is able to transcend the legendary fragmentation of the Protestant religion (Boal, Campbell and Livingstone, 1991) by providing those functions relating to group definition. Evangelicals are therefore an electoral liability rather than an electoral asset. Their congregations are smaller and the more conservative fundamentalist they are (such as Paisley's supporters), the less likely they are to engage with other types of Protestant denominations (Boal, Keane and Livingstone, 1997, 83 and 103). They therefore have less social capital that can be used for electoral advantage. There have been some advantages to the close connections between the Free Presbyterian Church and the DUP, as Smyth has pointed out. The church resources such as minibuses for election use are not to be underestimated (Smyth, C., 1986). However, the religious morals of the members have also imposed limits on the type of fundraising the party can undertake. Activities involving gambling and dances have been ruled out. More specifically, the religiously informed politics and conservative morality have created difficulties for the DUP on occasions. In an infamous case, Ballymena DUP councillors banned Electric Light Orchestra (ELO) from playing a concert in Ballymena Showgrounds because it would lead to what one DUP councillor termed the '3 Ds': the devil, debauchery and drunkenness (*Ballymena Guardian*, 3 March 1993). This was widely credited with leading to the defeat of the DUP in the 1993 local government elections for the area for the first time in 16 years.

Nevertheless, the initial success of the DUP in Ballymena involved overcoming these obstacles by using the social networks of the Orange Order for party political gain. The clearest example is in how the DUP transformed Orange rituals into DUP platforms. The Orange Order's main public displays occur on 12 July when the members of the Order parade in major towns across Northern Ireland. The parade marches to what is referred to as 'the field' where the marchers and the supporters eat and drink before the return march. During this break at the field there are speeches from a temporary platform, which is usually given by a religious minister, a local Orange official and a prominent UUP politician, usually the MP for the area. However, the 12 July parades are preceded by a month of other locally organised events linked to the Twelfth and towns and estates are decorated by bunting and 'Orange Arches'. In Ballymena, the DUP have turned some of these events, particularly the erecting of the Orange Arch for the relevant housing estate into opportunities for public meetings and these platforms are always populated by DUP politicians, usually Paisley, linking the DUP to the Orange Order in a manner which it is not in the rest of Northern Ireland. Significantly, the main meeting place for the Order in Ballymena is not an Orange Hall but a 'Protestant Hall' and the DUP use this hall for their meetings, the only example I can find of the DUP using such a facility.

Thus, academics have, at best, missed an important aspect of DUP organisation and political support and, at worst, have misinterpreted how the DUP functions as a political party. The success of the DUP has been heavily conditioned by its level of integration into the social networks of Ulster Protestants. This now raises important questions about the nature of political change within Ulster Unionism, which will be addressed in Chapter 5.

Relationships with nationalism

As in the macro-level politics of Northern Ireland, there are many issues which have the potential to be contentious and these can be of a symbolic or a substantive nature. Before the cases and nature of these contentious issues are documented, it is worth reflecting on the balance between contentious and non-contentious, or even harmonious, politics. As we noted earlier, many local councillors have argued that party politics is not relevant to local government and that even the divisions in Northern Ireland are frequently absent from council work. It is, of course, easier to measure and document controversy and by examining instances of controversy we run the risk of over-representing its occurrence. It may also be the case that local newspapers are more likely to report controversy and conflict rather than harmony. Nevertheless, coupled with the widespread issues of political recognition, the specific instances of controversy are significant enough in magnitude to merit consideration.

There are too many issues of contention within each council to document each one or even to examine the most important from each. Instead, Table 3.1 gives a taxonomy of the types of issues which occurred across the study, the nature of the claims made and the methods that were used to try and rectify them. As we can see, there are two main types of claim: recognition and material. Material claims concern matters such as employment or funding controversies. Recognition claims are usually taken to include questions of identity expression and related to the ways in which the identities of social groups can be misrepresented or misunderstood.

Recognition

Conflict can be and is local, as Harvey Cox observes about the Drumcree dispute: 'What is going on in Portadown is not *simply* a facet of the Ulster conflict. The conflict in Portadown is a conflict *about* Portadown' (Cox, 2002, 154). For Catholic residents in Portadown the conflict over Drumcree is about their position within the town (Garvaghy Residents, 1999; Ryder and Kearney, 2001); in Ballymena local councillors called for protestors to end the picket of the Roman Catholic Harryville chapel

Table 3.1   Taxonomy of contentious issues in local government

Issue	Council	Nature of claim	Methods used	Recipient of claim
Sport	DCC, CBC	Material Recognition	Direct action Judicial action	Other community
Symbols/ Commemoration	DCC, CBC FDC, BBC	Recognition	Publicity Boycott	Other community
Employment	DCC, CBC	Material	Publicity Judicial action	Government
Investment	DCC, FDC	Material	Organisational Publicity	Other community/ Government
Position in City/ Borough/District	DCC, CBC FDC, BBC	Material Recognition	Organisational Publicity	Other community

because they had no control over the linked dispute in Dunloy, a neighbouring village in Antrim Borough Council area; in DCC, long-running Unionist complaints were intimately grounded in local government politics. Matters are not aided by the reluctance of local politicians to make explicit links to similar situations in other parts of Northern Ireland; each area is seen as having its own unique development and characteristics. Therefore the position of the minority community in the city, district or borough had the potential to be the most significant issue. In Fermanagh, where political relations were heated at times but were generally courteous, symbols became the ground upon which these debates took place. In Derry or Craigavon, however, symbols were only a small part of a dense network of grievances that centred on a larger question, such as the one asked by the Waterside Think Tank: 'Are we not part of this city too?' (Waterside Think Tank, 1999)

   This section will argue that political controversy in local government was largely the result of the attitude of the majority segment towards the minority, no matter which community occupies either position. These controversies have, at root, a particular type of claim that the different communities are making. National groups usually make claims to self-determination, although this may not be complete statehood, and these claims are usually externally legitimated (Keating, 2001, 1–28). These maximal claims are obviously inappropriate at local government level where it is not a form of self-determination which is sought, even though this could be realised by some form of communal autonomy. Instead, the claims of recognition are something more intangible, almost psychological, and go beyond mere partnership. More importantly, they are being made of the other community grouping.

The common approach to the resolution of these issues was to place them in the context of the resolution of the wider conflict and address them through inclusion in political structures. However, as the only site of local political influence, local government became contested as a model of how Unionists and Nationalists could relate to each other at the macro-level. The SDLP were the most vociferous in drawing conclusions and parallels and held DCC up as its model of a future, agreed, Northern Ireland. For example, the party's 1993 local government manifesto stated:

> The contrasting ways in which the two major urban centres in Northern Ireland are governed at a local level makes the case for partnership and dialogue in the Councils more clearly than any election manifesto ever could. Derry, with an SDLP majority, rotates the position of Mayor and this is currently held by a member of the DUP. More important than the sharing of positions however is the way in which Derry City Council is able to project a positive constructive image to the wider world . . . Belfast City Council, on the other hand, controlled at present by a Unionist coalition, has become a by-word for sectarian, obstructionist politics of a kind that most of us, of whatever political persuasion, hoped we had seen the last of over twenty years ago. (SDLP, 1993)

This depiction of DCC as a haven of political co-operation and peaceful coexistence does not stand up to any serious scrutiny and the issues that contradict the SDLP description are common to almost all local government areas. Therefore, even at a purely symbolic level, the importance of local government should not be underestimated.

While the council chambers were characterised by conflict and polarisation in the 1980s (Connolly and Knox, 1988), political relations between Unionists and Nationalists in local government in Northern Ireland have gradually improved. Councils used a variety of mechanisms to take 'politics' out of the council chambers. Frequently there was an understanding that they would not bring forward motions for debate which were outside the council's remit. This prevented divisive debates and bad feeling but the more effective mechanism was to remove the annual elections for the ceremonial positions from the realms of political deals and majoritarianism, such as when Fred Crowe in Craigavon was going to offer the SDLP the position of Deputy Mayor but saw its councillors 'laughing and consorting' with the SF councillors and promptly offered the position to the DUP (*Portadown Times*, 11 June 1993). Many district councils have introduced some kind of power sharing arrangement but the type of arrangement varies substantially and many have only emerged organically and sporadically in the 1990s (McKay and Irwin, 1995, 30–2). In local government, power sharing rarely meant the actual sharing of real power but merely a symbolic recognition that minorities were valued within the civic system. For our purposes here, however, power sharing has to include representatives of both communities and can be limited, involving rotating the ceremonial positions of Lord Mayor, Mayor, or Chairman and their deputies, or can be extended, which was also commonly practiced, and involves sharing the chairmanships and vice-chairmanships of the council's committees. Moreover, these arrangements could be formal or informal, codified or uncodified and the distinction was frequently crucial. The one recurrent theme of the experience of power sharing is that of representation. The issue does not change between councils. Whether it is a Unionist minority or a Nationalist minority, the criticism of the power sharing system is that, on a frequent basis, the majority segment chooses 'acceptable' candidates with whom to share power regardless of the wish of the minority segment in the council.

In Derry, until 2001, the only aspect of the local government structure that was involved was the Mayoralty. The SDLP operated the policy in which the Deputy Mayor one year would become Mayor the next year and so power sharing effectively worked a biannual cycle and Unionists, until 1997, held the Mayoral position every other year. This allows Knox to describe DCC as a 'majority council which adopts power sharing characteristics' (Knox, 1996, 13) but this ignores the very real issue of representation that has dogged this informal system. From 1981 the DUP was the largest Unionist party on the council but the SDLP refused to give the Mayoral position to the party until 1991 and only then after an in-party dispute over the issue. Previously, the SDLP used a tactic not uncommon to majority segments and elected independents to the top positions. This only superficially implemented a power sharing model because the basis for representative electoral politics, and therefore key to local government (and also a key component of Lijphart's consociational model (Lijphart, 1977)), is party politics.

For example, the SDLP elected Jim Guy (an independent Unionist) Deputy Mayor in 1986. However, Unionists interpreted this as the SDLP choosing 'their man'. After the meeting Gregory Campbell (DUP) said:

> The average Unionist has realised that for a number of years the SDLP have required a token Protestant in a high position in order to bolster the false impression that Protestants would be well catered for under the SDLP's version of a new Ireland... What better way to deceive outsiders than covertly to make life difficult for Protestants in the city while overtly putting a Protestant in the position of second citizen? (*Londonderry Sentinel*, 11 June 1986)

The view was that the SDLP wanted a 'token' Unionist who would not cause trouble. In 1993 the SDLP wanted John Adams (UUP) to be Deputy Mayor but he refused (*Londonderry Sentinel*, 10 June 1993). The SDLP then chose Jim Guy to serve a second spell as Deputy Mayor. Unionists were furious, arguing that the SDLP had no right to choose their representatives. The following year the two Unionist parties combined to propose Joe Miller (DUP) for the Mayoralty but the SDLP still elected Guy as Mayor. William Hay (DUP) said, 'We can't allow the election of Councillor Guy to go unchallenged. Joe Miller is the person whom the vast majority of unionists in Londonderry want to be Mayor' (*Londonderry Sentinel*, 9 June 1994). Richard Dallas (UUP) asserted, 'The SDLP say this is a power sharing model. That's a sham, and we are giving them the opportunity, with the proposal of Joe Miller, to show whether it's a sham or not' (*Londonderry Sentinel*, 9 June 1994). The argument was clearly that party politics should be a constituent element of any power sharing arrangement.

Since the 1997 election there has been change in how the positions are allocated, although Unionists still find this scheme unsatisfactory. The SDLP has altered the system to include SF but the principle of power sharing has also altered. The positions no longer rotate between political traditions but are shared out by political party. Paradoxically, the recognition of the importance of the political party as an agent of representation has diminished the claims that Derry can be considered a power sharing council. Unionists argue that the introduction of d'Hondt for committees is long overdue and have no objections to its use here but argue that the Mayoralty is an issue that should be dealt with separately (Interview with Gregory Campbell, 26 February 2002). Under the present arrangement, Unionists have been reduced from two Mayors and two Deputy Mayors every 4 years to one Mayor and three

Deputy Mayors. Drawing the analogy with the First and Deputy First Ministers in the Northern Ireland Assembly, which are not elected by d'Hondt, Gregory Campbell argued that power sharing requires an equal share between Unionists and Nationalists because of the prestige of the posts (Interview with Gregory Campbell, 26 February 2002).

In Fermanagh District Council the issues were the same, although the positions were reversed. In this case the UUP was the largest party in the council, although it did not have overall control, as the council was finely balanced between Unionists and Nationalists. Nationalists controlled the council from 1985 to 1989; Unionists controlled it from 1989 to 1997 and in 1997 the council had no overall control as Unionists and Nationalists were equal, and Independent Davy Kettyles held the balance of power. However, the debate about power sharing emerged after the 1989 election. There was little Unionist–Nationalist co-operation between 1985 and 1987, as the SDLP supported SF and those two parties rotated the chairmanship position. This changed with the temporary UUP–SDLP *rapprochement* after the 1987 Irish Republican Army (IRA) Enniskillen Poppy Day bombing. The two parties passed a motion of no confidence in the SF Chairman and then in June combined to elect an SDLP Chairman and UUP deputy. The new council in 1989 started in a similar fashion as the SDLP and UUP again supported each other's nominations for the top posts and pledged to work together (*Impartial Reporter*, 8 June 1989).

However, for Nationalists, this was short-lived as in 1990 the DUP and the UUP combined to elect Caldwell McClaughry (UUP) Chairman while relegating Fergus McQuillan (SDLP) to the deputy post for the second year in succession. Nationalists condemned the Unionists but Raymond Ferguson (UUP group leader) defended the Unionists' actions and was to set the tone for the Unionist rationale for the next 8 years: 'The electorate has chosen what colours it wanted its council to be for the next three years and it wants a Unionist council' (*Impartial Reporter*, 7 June 1990). The only time that a Nationalist was elected Chairman during the period of Unionist control was in 1994. Gerry Gallagher (SDLP) was not elected because there was a mood of co-operation and partnership in the council but because of intra-Unionist politics. In order to elect a UUP Chairman every year, the party had relied on DUP votes at the annual election but in 1994 the DUP decided to flex its political muscle and abstained, allowing the council to elect Gallagher Chairman. The press and the UUP were condemnatory, thereby dispelling any suggestion that this was partnership governance in embryonic form. Nevertheless, the controversy did disguise the principle upon which the UUP had been working since 1989. The DUP abstained because they complained that Sam Foster (UUP) had told them that the UUP was giving the Vice-Chairman position to the SDLP and there was no place for the DUP (*Impartial Reporter*, 9 June 1994). Unlike Craigavon, where the UUP held onto both positions for as long as possible, Fermanagh UUP felt it important to provide some role for Nationalists in the district and consistently elected an SDLP councillor Vice-Chairman.

Following the 1994 chairmanship election, the UUP utilised the same tactics of the SDLP in Derry. They elected independent Nationalists to the key positions, thereby circumventing the problems of DUP dissent and avoiding dealing with the SDLP. When the council re-elected Foster and Patrick McCaffrey (Independent Nationalist) as Chairman and Vice-Chairman in 1996 respectively, Foster received both DUP votes for the first time in 3 years while McCaffrey defeated McQuillan by eleven votes to seven, with five abstentions – two UUP, two DUP and one SF. Raymond Ferguson suggested that McCaffrey join the UUP while John O'Kane (SDLP) called him a 'token taig' and 'Conor Cruise McCaffrey' (*Impartial Reporter* 6 June 1996).[4] The attitude of the Nationalist Independents towards Unionists changed as their role increased on the council and they were less tolerant of the SDLP's protestations on proportionality and power sharing, probably because they would have lost out under those systems.

The elections in 1997 changed the context for power sharing in Fermanagh. SF became the largest Nationalist party again while the council came under independent control. This gave the key role to Davy Kettyles, who had sat as an independent Progressive Socialist since the Workers' Party split of 1992. Kettyles produced a document outlining a 4-year rotational and proportional scheme for the council and it was implemented in the first year without a 'whimper' (*Impartial Reporter*, 5 June 1997). The council elected McCaffrey Chairman and Bert Johnston (DUP) Vice-Chairman on a 6-month basis and the committees were elected on a proportional basis (*Impartial Reporter*, 5 June 1997). The rotation policy saw a successful first year when the 6-month changeover went smoothly as McCaffrey and Johnston resigned and were re-elected. In a remarkable *volte-face*, Bert Johnston explained his conversion to power sharing, when he said his resignation was:

> Nothing to do with agreements among fellow members, but rather it is my conviction that the post should rotate among UUP, SDLP and

independent members...I support the idea of rotation as one who has suffered. In 20 years on the council I never got anything until six months ago. (*Impartial Reporter*, 4 December 1997)

At this stage Foster made it clear that the UUP opposed the system and was operating it under duress (*Impartial Reporter*, 4 December 1997) and therefore when a SF Chairman was necessitated by the plan in 1998 power sharing disintegrated. Instead Patrick McCaffrey was elected Chairman and Kettyles Vice-Chairman for a full 12-month term. However, the proportionality system was maintained for the committees (*Impartial Reporter*, 4 June 1998).

Fermanagh illustrates many of the same issues that arose in Derry. Party politics was essential to the composition of the council and yet when these informal power sharing arrangements emerge, majority segments attempt to deny this and use independents as the representatives of the minority community. In Fermanagh, the UUP was using the party system before 1994 to choose the Vice-Chairman. The UUP councillors usually abstained and allowed the largest Nationalist party (the SDLP at the time) to elect their candidate. When the UUP deviated from this system, Nationalists levelled the same accusations at the Unionists and the independents that the DUP was making in Derry, and a similar picture emerges in Craigavon.

Craigavon was a Unionist majority council that was dominated by the UUP but power sharing was only intermittently on the agenda. The UUP was unwilling to rotate even the deputy post, which Fermanagh Unionists felt should go to Nationalists every year. Between the formation of the council in 1973 and 1998, there were only two non-UUP mayors: James McCammick in 1974 for the Vanguard Unionist Party and Hugh Casey in 1998 for a period of 6 months for the Labour Party. In addition, there were only 12 non-UUP deputy mayors out of a possible 24 and only 4 were Nationalists. The UUP engaged in complicated political manoeuvring in order to hold onto the top positions after the 1993 elections when they were left just short of overall control. Joy Savage (UUP) was elected Mayor and Ruth Allen (DUP) Deputy Mayor. This move should be seen as part of a complicated political game by the UUP to retain the Mayoralty and not, as a number of studies have, as power sharing (McKay and Irwin, 1995; Knox, 1996). The following year it joined with the SDLP and Sean Hagan (APNI) to elect Brian Maguinness (UUP) Mayor and Sean McKavanagh

(SDLP) Deputy Mayor. However, the SDLP made it clear that it co-operated with the view of obtaining the top post the next year (*Portadown Times*, 24 June 1994).

The UUP reneged on this agreement in 1995 and elected Meta Crozier (UUP) Mayor and Hugh Casey Deputy Mayor (Casey had recently left the SDLP when he accepted an MBE). His election sparked angry scenes as SDLP councillors criticised Casey and the UUP. The UUP was only able to hold onto the Mayoralty for 6 months the following year, sharing it with Casey. The 1997 elections marked a significant change for power sharing in CBC, although this was not readily apparent as the council elected a UUP Mayor and DUP Deputy Mayor. However, in 1998, the UUP made it clear that it was operating a rotational system and Mervyn Carrick (DUP) was elected Mayor and Delores Kelly (SDLP) Deputy unopposed but SF and the independents were excluded (*Portadown Times*, 12 June 1998).

The openness to power sharing was symptomatic of a more general difference in the attitudes of the Unionist political parties to Nationalists. While there was no coherent DUP policy on power sharing across Northern Ireland (they embraced it in Fermanagh and Derry), the most significant political difference in Ballymena between the UUP and the DUP was the attitudes of their representatives towards their Nationalist counterparts. The DUP prevented the election of the only SDLP representative, P.J. McAvoy, onto committees throughout its period of control of the council and as a result McAvoy was kept off the council committees until 1993. The DUP justification was given by Maurice Mills on one occasion in 1990:

> By democratic vote the council decided as a whole that Mr McAvoy would not be on the committees. We must also remember that if you take Ballymena Borough Council in relation to other councils in Northern Ireland, you will find the discrepancies that are raised here are exceeded by what goes on in other councils. (*Ballymena Guardian*, 18 July 1990)

When the UUP gained control of the council in 1993, it signalled a differing attitude towards Nationalists. The borough had a new Mayor for the first time in 15 years as Robert Coulter replaced Spence and the UUP then elected Gareth Williams (APNI) Deputy Mayor. However, the SDLP councillors were challenging the UUP's 'partnership' by November. They wrote to Coulter and Currie alleging that the UUP councillors were 'in office but not in power' and were reacting to and not controlling events. They argued:

> Councillor Coulter has committed himself to changing the face of Ballymena. If he is going to do this, in our view, he will have to create a real agenda for action and be willing to take some risks. (*Ballymena Guardian*, 10 November 1993)

However, the new council was trying to remove contentious political issues by trying to prevent debates on, for example, the Hume–Adams discussions and the DSD (*Ballymena Guardian*, 12 January 1994).

However, the most serious issue that exemplified the divergent attitudes of Ballymena DUP and UUP towards Nationalists in the borough was the Harryville protest. On 14 September 1996 Loyalists began a 14-month picket of Our Lady Mother of the Church chapel in Harryville, ostensibly a retaliation protest for Nationalist protests and the subsequent ban of an Orange parade in the nearby Nationalist village of Dunloy. Although neither of the political parties was involved in the establishment or the organisation of the protest, the DUP aligned themselves with the protestors while the UUP made its opposition very clear. The Ballymena Protestant Committee, who organised the protests, distributed leaflets in October urging a boycott of Catholic businesses, naming some specific premises. Maurice Mills' condemnation was heavily qualified:

> I have always condemned boycotts for I don't believe that it is a true Protestant ethic to do so. It is regrettable that these things have come to pass in our Province but we all know where this has originated from. The situation now is that there is a determined effort afoot by the pan-nationalist front to ethnically cleanse the Border areas of Northern Ireland of Protestants and also in local patches of certain other counties. (*Ballymena Guardian*, 9 October 1996)

Unionists in the council avoided discussing the issue.[5] However, the Mayor James Currie (UUP), the Deputy Mayor Des Armstrong (UUP) and UUP councillors Joe McKernan, John Scott and David Clyde stood with Protestant clergy and supporters of the Catholic parishioners and were duly vilified by the protestors on the other side of the road. Currie explained his position: 'I have come here tonight to show solidarity with the Catholics of Ballymena. They, like Protestants, have the right to go to their church and worship in peace.' Mills replied that: 'I believe that the people attending the church cannot be satisfied. I believe their aim is a united Ireland...In a democratic society people should be allowed to protest so long as it is done in a rational and controlled manner' (*Ballymena Guardian*, 11 December 1996). In comparison to the UUP attitude, the DUP selected Davy Tweed, an ex-international rugby player and Harryville protestor, as a candidate for the local government elections (*Ballymena Guardian*, 2 April 1997; *Ballymena Guardian*, 23 April 1997). He stood in Ballymena South against James Currie and Declan O'Loan (SDLP) but the election was inconclusive as all three candidates were elected on the first count and all exceeded the quota by a considerable margin (*Ballymena Guardian*, 28 May 1997). The Harryville protests marked the lowest point in relations between Unionists and Nationalists in the borough, although it was largely independent from council politics or control and the UUP defended its policies of full party political participation in the council (*Ballymena Guardian*, 21 May 1997). In 1998, it finally elected McAvoy to the chairmanship of a full council committee when he replaced Mills as chair of the relatively powerful Finance, Policy and Resources Committee (*Ballymena Guardian*, 24 June 1998). Mills called it a 'vindictive attack' on the DUP and a statement by the party is telling in how the DUP saw such issues:

> It was very ominous to see what is now official strategy in the Ulster Unionist Party carried through in the voting into the chair of a major committee of council an SDLP member, thus ousting from the position the true, traditional Unionist in the person of councillor Maurice Mills, a professional in the financial field who had held the position with fairness and honour for a number of years. (*Ballymena Guardian*, 24 June 1998)

In the Unionist-controlled councils examined, it was the electoral composition that was the important determining factor that explained their willingness to countenance power sharing. Fermanagh Ulster Unionists' reasoning behind their policy on the Vice-Chairman post explains, at least in part, the problems with power sharing. From the beginning of the 1990s Sam Foster's views appeared in the ascendant in the grouping and the clearest exposition of these was his defence against Nationalist criticism in the 1992 annual meeting:

> This is not a Chamber of Commerce. It is a forum of political parties. We were elected to carry out the Unionist mandate and we have the

greatest and strongest block in the council chamber... We are twice
as large as any other party... We have a right to vote for our own
party... We have no apology to make for doing what we did... We
are an expression and reflection of the electorate which put us here.
(*Impartial Reporter*, 4 June 1992)

This defence of a Westminster conception of democracy has been
widely criticised (Todd, 1995a) and has led to accusations of bigotry
and discrimination. This does, however, miss an important point. In
Craigavon and Fermanagh, the UUP had double the political representation of any other party and it was therefore able to control the
destiny of the top positions. Craigavon introduced a rotational system
following the 1997 election. Until that time, the UUP had endeav-
oured to maintain its hold on *both* positions on the council and had
conceded a post only in order to hold onto the other. The fact that
both councils introduced a power sharing system in 1997 that would
be recognisable to readers of Lijphart's consociational theory is not
coincidental. The election saw a slight drop in the UUP vote and
councillors and a slight rise in the Nationalist vote and councillors in
both areas. The shifting electoral balance was not large but the shift
was significant and enough to push Unionists towards a formalised
power sharing system.

This does not mean that there was no dissent within the Unionist
groupings, as there were prominent politicians consistently arguing for
power sharing prior to this. Raymond Ferguson, who was the UUP
group leader in Fermanagh, argued for power sharing in 1992. He
abstained in the annual meeting in 1992 and 1993 and resigned as
group leader in 1992 as he was unable to persuade the party of his
position (*Impartial Reporter*, 4 June 1992). However, Ferguson was not
advocating power sharing but generosity towards the Nationalist
community; he did not see the SDLP holding the position other than
for 1 year in the 4-year term of the council. In Craigavon, there were
also prominent dissenters in the early 1990s. In 1990 three UUP councillors, James McCammick, Sydney Cairns and Mildred Moore, left the
council grouping and McCammick stated:

A caucus within the group decided that Councillor Fred Crowe
[UUP group leader] was the runner without consulting the three
of us... The three who have resigned want an SDLP deputy to
share around the posts of responsibility (*Portadown Times*, 1 June
1990).

McCammick and Cairns voted for the SDLP nominee in 1990, 1991 and 1992. Following the 1992 election McCammick and Cairns were denied the party whip, which drew this response from Cairns:

> This is the worst group of councillors I have ever worked with, and frankly I'm not much troubled by their puerile ban. They're worse than children, and when you look at councils like Londonderry who can appoint a DUP Mayor in an SDLP majority and Dungannon who share the post on a six-month basis between the parties, it shows how bigoted this crowd of ours is. I voted for Ignatius Fox because the time had come to give the SDLP something – and let's face it, being Deputy Mayor of Craigavon isn't exactly a position of power. (*Portadown Times*, 19 June 1992)

However, these dissenters have had limited impact, despite their profile, on UUP policy on power sharing.

The role of the DUP is interesting because, while they officially opposed power sharing, they were the immediate beneficiaries of the system in all three councils. As the largest Unionist party in Derry, the SDLP eventually accorded them that status. In Fermanagh, Bert Johnston became the first DUP Chairman of the council only because of the introduction of a rotational scheme that the party had opposed. In Craigavon, an identical picture pertained except that the DUP had previously held the Deputy Mayor. There have also been subtle changes in DUP attitudes towards power sharing on a more general level, perhaps because of the impact of the local government experiment and the principle of a proportional distribution of ministerial posts has been a relatively uncontentious aspect of the Belfast Agreement.

However, power sharing in councils, despite the analysis of Colin Knox (1996), was, by itself, an insufficient form of recognition for minorities. This was as important for Unionists as it was for Nationalists. This is most clearly shown by Unionists in Londonderry. The theme of Unionist politics in the city revolves around the question of their place in an area which has a Nationalist majority. The Nationalist ethos of the city and the council was compounded by the dramatic reduction in the numbers of Protestants in the city. Joe Miller described the biggest challenges to Unionism in Londonderry as fairness and confidence:

> Confidence is still lacking for many unionists who feel unsafe or don't want to cross the bridge or I think at the bottom you know feeling part of the city and being made to feel part of the city and not just an

outsider looking in...I think that if you had to go to the core that's what probably have been the basis of it all...but it all came up to the acceptance of our culture and our people and feeling you belong there and not under threat. (Interview with Joe Miller, 16 September 2002)

Therefore, many of the political controversies and debates were on issues of grievances of the Unionist population. Many asked: 'Is there a place for Unionists in Londonderry?' Gregory Campbell thought:

I suppose I'm saying yes to *should* there be rather than *is* there. There is a place for Protestants but I don't think Nationalism has created sufficient maturity to allow Unionists to exist in Londonderry. It's almost a grace and favour existence you know you will be allowed to exist...on our terms and that's not acceptable... 'we will allow Unionism to exist in Londonderry but on our terms, we will negotiate, we will determine, we will be magnanimous and generous but at the end of the day we are deciding what sort of space Unionism will fill.' That's not on our agenda. Yes there is a place but it has to be a place defined by Unionists not defined and permitted by nationalists. (Interview with Gregory Campbell, 26 February 2002, emphasis in original)

Whereas Londonderry Unionists most clearly accord with the description 'under siege', Fermanagh Unionists are not characterised by the same insecurities. Despite the close electoral balance between the communities in Fermanagh, the dominance of the UUP on the Unionist side contrasted with fragmentation on the Nationalist side and thus the positions on the question of political recognition were the reverse of those in Londonderry. The debates and decisions that Fermanagh Unionism have engaged in or made have been driven by the demographic circumstances in the county. A combination of insulation from party political threats due to the weak DUP position, and a pragmatic attitude towards the conflict with Nationalists due to demographics and the integration of the county gave Fermanagh Unionists the political space in which to engage in initiatives and thinking that does not seem to have been possible in other areas. They also had the most relaxed view towards Nationalists and the most flexible attitude towards SF than any of the Unionists in other areas in this study. Raymond Ferguson described the general desire of border county people:

People sort of expect the people who live in the west to be backwoodsmen, politically and every way and to hold on to loyalties long after their relevant but the reality is that . . . there's a much better consciousness of the fact that to make the society cohesive you want as little area of friction as possible, you don't want faction fights like we used to have in the nineteenth century. (Interview with Raymond Ferguson, 9 October 2002)

The nature of politics in Fermanagh is certainly shaped by the type of society and its accompanying attitudes, which would disadvantage the confrontational style of the DUP. Ferguson described how Fermanagh, and Enniskillen in particular, had remained a fairly integrated society (see Doherty and Poole, 1996). Bertie Kerr and Ferguson pointed to how the politicians and the churches had kept Loyalist paramilitaries out of the county (Interview with Raymond Ferguson, 9 October 2002; Interview with Bertie Kerr, 8 October 2002) and this, in turn, has been reflected in the lack of serious inter-communal violence or tension that is, in contrast, a strong characteristic of Craigavon. Local Unionists were therefore able to experiment and reflect in ways that other Unionists who felt less secure in their position could not. Fermanagh UUP members frequently appeared on television in the Republic before this was the norm and revised certain aspects of Unionist thinking, particularly on the AIA.

Material issues

As the powers of local government were circumscribed, the majority of controversy centred on issues of recognition but this did not prevent material concerns from becoming issues of conflict. By 1985 the most contentious areas of material conflict, such as housing, had been removed from local authorities for a significant period of time. Nevertheless, within the local government remit there were still areas which had the potential to affect material concerns. Primarily these were employment and investment. Unlike recognition issues some of these claims were made against the government, rather than the other community but it is these latter claims which will be considered here.

Local government employs 8678 people (Birrell and Hayes, 1999, 134) and a recurring theme in the conflicts between Unionists and Nationalists was differentials in employment rates. As in most issues in Northern Ireland, criticism was from both sides. In Craigavon, Unionists were criticised for being slow in implementing fair employment practices, and the Fair Employment Agency (FEA) report on Craigavon stated that the employment record of the council was heavily biased against Catholics (*Portadown Times*, 30 September 1988). However, in

Londonderry Unionists were more than willing to use fair employment as a weapon against the council; for example, Gregory Campbell stated:

> The media have portrayed Portadown as a predominantly Protestant town where Roman Catholics are confined to several areas and are unable to venture into the town centre at night. Here in Londonderry there has been no effort to highlight the predominantly Roman Catholic city where the Protestants must face the plight of being unable to work or live in vast areas of the city of their birth. (*Londonderry Sentinel*, 23 July 1986)

Indeed, Campbell was so effective at this that he was made the DUP's employment spokesperson. The FEA investigated the council in 1987 but exonerated it of religious discrimination. However, it did find that:

> The headquarters of the Council and the majority of the population and employment are on the Cityside. The patterns shown ... show a marked reluctance for people to apply for any job they consider to be on the 'other side.' This reluctance is particularly strong in the Protestant community with few applications for any posts on the Cityside. If this pattern continues the reasonable balance in the council's workforce will be upset and recovery will be difficult. (Fair Employment Agency, 1989, 14)

Unionist claims of material discrimination were not limited to employment. Unionists, and particularly DUP councillors, were able to point to a plethora of decisions made by the council to support their case. The 1990s saw a reduction in specific Unionist grievances but there was a general feeling that the Waterside received fewer resources than the Cityside. William Hay was at the forefront of this campaign:

> They [the Council] often harp on about discrimination against Roman Catholics by the former Corporation but I believe the clock has turned full circle and it is this council who are guilty of discrimination ... I now challenge the council to list the number of amenities provided in the Waterside, compared to other areas of the city. (*Londonderry Sentinel*, 10 January 1990)

Ian Paisley even took the disparity in East–West Bank funding to the Secretary of State (*Londonderry Sentinel*, 16 February 1995).

These types of issues were replicated by the Nationalist communities in Craigavon and Ballymena but the contentious nature of material issues in these areas can be contrasted with the lack of any significant controversy in Fermanagh. Here, geography was a significant issue in that councillors of different persuasions were required to work together to attract investments and jobs to relatively peripheral areas of Northern Ireland, which did not have any of the advantages of Derry. Moreover, there were frequent struggles with neighbouring Tyrone for the location of schools and acute hospital provision. When this was combined with the lack of any significant housing segregation, it removed material issues from the realm of political conflict.

Conclusion

Party politics has been conditioned by local factors. The character of political parties varies greatly from one area to the next and political strategy is largely dependent upon local conditions. The DUP organisation has, until recently, attracted more analysis than the UUP and while class and religion are both important parts of the DUP appeal, it has not been appreciated how the UUP has been tied into Protestant social structures and, in turn, how this impacts upon the DUP. This theme will be revisited in Chapter 5.

More significant is the observation that politics in local government displays none of the preoccupations with ideology or the construction or articulation of national identity evident in the broader debates in Northern Ireland. It was only briefly after SF entry into the council chambers in 1985 and after the AIA that these came to predominate certain councils. The concerns of local government politics are more mundane, which allows for a certain level of flux in the definition of communities. This observation is tempered by the prevalence of ethno-national party politics but does give credence to the widely held view that once politicians talk about 'bread and butter issues' the identity questions will recede in importance. More importantly, the evidence clearly shows that these communities are in constant dialogue with the 'other' community and are attempting to find a negotiated space within the relevant areas.

Thus, the evidence from local government challenges some of the fundamental premises about politics in Northern Ireland. Local government politics, while marked by political controversy, is not a zero-sum game, where one side loses and the other side wins. On occasions this has happened, such as the name change in Derry, but it has been followed by a, sometimes protracted, period of negotiation between the two communities. This opens the possibility of a liberal approach to the resolution of Northern Ireland's conflicts. Unlike Knox, who argued that the institutions of power sharing in local government offered a potential avenue for conflict resolution, and O'Leary and McGarry, who take a similar institutional approach, it is argued here that the possibilities are to be found in the claim and counter-claim that Unionists and Nationalists make of each other. That these claims are articulated in a liberal framework concerning recognition, equality and human rights is as significant as the recipients of the claims.

The fact that Unionists, when in a minority, have been articulating the same claims as Nationalists indicates that there is a common set of issues relating to minority communities which Unionists can appreciate. The difficulty has been to translate the micro into the macro. Thus, the tendency in Northern Ireland to define communities in very small areas, which are usually coterminous with ethnic cleavages, is a significant difficulty and many of the tensions in the political behaviour of elites (such as that between communal representation and civic responsibility) and the tensions on the ground arise from this definition; where a wider territorial definition is used, such as in Fermanagh, communal tensions are less obvious. Thus the distinction between an ethnic nationalism of the DUP and a civic nationalism of the UUP is not satisfactory as this is not reflected on the ground. The relationship with Nationalists is a key issue for this distinction and is more important than a civic definition of nationhood. The political negotiation of that relationship leads to a more pragmatic and inclusive discourse of politics.

4
Unionism and the Peace Process

So far we have seen how the parameters of the relationship between Unionism and the peace process were established and developed. New ideas provided an impetus for political change and the AIA was important in framing strategic objectives for Unionists, while simultaneously creating a disjuncture between British Government policy and Unionist interests. At the same time, relationships between Unionists and Nationalists at a local level were changing and becoming less conflictual. Thus, the backdrop to what is commonly understood as the 'peace process' (paramilitary ceasefires and all party talks) is an alternative process which conditions reactions to these 'peace process' events. These reactions are the subject of this chapter but before we analyse these it is important to recognise that there are several dominating intellectual orthodoxies about the peace process.

The most pervasive is the orthodox narrative within which academics studying Northern Ireland work. Journalists who have written extensively on the Republican movement and its politics have constructed this narrative and broadly speaking it runs thus: the Provisional IRA had come, by the early 1990s, to a military stalemate with the British government, they could neither win nor lose. Enter the actions and thinking of John Hume, who met, engaged with and persuaded Gerry Adams that the traditional Republican analysis had been overtaken by events. In particular, Hume argued that the 1985 AIA demonstrated that Britain was neutral on the question of whether Irish unity would occur. The Hume–Adams conclusions were then shown to the Irish government, which then negotiated the DSD with the British government, essentially changing the paradigm in which the politics of Northern Ireland functioned and thereby drawing Republicans away from violence (Mallie and McKittrick, 1996, 2001). After a protracted period during which negotiations stalled on decommissioning and the breakdown of the IRA ceasefire, all party talks were held and led to what is known as the Belfast Agreement of Good Friday 1998 (Hennessey, 2000).

My intention here is not to dispute any of the central tenets of this narrative, although Paul Dixon has already argued that this version has a poor understanding of the role of the British government (Dixon, 2001a, 278–9; 2002a); nor is it to write a kind of meta-narrative of the 1990s, which could be useful for our understanding, but to suggest that the Unionist narrative has been missing from the analysis and this is important as to how we analyse the peace process. This is significant because there is a general confusion as to what the peace process is actually about. Joseph Ruane has identified three possible readings: first, the Agreement represents the end of the centuries-old conflict between Britain and Ireland; the second reading locates the Agreement in the dynamics of the traditional conflict and so is simply a period of low intensity violence; the third reading is similar to the first but differs on whether the Agreement will end the conflict (Ruane, 1999). Ruane ultimately concludes: 'the one consistent feature of the peace process since its inception has been change, contradiction, uncertainty and unpredictability. This suggests that a model based on the readings as complementary, partial approximations to a contradictory reality may offer the best account of the current conjecture' (Ruane, 1999, 169). A contradictory reality is a key dynamic in the process, for example, Norman Porter, making a normative claim for the virtue of reconciliation in Northern Ireland, argues: 'The possibilities of an inclusive citizen belonging suggested by a notion of strong reconciliation are encouraged by the Agreement, and yet also discouraged by conflicting understandings of its meaning and resistance to implementation' (Porter, 2003, 216–17).

Most commonly, however, the peace process is understood as simply an absence of violence, Trimble has stated: 'The Agreement is nothing if it is not about peace' (Trimble, 2001, 140) and the most frequent passionate defences of the Agreement are premised on these grounds. This is somewhat of a disservice to the other changes in Northern Ireland that have been important in altering society (see Cochrane and Dunn, 2002) but this is the dominant analysis in the political arena. Unionism has not broken out of the peace/absence of violence orthodoxy but this is instructive about the difficulties with the process and will be discussed later. This chapter therefore has two aims: first, it will outline and examine the Unionist analysis of the peace process as a means of widening the orthodox narrative, although within its own limitations, as an explanation of political change; second, it will show the limits to the Unionist vision for a post-conflict Northern Ireland and how the process and the Agreement have not been emancipatory for Unionism. Throughout this chapter it is argued that the divisions within Unionism are slightly illusory because there is a common interpretative framework and common limits to what Unionists desire from any agreement and therefore the divisions are merely of a tactical nature.[1] This is a means of challenging the analysis of Unionist divisions that was outlined in the Introduction and developing the analysis which was formulated in Chapter 3 in order to assess the extent of the change which has occurred. This will be further developed in Chapter 5 but it is sufficient to recognise here that the tactical nature of the division is a new development and signals the beginning of a shift away from the parameters of the system which Chapter 3 identified.

The Unionist analysis of the peace process

Unionists have been more divided over the Belfast Agreement than Nationalists and those Unionists who support it are more ambivalent in their support than Nationalists (Hayes and McAllister, 2001a). Therefore the Unionist understanding of the peace process enables us to look at how we analyse it in constructive new ways. The Unionist experience of the peace process has been substantially different from that of Nationalists and their attitudes and perceptions offer an important way of examining the exact nature of the political changes in Northern Ireland, particularly in the 1990s.[2] The first and perhaps most important question that confronts us, which does not necessarily arise when studying Nationalism, is 'what is the peace process?' The possible different interpretations have been discussed above but in a practical sense the dominant ethnic conflict paradigm tells us that the peace process is about the resolution of the conflict between two rival ethno-nationalisms: Unionism and Nationalism. Yet for much of the conflict the ideological rationale for violence was far from this position and Republicans have not wholeheartedly embraced this definition of the conflict (Moloney, 2002, 146). Unionists have keenly felt this ambiguity over whether the peace process was a process towards a historic compromise between Unionism and Nationalism or an attempt to end the conflict between Britain and Ireland. Indeed, Unionists are uncomfortable with the very term 'peace process', even those Unionists who have been broadly supportive of the Belfast Agreement. They tend to differentiate between a 'peace process' and a 'political process'. The distinction appears straightforward but refers to policy arenas rather than an analysis of the conflict. Thus, while it mirrors Torkel Opsahl's observation that 'the distinction between conflict and violence is crucial' (Pollak, 1993, 3), it is qualitatively different.

Unionism has been divided into four political positions on the issue of the Agreement: a principled yes, a pragmatic yes, a pragmatic no and a principled no. The 'principled yes' position is held by those who believe that the Belfast Agreement represents a positive and important development for Northern Ireland. They agree with the broad ethos of the Agreement, particularly government by consensus. There is the commitment in this position that surpasses a 'Unionist' analysis; the Agreement is interpreted from an appeal to the general populace of Northern Ireland, not just the Unionist community. The 'pragmatic yes' position takes a more partisan view of the Agreement. They support it but interpret it from within a Unionist perspective. By this reading, the Agreement is a positive document but only because it represents a 'good deal' for Unionists, the 'best deal' for Unionists or because, on balance, it contains more positives than negatives. The 'pragmatic no' position has a similar reasoning to the 'pragmatic yes' but concludes that the Agreement is a 'bad deal', not the best possible deal or because, on balance, it contains more negatives than positives. Those who espouse the 'principled no' position argue that the Agreement is inherently bad because, among other things, it involves compulsory coalitions with terrorists, releases prisoners and contains other clauses and conditions which are found to be morally repugnant.[3] It should be noted that these positions can exist independently of any ideological positions; it is possible for a 'liberal' Unionist to hold a 'principled no' position.

The interviewees for this book were asked for their definition of the peace process and the following four responses from the spectrum of Unionist opinion on the Agreement would indicate that, contrary to common perceptions, the Unionist interpretation of the process is remarkably uniform. Duncan Shipley-Dalton (UUP):

> It's a dual process. The peace process is one thing the political process is separate. There's a peace process that involves the IRA and the British and Irish governments and then there's a political process which involves the political parties in Northern Ireland and the Irish, British governments...and I think the two are, to a degree they're intertwined but they're not co-dependent...the political process can collapse, it doesn't necessarily mean the peace process will collapse. The peace process is essentially a process of agreement,

compromise, negotiation between the British government and the Republican movement, those two groups of people fighting each other essentially, they have been working through a process of peace making between them (Interview with Duncan Shipley-Dalton, 27 September 2002).[4]

Esmond Birnie (UUP) put it:

I actually don't like the phrase [peace process] and I think you've probably found many Unionists, maybe some others, don't. We have a political process which I hope is contributing to achieving more peace but the problem with calling it the peace process is that it creates the impression that we're engaged in appeasement, that we're buying peace at all costs. I don't believe we should be doing that nor do I believe we are doing it but I think there is a danger of it happening so yes we have a political process of trying to obtain accommodation between parties who are still radically different which as I say I hope is generating more albeit imperfect peace than we had before. (Interview with Esmond Birnie, 4 October 2002)

David Burnside (UUP) described the peace process as:

Trying to get all peoples involved in the conflict to agree a form of institutional relationship within the British Isles that restores some sort of normality and peace, and institutions were set up accordingly...the peace process is a political process. The present political process I'm not happy with, everybody's in favour of a peace process on their own terms. We need a peace process that modifies the present political process which I think is inherently unstable. Having all parties to the conflict involved with all the inherent contradictions I don't think has worked out. (Interview with David Burnside, 13 September 2002)

Mervyn Carrick (then DUP):

I suppose in a dictionary definition of the words peace and process you would think it's a series of steps leading to peace. However in the Northern Ireland political context the peace process has become corrupted by a *political* process, which if you come from the nationalist or republican side of the political equation means progress towards a united Ireland and that is a difficulty, the word [*sic*] peace process has become corrupted . . . We [the DUP] would see that [peace process] for what it is: a republican agenda, a nationalist agenda towards an undermining of the British link and the establishing of a united Ireland. (Interview with Mervyn Carrick, 21 October 2002, emphasis in original)

Unionist interpretations of the peace process which have distinguished between a peace process and a political process are dependent on their narrative of their experience of the process by which Republicans were persuaded to end violence and in particular the way it has been presented.[5] In the words of Martin Mansergh, the peace process has been an 'Irish peace initiative, which the British government was persuaded to opt into in modified form, that led on to the cease-fire and eventually to peace' (Mansergh, 2002, 106) but it is necessary to go further and argue that it has been a Nationalist-driven peace process and this has had an important and neglected dynamic on the implementation of the Agreement. Ruane and Todd argue that the repositioning of the British state has encouraged Unionist interaction with Nationalists and also opened up the possibility of Irish unity with Protestant consent (Ruane and Todd, 2001, 927) but British policy has left Unionists isolated from major policy initiatives since the AIA. Peter Robinson has argued:

It isn't Unionists who are calling the tune. Unionists are left to react to events because they haven't got an attainable goal. The only time you have an attainable goal is when you set your sights on something you can achieve by your own power and not be dependent on the British government and the crumbs that come from their table. What we want we can only have on terms that somebody else gives us. (quoted in O'Malley, 1990, 38)

Perhaps least importantly there is a general feeling of anger within all sections of Unionism that Hume was always willing to speak to 'those well known democrats in the Army Council' while refusing to engage with Unionists in, for example, the Brooke and Mayhew talks (Unionists unanimously blame Hume for the collapse of those talks),[6] the Northern Ireland Forum for Political Dialogue (King, 1997a) or even with his own party (Dixon, 1997). For them Hume had presented his role throughout the peace process as benign and virtuous, 'a disinterested pursuit of an end to political violence' (Roche, 1997). Steven King, reviewing Hume's *Personal Views*, observed that 'Hume offers a bland repetition of jumbled nostrums as if wanting peace, agreement and equality of treatment was his exclusive preserve' (King, 1997). Roche argues that there is more to this projection:

> The peace rhetoric is intended to give substantive credibility to the perception that nationalist leaders – particularly Mr Hume and Mr Adams – are primarily concerned with the achievement of peace rather than with the atavistic goals of Irish Nationalism. However, the reality of their position is that peace in Ireland can only be secured when Irish unity has been achieved. (Roche, 1997)

The language of peace has been a key part of the political changes in Northern Ireland. Chris Gilligan has argued that the concept of peace is a morally loaded term and this often prevents dispassionate analysis which has been central to the process (Gilligan, 1997), while Shirlow and McGovern have shown that the adoption of the language of 'peace' by SF was a key factor in allowing the Republican movement to escape from the 'containment strategy undertaken by the British and Irish States' which controlled language and therefore the presentation of SF and the IRA (Shirlow and McGovern, 1998, 180–2). Unionists have not been adept at using such language and indeed frequently they express opinions qualifying the desirability of peace; for example, William McCrea stated:

> Now many people on the Unionist community went in favour of the Belfast Agreement because ... they were promised peace and many after 30 years or so were war weary and would take peace at any price. I have to tell you that I do not believe in peace as an end in itself because I believe there's another one [end] which really brings genuine peace and that's freedom. (Interview with William McCrea, 26 November 2002)

Paul Berry voiced his frustration at the perception which such an attitude has generated, showing the potency of 'the language of peace':

> The only problem I have with it is: is that those that were against the so-called peace process and that's many times what's quoted, the people that's against the peace process, the perception out there is that we're against peace, that we're bigots, that we hate Catholics, that we don't want peace, we just want the conflict to continue and I think that's maybe where ourselves on the Unionist side who had

rejected the Agreement had a problem with getting our message across because we're seen very much against peace, which couldn't be further from the truth. We want peace, we long for peace, a lot of our people, a lot of our friends and relatives have suffered as a result of terrorism and we certainly don't want to go back to that and there's this whole thing that you're against the peace process, we're against the process, we're not against peace. (Interview with Paul Berry, 13 November 2002)

Peace itself has been inadequately defined, perhaps deliberately so. It is unclear whether peace simply means an absence of violence or whether peace is some grander concept connected with a process for ending ethnic conflict.

Unionists have not exerted much intellectual energy in constructing a vision as to where the process should be going. They take their lead from the two agendas which they perceive as driving the process: the British agenda and the Nationalist agenda. Traditionally, the British agenda in Northern Ireland has been the most contentious. Indeed, for Republicans it was their interpretation of the British agenda which sustained the ideological rationale for armed struggle. Unionists have had a more complex relationship with Britain, as has been noted on many occasions in these first three chapters, but before considering the interpretation and impact of government policy it is worth briefly outlining the academic analysis. The debate on conflict resolution has been split over 'bottom–up' (Ruane and Todd, 1996; Todd, 1995b; although also see Ruane and Todd, 2004) or 'top–down' initiatives and the latter debate has been split over a large number of potential options (see McGarry and O'Leary, 1990) and connected to this debate has been a further debate on the British government's policies and preferences. O'Leary and Dixon, for instance, have debated whether British government policy has been characterised by consistency or 'ethno-national conflict learning' (O'Leary, 1997; Dixon, 2001b) but this debate has been over their approach to constitutional options for Northern Ireland. There is a further debate over the compatibility of government policies which essentially attempt to address both approaches to conflict resolution. Therefore this dual strategy of encouraging the growth of civil society while simultaneously encouraging political compromise between the two rival groups in Northern Ireland has been seen as both complementary (Bloomfield, 1997) and contradictory (Guelke, 2003). Nevertheless, it is the constitutional policies and strategy which political actors have scrutinised most carefully and which have had the most dramatic political effects; we have already noted the political impact of the AIA but at least one commentator has argued: 'it is not imprudent to...argue that the overriding policy of *successive* British governments has been to render ineffectual the military capacity of the IRA' (McIntyre, 1995, 103). Academics have been reluctant to fully explore the relationship between Republican violence and British policy. However, the contention that the British policy in Northern Ireland can be influenced by Republican violence has been a key part of the political analysis of both Unionists and Republicans.

It would be problematic to consider British policy as following the myopic approach to obtain the single aim of ending Republican violence, as some such as Robert McCartney have argued:

> To fully appreciate the current political situation and to forecast where it could lead us, it is necessary to understand certain funda- mental principles of government policy...The Agreement's real purpose is to further the government's policy of disengagement from Northern Ireland and to protect the lives and property of its 'first class' British citizens on the mainland. It represents the terms of a conflict resolution treaty between the Sinn Féin/IRA and Britain. (McCartney, 1999)

However, the Unionist analysis, combined with academic interpreta- tions, does demonstrate the utility of identifying three policy arenas: encouraging civil society and therefore 'bottom–up' conflict resolution; a political compromise between the leaders of Unionism and Nationalism, 'top–down' conflict resolution; and ending Republican violence through political and military means. It is useful to see the policy of encouraging ethnic compromise as distinct from that of ending Republican violence because the two have required different strategies, which have had implications on each other and it is here where the Unionist analysis becomes particularly pertinent because they, perhaps exclusively, feel pain in one and strength in the other.

Arguably the greatest political changes occurred within the Repub- lican movement as they revised the important articles of ideology that had sustained the conflict but this was not a voluntary process[7] and Unionists have had little control or input into the process by which the Republican analysis was challenged. Indeed, challenging Republicans involved endorsing a view of the conflict which isolated Ulster Union- ists and therefore there is the very real sense among Unionists that much of the peace process does not belong to them. Moreover, it is suggested here that the statements of the British have had as important an effect on Unionists as they have on Republicans. The DSD is important in this regard. It confirmed the British government had 'no selfish strategic or economic interest' in Northern Ireland. Unionists refer to this document as the 'Declaration of Disinterest in the Union' (McCartney, n.d., 6)[8] and this is perhaps more important than the offence that some Unionists have felt at SF's apparent reward for the IRA's campaign of violence. Duncan Shipley-Dalton demonstrates that even pro-Agreement Unionists feel a certain detachment from British government policy:

> I don't think that republicans are going back to war and I don't think the British government is going to sacrifice its own interests in favour of Unionism, it will continue to make peace with republicanism; that's what it wants to do because that's in the best interest of all of the people of the United Kingdom. HMG [Her Majesty's Government] has a responsibility to represent all the people of the United Kingdom, not just the awkward group in the top left hand corner...we're 1 and a half million people here in Northern Ireland, Unionism is less than a million people, more people than that live in Birmingham. What does it mean to the British government if 1 million of its citizens aren't particularly happy with something that 54 million of them are happy enough. Why would they change their policy? (Interview with Duncan Shipley-Dalton, 27 September 2002)

Shipley-Dalton went on to explain that the Assembly was crucial as a mechanism for increasing the level of influence that Unionists had on a variety of national and international stages. The DUP appear more affected by the effects of the British government's overtures to Republicans than the UUP. The title of an August 1994 policy document needs little explanation: *What's the British government up to? Tampering with Ulster's constitutional position* (DUP, 1994). Mervyn Carrick goes further:

> There's a Unionist sense of alienation, there's a Unionist sense of being let down, there's a Unionist sense of not being wanted, there's a Unionist sense of mistrust and if you mean by siege that we don't appear to have too many friends, influential friends, in support of our continued part of the Union then the answer to your question is yes but we have sufficient confidence in ourselves in the Unionist population to be able to say yes things are going against us but when it comes to the crunch we will not be the pushover that you thought

we would...A Union is, if you like, a bridge between two stable points and if in the documents released by Westminster that they say that they have no selfish strategic or economic interest what am I to take out of that? They are no longer interested and that is the problem that Unionists have, the second leg of their union is built on sand, they don't want you. (Interview with Mervyn Carrick, 21 October 2002)

Unionism has always had a complex and slightly ambiguous attitude towards nationalism and particularly the type of nationalism on offer to those members of the British national community (see Introduction). However, the British government, in its attempt to bring Republicans into the process, sent a signal to Unionists particularly through the DSD that not only was Northern Ireland a conditional part of the UK state but they were a conditional part of the British-imagined community, perhaps best summed up in John Dunlop's striking phrase, 'a precarious belonging' (Dunlop, 1995).[9]

Consent

If Northern Ireland was this hotbed of conditionality the only mechanism that therefore guaranteed Unionism's political survival was the principle of consent, and many commentators have interpreted consent as the key issue of the peace process for Unionists (Bew, 1998a). Indeed, some have seen it as the only issue for Unionists: the argument runs if it contains consent then Unionists can have no real objection to whatever political declaration is in front of them. But the question legitimately arises as to the definition of consent. MacGinty, Wilford, Dowds and Robinson have identified four distinct interpretations. In the first it is a guarantee, acting as a stabilising force and a safeguard against an executive *fait accompli*. In the second, consent makes Northern Ireland a constitutional anomaly by making its position conditional and stops the parties from working towards an accommodation. In the third, it allows the governments to present themselves as neutral arbiters and allows Britain to point to an easily legitimised source of power. Finally, Nationalists argue that consent simply amounts to a veto but, furthermore, point out that consent does not necessarily mean consent to the *status quo* (MacGinty *et al.*, 2001). The origins and development of the principle of consent are instructive because they illustrate how interpretations have changed and how the principle itself has altered and become a political dynamic. Martin Mansergh claims that consent has been at the heart of Irish government policy on Northern Ireland since the 1920s (Mansergh, 1997) but the first exercise of consent was incorporated into the 1920 Government of Ireland Act where the Northern Ireland Parliament was given the option of opting out of a Parliament for the whole island. It was restated in the 1949 Ireland Act but changed in the 1970s from the Parliament of Northern Ireland to the people of Northern Ireland. However, its application and definition to the peace process can be found in the AIA of 1985. Here it was stated that: 'the two governments affirm that any change in the status of Northern Ireland would only come about with the consent of a majority of the people of Northern Ireland' (Hadden and Boyle, 1989). However, this consent was limited because the only envisaged change in Northern Ireland's constitutional status was if it wished to become part of a united Ireland. The AIA also marked an implicit boundary to the principle of consent in that it clearly said that a united Ireland was to be the only opportunity for that consent to be exercised and it is from here that Unionism's ambivalent relationship with consent begins.

Adrian Guelke has pointed out that the use (and abuse) of the consent principle by the two communities in Northern Ireland has effectively amounted to a veto claim; each should have the right to consent to or, perhaps more importantly, to withhold consent from possible political arrangements (Guelke, 1996a). Thus Unionists argued the AIA changed Northern Ireland's constitutional position and used a number of methods to demonstrate that they did not consent to it (Chapter 2). Consent as a veto claim can be extended to a demand for self-determination for each community, a demand which Gallagher describes as a 'chimera' because neither side can effectively appeal to international norms and practices to support their position (Gallagher, 1990). Nevertheless, consent has become an accepted part of the peace process (MacGinty *et al.*, 2001) and on a six-county territorial basis. As such, Unionists see consent as a constitutional guarantee; Jeffrey Donaldson gives the clearest expression of this view:

> In the end the Union will be secured and will continue to be secured by the votes of the people of Northern Ireland, that is the only bulwark, it's the only defence. I, as a Unionist, am not relying on the British government to safeguard the Union, I think successive governments have made it clear it's up to the people of Northern Ireland and that principle is embodied within the Agreement recognised now by not only the SDLP but also by the Irish government ... and by the republican movement whether implicitly or explicitly so the

principle of consent...is the only safeguard for the Union. (Interview with Jeffrey Donaldson, 11 November 2002)

The acceptance of consent has been a significant change in Northern Ireland's political landscape. If Nationalists and Republicans accept the principle then, implicitly, that was the recognition that, first, Northern Ireland was a legitimate entity and, second, the possibility of a United Ireland was remote. Adrian Guelke has argued that part of the intractability of the Northern Ireland conflict was due to the lack of legitimacy of the partition because of Nationalist assumptions about a 32-county unit (Guelke, 1985). Such legitimacy now appears to have been granted to Northern Ireland as an entity. However, despite its real importance to Unionism, at no stage in the course of the peace process since the AIA have Unionists been involved in shaping its definition and exercise. Thus Arlene Foster remarked, somewhat self-pityingly:

> The whole reason for wanting to give Ulster a devolved Assembly and all its attachments *a la* Framework Documents is to slide us slowly towards a united Ireland. The Government will say that this is not the case at all and cry 'what about consent?' One cannot help thinking that it is to the speed of unification to which we have consent and not staying within the Union. (Foster, 1997)

Peter King warned during the negotiations that problems with the definition and exercise of consent meant, 'if you were not nervous about consent then you should be' (King, 1997b). Hume's efforts in the 1990s were to reconcile the Nationalist demand for Irish self-determination and the Unionist demand for consent but this formulation was rejected by Unionists because it rested on Nationalist assumptions about the unity of the island (Cunningham, 1997). More importantly, the consultations on this fundamental principle of the peace process did not include any Unionists. Indeed, the only time when Nationalist Ireland gave Unionism an active exercise of consent was a drafting oversight by Dick Spring when his speech outlining six principles for a peace process erroneously included the phrase 'Unionist consent' rather than 'majority consent' (Mallie and McKittrick, 2001, 206–7). Nationalists are as equally ambivalent about the use of the two as are Unionists. Recognising that 'majority' consent contains at least the possibility of constitutional change whereas simultaneous Unionist consent and Nationalist consent does not, they have been ambiguous as to the exact nature of their use. They claim, as do Unionists, the right to withhold consent to particular government structures but claim the importance of majority consent to the crucial issue of a change in sovereignty. The Belfast Agreement contains both of these contradictory formulations (see also Pollak, 1993, 9–21).

So, if both political blocs use consent to strengthen their particular case then what importance does it really have? Consent as a guarantee can also be read in an alternative manner; the Unionist stress on consent is, to borrow a phrase, inextricably linked to broader Unionist insecurities, commonly known as the Unionist sense of siege. Roy Garland argued that the sense of siege was both his motivation for becoming involved in politics and:

> I think it's absolutely central... that's the core of Unionism [the sense of siege]. I felt that Derry in Unionist history is more important than the Boyne. I can always as a child remember identifying with stories of Derry and the suffering and eating rats and mice and cats and dogs, that survival and that determination. (Interview with Roy Garland, 18 November 2002)

We have already seen how British government policy impacted upon Unionism and this was compounded by their perception of the Nationalist agenda. Unionism's interpretation of Nationalism has always been rather impoverished (and the same should be said about Nationalism's views on Unionism) but for Unionists the peace process demonstrated unequivocally the unity of purpose of all Irish Nationalists. There was a pan-Nationalist front consisting of, as David Burnside described:

> John Hume, southern government, Catholic Republic [of Ireland], Catholic Democrat America, left wing of the Labour Party, SDLP, Sinn Féin, all those who are generally nationalists of one form or another, including republican. Very effective, big resources, especially with the government of the Irish Republic. That is what Unionism has got to fight against helped by Republicans being in the [United] States rather than the Democrats who are more traditionally linked to the Conservatives in the UK. (Interview with David Burnside, 13 September 2002)

Mervyn Carrick asserted:

> I have absolutely no hesitation in saying that there's a pan-Nationalist front. The Irish Republicans may be forcing the agenda at a quicker

pace, the SDLP and nationalism may be playing it more subtly but they each have the one clear objective and when it comes to the crunch they will collaborate and they will work together to deliver their objective. (Interview with Mervyn Carrick, 21 October 2002)

Duncan Shipley-Dalton, while rather scathing about this attitude towards Nationalists, did not dispute the dominant perception of such a front within Unionism (Interview with Duncan Shipley-Dalton, 27 September 2002). The question then is: How does this affect the dynamics of Unionism?

Unionists have always felt threatened by Irish Nationalism. The siege mentality was a product of the existence of a minority committed to changing the constitutional position of Northern Ireland through, if necessary, violent means. In recent times Unionists have stressed the IRA campaign and the irredentist aims of the Irish state. Referring to the importance of Articles 2 and 3 of the Irish constitution, Chris McGimpsey stated:

> It gave spurious justification to the IRA campaign and what it gave was the foundation of the Irish state which denied the legitimacy of Northern Ireland...and the big line is that we talk about our siege mentality, lift the siege, we'll not have a siege mentality if you stop besieging us. (Interview with Chris McGimpsey, 6 June 2002)

The pan-Nationalist front was perceived as merely the next stage of this ongoing attempt to try to force Unionists into a United Ireland, as an article in the *New Protestant Telegraph* explained:

> The pan-nationalist axis of Dublin, the SDLP and IRA/Sinn Féin is trying to dictate terms for Ulster's surrender. This is what the 'peace process' is all about. It was born out of the Adams/Hume agreement which has never been revealed publicly and it has now been built upon by the Downing Street Declaration and the Framework Document which are blueprints for Ulster's destruction. (*New Protestant Telegraph*, September 1995)[10]

The general attitude that this fosters is one of defeatism and inevitability or, as Arthur Aughey describes, a 'culture of fatality'. Some Unionists recognise that this is a negative dynamic which causes many needless problems for Unionism and have attempted to alter Unionist political philosophy to move away from this fatalism, what Aughey calls the

Trancredi option, 'an attempt to make history rather than to dance to its fatalistic tune' (Aughey, 2001c, 189). Esmond Birnie argues:

> I would say that it is one of the things I would criticise within Unionism and within my party, there is a strand of undue pessimism almost a sort of school of thought of historical inevitability, we are beat, we are finished, woe is us and the problem I would say with that mentality is that leads to self-fulfilling prophecy. (Interview with Esmond Birnie, 4 October 2002)

One of Trimble's projects after his election as leader of the UUP was to try and change this philosophy within Unionism. In a speech, which contains many elements of the Trimble project, to the Young Unionist conference in 1998, he not only told the assembled delegates to go and read Karl Popper but said:

> It is not good enough to be passive, to adopt a tactic or an approach that consciously or deliberately leaves the decision in the hands of other people. At the end of the day, the more sensible thing to do is to be seriously engaged in the situation...there is another crucial point. You have to engage with a degree of self-confidence. The latter point is a serious reproach to many Unionists. Perhaps it shows that the republican campaign had more success than we realised. Many Unionists now seem to lack confidence in their arguments and in their abilities. Many have fallen into a self-pitying mode of saying 'everybody is against us, we are doomed to defeat and it doesn't matter what happens it is bound to fail.' But it is not necessarily so...There are no historical inevitabilities. It is, at the end of the day, up to ourselves, our own abilities. (Trimble, 2001, 46–7)

Trimble and others around him have actively tried to confront this defensive siege mentality and have set out to promote the Union, to try and give Unionists confidence and find a way out of this Unionist pessimism. Consent has traditionally been seen as the best method for this because it did not contain any dynamic within it, the majority was stable and it was therefore less of a live political issue. The UUP have sold the consent principle in the Agreement in these terms again. The UUP document 'Understanding the Agreement' states:

> This [article 1 of the Belfast Agreement] enshrines the principle of consent and the reality that the Union will continue for as long as

that is the wish of the greater number of people in Northern Ireland: if the people of Northern Ireland continue to vote to stay in the Union, that will be respected. (UUP, 1998)

Together with the change in Articles 2 and 3, the constitutional future of Northern Ireland should be secured and therefore Unionists should have no fears about their future and therefore there is a way out of the 'culture of fatalism'.

Unfortunately for Unionism and for Northern Ireland the experience of the peace process for Unionists has not enabled Trimble's or Birnie's optimism to triumph. Instead, John Reid, the then Secretary of State, has spoken of a 'Cold House' for Unionism (Reid, 2001). Reviewing this particular speech in which the Northern Ireland Secretary John Reid speaks of a need for a confident Unionist majority, John Wilson Foster argues that Reid was unable to adequately account for this phenomenon because of the implications for British policy. Foster unequivocally lays the blame on the door of the British government and its policy on Northern Ireland. Foster points to 'the ambiguity inherent in a longer-range, open-ended *process* over which unionists feel they have no control and the end of which they very much fear'. Moreover, Unionists 'require . . . an *ingenuous* and *convincing* recognition of their cultural and political Britishness in addition to their cultural Irishness' (Foster, 2002, emphasis in original). We have therefore returned to the foundations of the peace process, Hume's attempt to reconcile self-determination and consent which was adopted almost completely by the British and Irish governments. It emerges in clause 4c of the DSD, which states:

> The British Government agree that it is for the people of the island alone, by agreement between the two parts respectively, to exercise their right of self-determination on the basis of consent, freely and concurrently given, North and South, to bring about a united Ireland, if that is their wish. (HMSO, 1993)

The Unionist critique of this has been widely neglected but is acutely relevant to this discussion about the nature of Unionist confidence. Partly due to political circumstances in the House of Commons, the DUP were the sole unambiguous critics of the DSD and particularly of clause 4c. Gregory Campbell, in the DUP's official response to the Declaration, stated: 'We, rather than being a people within the United Kingdom family are regarded as one of the diverse traditions within

Ireland. Nothing could be clearer' (Campbell, 1994). The same argument emerges in the United Unionist 'It's Right to Say No' campaign against the Agreement. They state: 'We reject the abandonment of the United Kingdom's sovereignty over Northern Ireland in exchange for an amendment of the Irish constitution that renders Unionists a mere tradition in the Irish nation.'[11]

Trimble has attempted to counter this Irish-centric view of the relationships on the island with a greater appreciation of the East–West or archipelagic dimension but clearly the commitment to those structures has been less enthusiastic than to the North–South dimension and, as Arthur Aughey observes, 'The generality of Unionists read the trend of policy fatalistically' (Aughey, 2001c, 192). This had prevented consent fulfilling a liberating role for Unionists. McCartney, perhaps the most fatalistic of all Unionists, has argued that consent is meaningless within the context of the peace process:

> Few are fully aware of the ongoing process for modifying and diluting that principle [consent] to the point that it will present no obstacle to the unification of the island. The present policy of the British government is to disengage from Northern Ireland by creating and putting in place institutions of government agreed jointly with the Irish government. These institutions will gradually evolve into a factually and economically united Ireland that will render the final consent to the transfer of legal constitutional sovereignty a mere formality. (McCartney, n.d., 2)

This is therefore where the two agendas converge and demonstrate the difficulty with seeing consent as a principle which can be sold as a positive gain for Unionists. The fatalists' argument is that getting Republicans to sign up to consent is hardly a concession when consent, in the context of the peace process, actually means a united Ireland.

The limits of a settlement

The most ubiquitous criticism of anti-Agreement Unionists is that they have no alternative. Indeed, many are of the opinion that Unionism is incapable of producing a coherent strategy for a negotiating process so it is therefore necessary to examine some of their proposals for a settlement. The debate over devolution or integration has already been discussed, as has the widening of their traditional horizons of an 'internal settlement' but this section will discuss the wider issues of the peace process, in particular ending violence and possible frameworks for the inclusion of Nationalists and Republicans. These issues are, crucially, related to the Unionist interpretation of their 'practical' experience of the conflict and, in this, they are not detached from the broader Unionist community. Indeed, one of the features of the conflict that has received inadequate attention is the differing experiences of different communities. Fay, Morrissey and Smyth, in recent and valuable research that has begun to rectify this occlusion, have argued: 'There has not been one uniform conflict in Northern Ireland, rather the Troubles are a mosaic of different types of conflict. Accordingly, the "reality" of the Troubles is different for different people in different locations and in different occupations' (Fay, Morrissey and Smyth, 1999, 136). Evidence would suggest that Protestants have less direct and indirect experience of violence (Hayes and McAllister, 2001b, 909), which is supported by Fay, Morrissey and Smyth's research which demonstrated that the most intense areas of conflict had been confined to Nationalist areas or localised mixed areas. The majority of the east of Northern Ireland, which has the highest concentration of Protestants, was largely untouched by periods of sustained violence (Fay, Morrissey and Smyth, 1999, 141–55). Public opinion research about the issues in the negotiations illustrates this starkly. While Nationalist priorities in any settlement centred on human rights issues and reform of the police service, Unionist priorities were to disband paramilitary groups, have stronger and more effective anti-terrorist measures and bring about an end of the Republic of Ireland's territorial claim. Beyond these three issues, there was no other issue that more than 37 per cent of Unionists felt was essential to a settlement. In comparison the Nationalist 'shopping list' was much longer and included integrated housing and education and politics without a sectarian division (Irwin, 2002, 167–70). The Unionist vision for a peaceful Northern Ireland was just that – peaceful; there has been no broader vision of the type of society that Unionists would like to see. David Trimble has outlined this type of thinking:

> Our strategy was based on three key propositions. The first was that the principle of consent should govern the future of Northern Ireland and its relationship with the Republic. The second was that the notion of the British government 'facilitating' Irish unity must be abandoned. The third was that in order to secure the proper political atmosphere the Irish government should remove the territorial claim in Articles 2 and 3 of its constitution. (Trimble, 2001, 133)

These priorities are evident in the Unionist parties approach to the two constitutional talks processes in the 1990s: the Brooke and Mayhew talks of 1991–1993 and the all party negotiations of 1996–1998. One of the most important differences between these two sets of negotiations was the inclusion of SF in the context of an IRA ceasefire. The purpose of the latter talks was to find a conclusion that would cement the cease-fires and deny Republicanism a reason to return to violence. However, even during the Brooke–Mayhew talks, Unionists had been uncon-vinced that any political settlement would be able to fulfil such a role without it being laden with concessions to those previously engaged in violence. In their opening submissions to the Brooke talks in 1991, Molyneaux and Paisley both doubted that a successful conclusion would have an affect on terrorists. Molyneaux said:

> Colleagues will be aware that our modest level of talks has been labelled a 'Peace Conference.' That is an utterly false description and monstrously unfair to all of us who sit around this table. We are only too well aware that even if we achieve complete success, the effect on the terrorists will be *nil*. (Molyneaux, 1991, 3, emphasis in original)

Paisley said:

> It is a fact, however unpalatable it may be to some members of the general public or even members of the delegations around this table, that even if these talks attain political agreement, our war torn, and carnage ridden Province will not be rid of its greatest scourge – the scourge of IRA terrorism, and other terrorism resulting, nor can these talks give to the people of Ulster its greatest goal – the goal of peace. We would do well as we enter these proceedings to keep those stern truths firmly to the forefront of our minds. No political agreement at these talks, short of the impossible, that is surrender to the IRA's demands for a 32 County Republic, will cause the IRA to go away. (Paisley, 1991, 1)

When talks did eventually reach the stage where SF and the loyalist paramilitary parties were represented, the DUP and the United Kingdom Unionist Party (UKUP) still refused to countenance a settlement based on their participation. Robert McCartney argued:

> It is wrong, absolutely and always, to negotiate with armed and unre-pentant terrorists in a democracy. Northern Ireland is not South Africa, where the great majority had no vote. Democracy always has to

be defended, and violence must never be rewarded, either while that violence is being perpetuated or after its perpetuators have ceased. Difficulties in defeating violence are no excuse. A failure to eradicate the Mafia or to prevent the activities of drug dealers does not lead to offers to negotiate with the godfathers. (McCartney, 2001, 106–7)

This argument is still widespread and influential within Unionist circles, sections of the Dublin media and those hostile to Republicanism and can be termed 'the peace process as appeasement' interpretation (see also Skelly, 1999; O'Brien, 1994, 174–97; Myers, 2000, 120–48). It links the Unionist analysis of the process and their thinking on the limits of a settlement because it is concerned with the question of violence, thus the asymmetry in Unionist involvement in the two 'arms' of the process. Unionists could be and were persuaded on certain political issues but their answer on how to end violence was deemed either impractical or incommensurable with the political agendas of the other political actors involved.

The answer Unionists commonly gave to the question as to how to end violence was that it should be defeated militarily. The DUP was the most unambiguous in its conviction that military measures were the only solution. Robinson stated: 'You don't get peace just because you ask for peace. You have to get out there and defeat terrorism' (*New Protestant Telegraph*, April 1993). In a 1993 manifesto they argued:

The essential factor in the attempt to realise peace and stability in Ulster is the defeat of terrorism. Nothing short of the elimination of the IRA will suffice. As the Chief Constable said, the defeat of the IRA would bring about an end to all other terrorism as well. PIRA will not be talked out of existence nor will any constitutional device cause them to go away. They must be militarily defeated. The starting point must be the scrapping of the present failed and blood-soaked security policy. (DUP, 1993, 3)

Its policy for the defeat of terrorism was a twelve-point plan that included: sealing the border; removing security constraints and allowing the RUC to go on the offensive against the IRA; recruitment of 50,000 civilians into a force equivalent to the 'C' Specials; a 'ring of steel' around areas known to be the 'haunts' of terrorists and therefore stopping explosive devices at source rather than in transport; search and seizure operations; introduction of identity cards for everybody over the age of 14; intelligence gathering; proscription of SF; curfews 'on those areas where this [terrorist violence] illegal and disruptive activity takes place'; monitoring the movements of suspected terrorists; internment; tougher sentencing; and the government should step up its propaganda war and extend it overseas. The most important aspect, however, was that the government should have the 'will to win', a quality the DUP felt had been lacking (DUP, 1993, 11–14).

The UUP did not advocate such draconian measures but did express its 'dissatisfaction' with the government's approach. It argued that:

> Restoration of the Rule of Law is dependent on the early destruction of the higher echelons within terrorist organisations and on the disruption of their lines of communication. Ulster Unionist Members of Parliament will continue to press the next government to define a proper strategy for dismantling the senior command and control structures of paramilitary groupings. (UUP, 1992b, 4)

The UUP policy documents displayed more interest in political structures than in security measures as a means to defeat terrorism. They advocated political arrangements that would end constitutional uncertainty and provide a meaningful role for elected representatives and accountable democratic arrangements for Northern Ireland (UUP, 1994). The problem with the proposals of the two governments in the DSD and Framework Documents was:

> The two governments' current plan is deficient as it is totally theoretical and offers no scope for the development of those practical *'confidence building measures'* which will be necessary if real *trust* is to develop. (UUP, 1995, 4, emphasis in original)

Trust was the crux of the problem of establishing political structures (UUP, 1995, 2) but these structures had to be firmly within the Union and as applicable to Scotland or Wales as to Northern Ireland. Thus the UUP promoted both a Northern Ireland Select Committee at Westminster and a devolved Assembly for Northern Ireland (UUP, 1994). The Union was to be the framework for any possible settlement because, as Molyneaux stated at the start of the Brooke talks:

> The whole process in which we are presently engaged will be futile unless there is a recognition of the solid fact that the greater number of people of Northern Ireland do not wish to leave the United Kingdom. (Molyneaux, 1991, 2)

Molyneaux's project was to try and end the 'arms length' policy of successive British governments towards Northern Ireland (UUP, 1992b, 1) and argued:

It is now surely incumbent on HMG to re-establish, and as quickly as it can, a clear understanding of the Union, and to reinforce this with constitutional arrangements which show that the supreme body is presently, and will remain, the Queen in Parliament. Furthermore it must be demonstrated that the citizens of Ulster are, like their colleagues in England, Scotland and Wales, citizens of the United Kingdom with all the rights and obligations which go with that status. Ulster, in the political sense and more recently in the economic sense, has been quarantined for far too long from the mainstream of life in the United Kingdom. (Molyneaux, 1991, 1)

Such integration into mainstream British political life was going to be resisted by Nationalists but Unionists, and particularly the UUP, disagreed that this was any threat to Nationalists. The UUP challenged the SDLP's analysis that the conflict was about identities:

We...would maintain that identities are far more subtle and complex, and have far less impact on the political life of a country than the SDLP believe. Political institutions and systems cannot in themselves cater for perceptions of identity by any sector of the population. (UUP, 1992a)

It instead began to look to international analogies to see how minority identities could be recognised. Its *Blueprint for Stability* developed some of these ideas. It argued that 'machinery would be established to deal with and correct grievances, and to provide for further entrenchment of individual and community rights. This would include a Bill of Rights, which could not be amended by the Assembly' (UUP, 1994, 5). More importantly, they referred to the Conference on Security and Co-operation in Europe (CSCE) in the Vienna Accord (1989) and the Charter of Paris (1990) and argued:

The CSCE has, in these documents, devised a code of practice on the rights of communities and minorities. These European standards were developed with regard to the many ethnic and community problems in Europe. Institutions have also been created to monitor the application of these standards. The CSCE standards should be adopted as the criteria for law and practice in Northern Ireland. The methods by which the United Kingdom and the Irish Republic could co-operate on the implementation of the standards, within the institutions of the CSCE, should be explored. It is noted that the Council of Europe is preparing a Convention on national minorities, with a view to adding a protocol on that subject to its European Human Rights Convention. The protocol, when adopted, will apply to Northern Ireland. (UUP, 1994, 7; see also Trimble, 1996; Nesbitt, 2002)

This was used to buttress the Unionist case against Articles 2 and 3 of the Irish constitution. Unionists argued, 'The "constitutional imperative" must go. Unilaterally made, it must be unilaterally withdrawn' (DUP, 1993, 2). They argued this for several reasons. Members of the UUP pointed to the importance of the recognition of sovereign borders in the international system. Molyneaux had addressed this during the 1990 Gulf crisis. In a letter to grass-roots party officers he stated that the crisis had demonstrated how territorial claims could be aggressive and accused the European Community of turning a blind eye to:

Irish defiance of the requirements that nation states respect the integrity of each other's territory ... If the EC refuses to impose its own rules, then the Security Council must eliminate the only remaining territorial claim anywhere in Europe. (*Belfast Telegraph*, 23 August 1990)

At a Royal Black Institution demonstration in his constituency in Lisburn, he went even further:

Until 1990 Iraq laid claim to little Kuwait, but the world chose to regard that as a mere political aspiration, and in the United Nations talking shop no one had the courage to repudiate the claim. President Saddam Hussein decided to make it a constitutional imperative; seized Kuwait and brought us all to the brink of war. Iraq is providing a terrible example of the dangers inherent in claiming the territory of others. In our own land, it is a crime against humanity for politicians to assert a territorial claim and leave the IRA to enforce it. (*Belfast Telegraph*, 25 August 1990)

Martin Smyth argued:

The Unionist people are asked to forego their right to be British citizens or continue to face 'ethnic cleansing' by the IRA and their supporters. Surely, if Croatia and Slovenia, with large minorities, have been accepted internationally, Northern Ireland should be so recognised and the improper claim by a European partner over part of the UK forthwith dropped in keeping with international obligations. (*News Letter*, 18 September 1992)

The DUP had more pragmatic reasons for a removal of the two articles. Their submission to Strand 2 of the Mayhew talks, *A New Start*, cited Articles 2 and 3 as 'the key issue' and argued that:

> If our two countries were to sit side-by-side, in continuing hostility, then unionists would condemn the territorial claim but they would not require it to be removed. If, on the other hand, we are to establish a proper neighbourly relationship between Northern Ireland and the Irish Republic, as we earnestly wish, then the removal of that claim is not just a matter for consideration but an imperative. (DUP, 1992)

They were keen to widen the area in which these matters were considered to 'an all-encompassing British-Irish axis, albeit compartmentalised to satisfactorily deal with matters which could be more appropriately considered in that way' (DUP, 1992). They envisaged a dramatic political transformation would flow from such a move and ended on a positive note:

> Our hope is that the removal of the territorial claim and the creation of contact consistent with a normalising of neighbourly relations, would develop a new spirit of cordial co-operation and friendship, bringing a united effort for the common good. Such a process must inevitably tend to remove prejudices and allay anxieties and to promote better understanding.
> The divisions between the two traditions in Northern Ireland are very deep and we cannot estimate to what extent, if any, such new understandings as we have mooted might valuably assist in reducing or eliminating the distrust that has flowed from this division. However, we were asked by the SDLP to consider how we might provide for an outlet within which they might express their identity. It seems to us that this represents the limit that can be reached, consistent with the constitutional reality which every delegate has acknowledged. We contend that such a development has the potential

of being a turning point in Irish history, and we stand ready to make a sincere and generous contribution to the ongoing co-operation.

We desire that we might live as two countries on this island at peace and in friendship, respecting each other's right to exist and co-operating to our mutual advantage. (DUP, 1992)

Nevertheless, despite this 'positive' attitude, the DUP still had problems engaging with Strand 2. The DUP view on the Strand 2 negotiations was conditioned by its understanding of what they were meant to achieve. Fundamentally premised on the idea of two states, the purpose of Strand 2, in DUP eyes, was to normalise relations between states and not, as was understood by the Irish Government and the SDLP, to provide institutional recognition of the Nationalist identity.

The approach that Unionists adopted in the various stages of negotiations has been criticised in the political theory literature on Northern Ireland. O'Neill argues, in Rawlsian terms, that expression of national identity should be a primary good and therefore Unionists should be more open to means of expressing this right (O'Neill, 1994). Porter has gone further and argued that Unionists have substituted a variety of confrontational tactics for substantive dialogue and this not only violates normative political theory but simultaneously is a barrier to reconciliation between the two communities in Northern Ireland (Porter, 2003, 119–20). Therefore, for these normative theorists it is probably spurious to distinguish between Nationalists and Republicans. However, not only is this common among Unionists, regardless of their opinion of the Agreement, but it also illustrates the changes in Unionist attitudes. Admittedly, Unionists held out against power sharing until the very last stages of the negotiations (Hennessey, 2000, 167–8; De Bréadún, 2001, 130) but power sharing is no longer the contentious issue that it has been in the past and Unionists have been more open to accommodating the Nationalist minority. As Donaldson noted:

This notion that's put about by republicans that Unionists don't want a 'Fenian about the place' is completely wrong. That does not reflect the position of either the UUP or the DUP who have made it clear that for them power sharing with Nationalists is a given but power sharing with Republicans who are still wedded to a private army is certainly not a given and that is the position Bertie Ahern has taken in Dublin. He wouldn't have Sinn Féin in an Irish Government until the IRA has disbanded and I think that for Unionism that is now the measure by which we will judge if the Republican movement Sinn Féin/IRA have made the commitment to exclusively peaceful means. (Interview with Jeffrey Donaldson, 11 November 2002)

David Burnside asserted: 'What you can't have is unreconstructed militant Republicans [in government]. Working with Nationalists in local government in Northern Ireland is no problem. What the present conflict is within Unionism is working with Republicans, militant Republicans' (Interview with David Burnside, 13 September 2002). William McCrea, probably the most hardline critic of power sharing in the Unionist community, said: 'personally I believe that majority... decide the rules of the game. However, to engage and to try and face a reasonable settlement within Northern Ireland, while personally I don't like it, I was willing to live with the constitutional Nationalists involved' (Interview with William McCrea, 26 November 2002). When he was asked how he proposed to include the minority, Jim Wells replied:

How do we convince more Catholics [that the future of Northern Ireland is in the Union]? By a negotiated settlement, a just settlement, which gives the nationalist community a far greater role in the internal affairs in this part of the United Kingdom than any other minority anywhere else in Europe, a revolutionary role, which would not be granted to the Basques in France or Spain or the Hungarian minority in Czechoslovakia or the German minority in Poland. Give them an enormously effective role but excludes those who reserve the right to kill people for political ends... You could have a coalition, this wouldn't be party policy, we haven't adopted a policy, but you could have a coalition, of Ulster Unionists, DUP, Alliance and SDLP. A coalition which would represent 80% of the people of Northern Ireland running this in partnership, no problem at all. You would say to the terrorists, 'you've excluded yourselves, you've reserved the right to go forward with the ballot box in the one hand and the armalite in the other and therefore until you resolve that dilemma and you genuinely prove that you're carrying forward with peaceful democratic means there is no place for you in government.' In the meantime the ordinary decent people in this Province, Roman Catholic and Protestant, can run this part of the United Kingdom for the good of everybody. (Interview with Jim Wells, 7 November 2002)

Trimble has also made speeches addressing the Nationalist minority and the importance of incorporating them and their experience into

Northern Ireland. In his Nobel speech, for instance, he stated: 'Ulster Unionists, fearful of being isolated on the island, built a solid house, but it was a cold house for Catholics' (Trimble, 2001, 62).[12]

Moreover, the confrontational tactic over, for example, decommissioning has been conducted with the aim of using the political process as a 'carrot' to Republicans. It is undoubtedly the case that involvement in mainstream political life and its concomitant benefits were in the thinking of both John Hume and Gerry Adams (albeit separately) when they began to move the Republican movement away from armed struggle and so the Unionist approach is not totally divorced from political thinking in Northern Ireland in general. Indeed, it seems that Porter's approach to reconciliation, while persuasive, has less grounding in the political life of Northern Ireland than Unionist confrontation. Jeffrey Donaldson, who walked out of the negotiations in the final few hours, demonstrated an anti-Agreement vision of the Agreement consistent with many of the core principles which shaped it in the first place – inclusivity and bringing the Republican movement into the political process:

I think where the Agreement was flawed and where it falls down is in the failure to pin down the linkages between the peace process and the political process that would have been essential towards ensuring long term stability...I think that you're looking at some reshaping of the institutions to make them more accountable, to make them more workable but in terms of the core principle – that it is still power sharing based on inclusivity – but firmly underwritten by a commitment to exclusively peaceful and democratic means with much more stringent measures to deal with those who fail to make that commitment...the problem is the IRA keep eating all the carrots that the SDLP and the British government offer them and it seems like they've got this conveyer belt of tinned carrots that keeps being put on order for P O'Neill and their approach is: 'we'll give as little in return as we need to in order to keep the supply of carrots coming.' Unionism has made it clear now that this conveyer belt has to stop and it is clear that the carrot is there but it will only be available to them in the event that they deliver on their side of the bargain. I said after the Agreement was concluded that for me the problem was the Agreement blurred the lines between terrorism and democracy and I think what we've got to do now is unblur those lines and I think actually that is what's happening. (Interview with Jeffrey Donaldson, 11 November 2002; see also Donaldson, 1999)

It is clear that Unionist priorities and strategies have been overtaken by those of other parties who have had a more effective method of achieving their aims. Unionists have seen the benefits in the outcomes of these strategies, a more peaceful society for instance, but without controlling the political ramifications, the only route open was a confrontational one in which they have been, nominally, in control.

Conclusion

This chapter has argued that there is a general uneasiness among Unionists about the future direction of Northern Ireland and this is directly linked to their experience of Northern Ireland's process of change. This uneasiness has reinforced the 'undue pessimism', as Esmond Birnie describes:

> The problem with this mentality is that once it's there it's very hard to shift and it changes form so that if there's violence people say 'oh well they're bombing us into a united Ireland' and then when the violence stops 'oh these wicked people have devised a new strategy now, it's much more subtle' so people are never convinced. (Interview with Esmond Birnie, 4 October 2002)

The problem with the peace process is that it has done very little to try and remove this attitude, and indeed the process by which Irish Nationalists and the British Government has attempted to end the political violence in the province has, in many ways, given an element of political logic to those who argue in fatalistic terms.

The problems that the Belfast Agreement has encountered stem from this experience of the peace process. Unionists have been largely outside the formative stages of the process: they had a very limited input into the DSD, no input into the AIA or the Framework Documents and no influence on the process of ending violence. There is therefore no real sense of ownership of the peace process within Ulster Unionism, even among those pro-Agreement Unionists and, moreover, this is compounded by the perception illustrated by Roy Garland: 'I think it is true that Trimble has borne the brunt of the pain in this process' (Interview with Roy Garland, 18 November 2002). This is reflected in Ulster Unionist attitudes towards the Agreement; almost all see the Agreement as a deal or a contract, as Trimble explains:

> The Belfast Agreement is a contract between the people of Northern Ireland. Of course, rather like Hegel's ideal marriage it is a contract

which aims to go beyond contract. What it aims to achieve is a condition of mutuality amongst the people of Northern Ireland as the basis of a stable political order. As a marriage, though, mutuality cannot be achieved if the contract itself is not properly honoured. (Trimble, 2001, 132)

The dogmatists argue that any deal under the terms of such documents as the DSD or the Framework Documents was always going to be inimical to Unionist interests but those pro-Agreement pragmatic Unionists share the same experience of the peace process and find it difficult to persuade others that their interests are best served in such a process. Therefore there is the contradiction that an agreement that actually offers many positive things to Unionism is not seen in such a manner. The assessment of the Agreement by a pro-Agreement Unionist, Duncan Shipley-Dalton is indicative: 'Well that's the problem as it's [the Agreement] quite a difficult thing to sell. Accept the reality of your weakness wouldn't be an attractive message to sell to people' (Interview with Duncan Shipley-Dalton, 27 September 2002).

5
Unionism and the Politics of the Agreement

The story of the conclusion of the negotiations which led to the Belfast Agreement of Good Friday 1998 is well known (Hennessey, 2000; Mallie and McKittrick, 2001; Godson, 2004), as are the structures which it established (O'Leary, 1999) and their weaknesses (Horowitz, 2001; Taylor, 2001). The divisions within Unionism over the Agreement did not seem to have been taken seriously by the two Governments or by Nationalists and Republicans. Nevertheless, April, May and June 1998 were marked by optimism and hope, although it was obvious there would be difficult times during the implementation phase of the Agreement. In the heady days of 1998, a pro-Agreement consensus was evident among academics, journalists, civil society and Government; indeed, everybody but the estimated 49 per cent of Unionists who voted against it. The Agreement was a supposed triumph for the SDLP analysis and justification of its political project for the previous 26 years. The Agreement was a triumph for liberalism, pluralism and revisionism (both Nationalist and historical). All roads seemed to end at Good Friday. Anti-Agreement Unionists were looking isolated nationally and internationally and the 1998 Assembly results showed Unionism was more divided than ever. Even pro-Agreement Unionist academics, somewhat condescendingly, were calling anti-Agreement Unionists 'rejectionists' (Bew, 1998b). Yet it seemed to go wrong very quickly. Decommissioning did not happen and the formation of the cross-community Executive was delayed when the UUP Assembly party was absent when the D'Hondt procedure was being run at Stormont (*Irish Times* 16 July 1999). Furthermore, Trimble was given a weak mandate for Executive formation when it did happen and was constantly having to battle and negotiate with elements of his own party to carry out his strategy.

The assessments of Trimble have been largely positive. While paying attention to his awkward and almost anti-social personality traits, he has been seen as giving courageous leadership and attempting to combine flexibility, secularism and liberalism with Unionism, acknowledging past mistakes and giving Unionism an articulate and fresh face on the international stage. All this is true but his critics argue that he has conceded too much without adequate reciprocation and that he has become detached from the grass roots. Nationalist critics say he has not sold the Agreement sufficiently. All this nicely ignores Unionist dissatisfaction with the peace process and the widespread exclusion of almost half of Unionists from the political decisions about the future of Northern Ireland. While it is possible to be sceptical of the political use that SF have made of the peace process, it is quite clear from its politicians that they have invested much political time and capital in it, have some control and have made compromises. This is not reflected in the statements of pro-Agreement Unionists. The lack of ownership for Unionists is palpable in direct contrast to that of Republicans. This is even clearer on key implementation issues such as policing.

There are various ways of measuring this dissatisfaction. First, it is shown in opinion polls, which have recorded a steady decline in Unionist support for the Agreement, although there is consistent support for power sharing and consent (MacGinty, 2004). The estimate of Protestant support for the Agreement in the 1998 referendum was low at about 55 per cent but the Northern Ireland Life and Times survey showed that it had declined to only 28 per cent in 2003. The second is in the support for political parties which are anti-Agreement. The third is the increasing violent incidents on the growing number of interfaces and between and within paramilitary groups. All these measures are manifestations of the processes which have been discussed in the previous chapters; an infusion of new ideas seeking to reassert the validity of Unionism but not necessarily advocating a compromise solution; a disconnection from British policy and therefore a measure of disconnection from the British State; and a further disconnection from political developments, including key ideas which formed the framework for negotiations leading to the Agreement. All these developments are common to Unionists and did not significantly alter Unionists divisions; we saw how there was a common interpretation of the AIA and peace process in Chapters 2 and 4. However, the significant difference between those two developments was in how Unionists reacted. It was argued in Chapter 2 that there was a greater level of unanimity among Unionists as to what strategy to pursue that has hitherto been appreciated. However, the taxonomy developed in Chapter 4 demonstrates that this was not the case in relation to the 1998 Agreement. This Agreement became an issue of contention within the Unionist party politics and allowed for the possibility that the nature of Unionist political divisions would change.

This chapter will first examine the most important reasons behind the continuing crises of implementation through examining decommissioning (the main issue) and substantive issues (such as policing, equality, human rights and community relations) in order to ascertain if the connections between Unionism and the process changed with implementation. The second section will focus on party politics and seek to explain the increased support for the DUP and to assess its importance.

The politics of the Agreement

There have been two general approaches concerning the relationship between Unionists and the political process since the Agreement. The first, and most common, argues that contingency has been the most important factor in explaining the declining Unionist support for the Agreement and, by extension, Trimble and the UUP. This argues that the UUP made short-term losses in the Agreement but these were balanced by long-term gains. This trade-off became unstuck when, in the medium term, Republicans did not decommission and the Patten Commission on Policing recommended significant symbolic changes to the RUC. For example, Jonathan Tonge argues: 'The paradox is that, while the union now appears to have been made safe, those unionists who brokered the deal that ensured this have been made vulnerable' (Tonge, 2005, 81). The second approach argues that the Agreement changed the structure of politics and the state in Northern Ireland. Thus, the equality provisions, changes to the police, changes in the judicial system and so on, all involved moving the state from being 'structurally unionist' to structurally neutral (Ruane and Todd, 2001). Both the approaches acknowledge, however, that the effect of this was deep anxiety in the Unionist community and a general sense of loss. Aughey argues that this anxiety was manifested in two ways: anxiety of process, whereby the passive acceptance of the constitutional status of Northern Ireland was contrasted with the active programme to address Nationalist grievances, and an anxiety of influence, whereby the positive aspects of being inside devolved structures and having influence were contrasted with the notion that this could mean being trapped in a logic which was inimical to their interests (Aughey, 2005, 124).

However, as Chapters 2 and 4 demonstrated, this anxiety about the state of the process has roots which pre-date 1998 and there are two important caveats that should be added to an analysis which argues that Unionism has had a pessimistic and fatalistic reading of contemporary events. The first is that the tendency of academics to use a dazzling array of dichotomies to describe Unionist divisions is recognition of the ideational struggles within Unionism and many of these dichotomous observations have revolved around a fatalist/empowered axis. This is partly because the leadership of the UUP since 1995 and the Loyalist political parties have explicitly stated that this is part of their project. The DUP has been seen as the repository for a fatalistic Unionist politics (McAuley, 2003). However, the DUP critique of the UUP negotiating strategy is also a critique of this accepted wisdom on the balance of fatalism within Unionism. We saw in Chapters 1 and 4 how ideas were important in Trimble's thinking on transcending a siege mentality and engaging with Nationalists but the DUP have also developed a thesis on this and, interestingly, argue that it is Trimble who is the defeatist. Most forthright in putting this argument has been Gregory Campbell, who, during the debate in the Assembly on the establishment of ministries, argued that there would be three elements of Unionism:

> First, the defeatist section of Unionism, who, for whatever reason, has decided that it cannot change anything, that the combination of Sinn Féin/IRA, the SDLP, the British Government, the Irish Government, the Irish Americans and the European Union cannot be defeated. People in that section have thrown in the towel and said 'Let's make the best of it.' That is the defeatist element of Unionism. They have cut their cloth, and there is no going back after this vote. I am not throwing my lot in with them, nor will I ever do so.

The second element contains those who had opted out and was shown by lower electoral turnouts in the east of Northern Ireland. The third:

> contains those of us who are realists. We know what is going on. We see the reality of what is happening, and we have determined to do something about it, irrespective of our party label – whether we be DUP, Ulster Unionist, UK Unionist, United Unionist, Northern Ireland Unionist, or part of the mass of Unionists who simply see the realpolitik in this building and outside and want a change. They

have said 'We do not like what we see. We do not want the status quo.' I have said here many times and outside the Chamber a thousand times that we do not want the status quo. Why? Because the status quo has brought us to where we are today. We want a dynamic, determined, confident, assertive Unionism, whatever its label, whatever party we belong to. We want that to enable us to bring about change for our people and for the Nationalist community so that together we can go towards the future and put the past behind us.[1]

This critique was formulated from an early stage after the Agreement and contains many of the same phrases and much of the same analysis of the state of Unionism, insofar as it was passive and defeatist, as the 'New Unionists' discussed in Chapter 1 and yet, contrary to accepted opinion, the peace process was symptomatic of this defeatism and not a way out.

The second caveat is that the institutionalisation of the Agreement has had important effects which have counteracted the lack of ownership of the process widely exhibited by Unionists. Duncan Shipley-Dalton illustrates:

> The position of influence and power that we get is through the Assembly, it's the one big gain that we've made. It's a great political institution in which we share power with other groupings that gave us an influence. It gave us the opportunity that within the context of Northern Ireland we could punch to our weight because for years we were just completely futile, politically impotent, at least then as part of the government of Northern Ireland we had some kind of system we could use to give us some influence. From that we had the opportunity to go forward, at the end of the day David Trimble is the First Minister of Northern Ireland, he's Northern Ireland's Prime Minister when he goes to England and he gets an influence and he gets a hearing that he might not have but for that and in that way we create an extra outlet for ourselves as well and the same internationally...so I think the institutions gave us a great opportunity to actually increase the influence that we had and that's why I think they're probably the most important part of it. (Interview with Duncan Shipley-Dalton, 27 September 2002)

The internal effects of this are most clearly seen in the decommissioning saga. From the ceasefires of 1994 through to the Agreement of 1998, successive agreements on the timing of decommissioning were reneged, so that decommissioning prior to talks became decommissioning during talks, which became decommissioning after talks in the context of the full implementation of the Agreement (Brown and Hauswedell, n.d., 8–47). There is little evidence of Unionist influence over these changes in policy, which were pragmatically driven to keep Republicans in the process. However, the potential Unionist influence over the fact and timing of decommissioning changes when the institutions of the Agreement are established. Connections are made between the Unionist demand for decommissioning and Republican participation in an inclusive Executive, although it was possible for other connections to have been made. The UUP ran an election campaign on the principle of 'no guns, no government' and Trimble explicitly linked the two issues when he announced the UUP would enter government: 'We have done our bit. Mr Adams, it's over to you. We've jumped, you follow' (Godson, 2004, 531). When this process occurs, there is the creation of informal links between the agendas of the parties and aspects of the peace process. Thus, theoretically, Republicans could have used their participation in the Assembly as a mechanism for extracting concessions from Unionists in the same way as Unionists attempted to do with Republicans.

David Trimble was essentially playing a tactical game with Republicans over decommissioning; he thought Republicans would decommission but did not expect them to do so without pressure, although it was ultimately international pressure and not pressure from Unionists that was important. In playing this game he was constrained by the arguments of Unionists for whom decommissioning was a more fundamental question relating to the form and substance of democracy in Northern Ireland and who doubted the sincerity of Republicans (McCartney, 2001, 151–76). Those who consistently argued that the principle of decommissioning was a make-or-break issue for Republican participation in governmental structures have seemed isolated for much of the period since the ceasefires, when a self-evident pragmatism was the dominant framework within which the two Governments, Nationalists and Republicans, operated. The pragmatics meant that the greater goal was peace and a degree of flexibility was required on the mechanics of getting there and Republican good faith was assumed. This was underpinned by an analysis which stated that the IRA was not able to go back to war. This argument has firm credentials (Ruane, 2004) and it is certainly the case, as many argued, that one of the implications of this analysis is that decommissioning was a red herring; the guns were useless if they could not be used. However, it is important to understand the *type* of argument that this is; it is a strategic argument based on the costs and benefits of the armed struggle. Why would Unionists agree with the optimistic implications that Republicans would not go back to war when this strategic analysis is premised on their own internal logic? As Trimble, who also seemed to agree with this analysis, argued at the review of the Agreement in February 2003:

> If republicans had acted from a realisation that violence was morally wrong, then we would not have had the ambiguity of the 'cessation of military operations' and the endless foot-dragging on decommissioning. Instead there would have been a ready willingness to end all aspects of the campaign and to genuinely embrace exclusively peaceful and democratic means. (Trimble, 2004a)

For Unionists, it was important that decommissioning happened, not merely that Republicans were unable to go back to war. The act of full decommissioning became invested with meaning which concerned Republican motivations; if Republicans decommissioned that indicated something more fundamental about the meaning of the peace process than the widely held view that Republican strategy was premised on the Tactical Use of Armed Struggle (TUAS).[2]

In order to maintain the credibility of this pragmatic reading there was a moral ambiguity over the connections between SF and the IRA, which was only periodically punctured prior to 2005, such as during the debates as to the suitability of SF for government in the Republic of Ireland (O'Donnell, 2004, 223–66). However, the pragmatic consensus came apart in a rather dramatic fashion in early 2005 after the alleged Republican involvement in the Northern Bank robbery and the murder of Short Strand resident Robert McCartney.[3] Senior Irish Government ministers openly admitted that they had adopted a pragmatic policy of 'constructive ambiguity' to Republican paramilitary activity,[4] and commentators not known for their Unionist sympathies articulated hostility towards SF (Finlay, 2005). In the Republic of Ireland this change did not seem to be a conversion to Unionist thinking but was partly led by Northern Nationalists, as shown by the McCartney sisters and their campaign, and the perceived threat to the southern state posed by the connection between IRA violence and crime and the growth of SF.[5] However, the pragmatic approach to decommissioning and Republican good faith was never a strong argument in Unionist circles and the idea of trust was an important theme after the Police Service of Northern Ireland (PSNI) raids on the SF offices in Stormont in October 2002.

One further aspect of the decommissioning issue is illustrative of how Unionists have related to the peace process in a different manner to Republicans and Nationalists. Michael Cox has argued that the ending of the Cold War had an important effect in reassessing the world view of Republicans and their interpretation of British interests in Northern Ireland and thus was an important background factor in the peace process (Cox, 1997). There have been some counterarguments (Dixon, 2002b), some evidence has been produced to say that international changes did not affect Republicans (English, 2003, 303–15), and the important international canvassing by John Hume from the 1970s pre-dates the Cox analysis (Wilson, 1995). However, the internationalisation of the peace process is not in doubt through the interventions of Bill Clinton (O'Clery, 1996; MacGinty, 1997; O'Dowd, 2002), various groups of South Africans (Guelke, 1996b, 2000) and the effects of international events (Farrington, 2004a). Each one of these aspects represents a different type of intervention by the international dimension: interventions by specific actors, Track Two diplomacy and the effects of changes in the international environment. For Unionists the most important aspect of this was probably the Track Two diplomacy, which took place outside Ireland and marked an important space for learning and dialogue (Arthur, 1999b). However, there was not the same degree of international pressure on Unionists as there was on Republicans. There have certainly been phone calls from American presidents to Unionist leaders at key points in negotiations (Godson, 2004, 352; *Irish Independent*, 27 November 2004) but it is not possible to argue that changing international environments (as opposed to specific international interventions) affect Unionist strategy, as they do not have the same international links with groups around the world or an ideology which has an explicit international dimension as Republicans. On the other hand, Republicans have been subject to such pressures, as was evident after September 11 and in relation to the Colombia Three (Farrington, 2004a). These events combined to produce an act of decommissioning and illustrate two things. First, as with the Northern Bank raid and the murder of Robert McCartney it was not Unionist pressure which brought movement from Republicans and thus proving the futility of linking decommissioning and executive formation. Secondly, it demonstrates the different worldviews of Unionists and Nationalists in Northern Ireland. There may be international comparisons to be made with other conflicts but apart from pro-Israeli sentiment in some Loyalist areas of Belfast (*News Letter*, 25 May 2002), there are not the same sentiments of solidarity with other areas and peoples from Unionists as there are from Republicans.

Aside from the use of the Assembly as a tool to achieve decommissioning, the institutions of the Agreement – the Assembly, the North/South Ministerial Council and the British-Irish Council – were relatively uncontentious. This was perhaps surprising, as Colin Irwin's opinion polls demonstrated that 40 per cent of Protestants said the idea of North/South bodies was unacceptable.[6] But, by 2000, the Northern Ireland Life and Times Survey found that only 16 per cent of Protestants opposed the creation of the North/South bodies.[7] This marked a change in the political arena. Prior to the agreement of the institutions much of the peace process had been concerned with ideological and institutional questions: How could consent be reconciled with self-determination? What institutions would reflect Irish Nationalist identity but be acceptable to Unionist ideas on a minimalist cross-border co-operation? After 1998 the contentious issues became substantive rather than institutional and included policing, human rights provisions and community relations.

The changes to the police as recommended by Patten were crucial, as changes to the nature of policing were essential if an agreement was to truly represent a 'new beginning' in Northern Ireland and changes to policing were consistently shown in opinion polls as contentious issues for Protestants.[8] The RUC was overwhelmingly Protestant in composition and had lacked legitimacy in the eyes of Republicans and Nationalists. However, the issue was so contentious that, in order to reach an agreement in April 1998, it was decided to give responsibility for recommending changes to an independent commission (McGarry and O'Leary, 2004, 371–4). The Commission recommended, among other things, that the name of the RUC should be changed to the PSNI, the badge should be changed and that recruitment should be on a 50–50 (Catholics: Others) basis to rapidly increase the numbers of Catholics employed in the force.[9] Apart from the 50–50 recruitment, for which the British Government had to get special dispensation from the European Union (EU), most of the issues were largely symbolic and not totally satisfactory to Republicans but yet they seemed to represent a significant defeat for Unionists, with no accompanying pay-off, as was the case with the Agreement. The UUP had very little influence over the Patten Commission, despite appointing one of the Commissioners, and both the UUP and the DUP failed to amend the legislation when it came before the House of Commons. However, the UUP bore the brunt of the blame within Unionism for the changes.

The question of human rights in Northern Ireland has been entangled in communal politics but not in the symbolic or zero-sum fashion of the policing question. The idea of human rights was not one which

Unionists were adept at using but it was not an idea which was seen to be intrinsically inimical to Unionist interests. Trimble did say: 'One of the great curses of this world is the human rights industry... They justify terrorist acts and end up being complicit in the murder of innocent victims' (*The Guardian*, 29 January 2004). However, most Unionists gave a qualified welcome to their enshrinement in law. For example, Robert McCartney stated:

> No democrat or pluralist could do other than welcome legislation or institutions that safeguard the civil and human rights or the citizens of the United Kingdom of Great Britain and Northern Ireland... [but] For any institution, or commission, to propagate the views that it was brought into being to promote, it must have the support of the entire community. One of the disadvantages of the Human Rights Commission is the widespread view, which I share, that it is unbalanced, unrepresentative and has not devoted itself to the human rights of the entire community. Since it was instituted, and in its entire modus operandi, it has done nothing to obtain the support of the majority community.[10]

The Human Rights Commission was obviously stung by such criticisms (see exchange between Foster, A, 2003 and Dickson, 2003) and made a concerted effort to go and talk to, for example, Protestant community groups. However, there were three issues related to the concept of human rights which represented fundamental problems. First, there was a debate over group vs individual rights and Unionists argued for individual rights to predominate (Foster, 2003). Secondly, there were the linkages which Unionists made between rights and parading, which were partly due to the perceived partisan use of rights by Nationalists. Unionists used a rights-based argument to try and secure traditional routes for Orange parades[11] but this was far from a clear case and was ultimately unsuccessful, giving further evidence for Unionists of the partial nature of such tools (DUP, 2003, 48–50). Thirdly, there was the historical legacy of human rights groups in Northern Ireland, which had focused on state violations of human rights; this coloured Unionist perceptions of the nature of the inclusion of the agenda and was combined with another argument concerning the treatment and analysis of victims of the Troubles.[12]

Chapter 4 distinguished between three processes which were occurring in the 1990s: a peace process, which involved persuading Republicans to end violence; a political process, which involved attempting to get an agreement between Unionists and Nationalists on political structures for Northern Ireland; and another process below the level of the political parties, which many working in the community sector consider the real peace process. This involves grass-roots peace building and was encouraged by the British Government in the early 1990s but became significant after the EU made funds available for such work, and most of this sector is now funded through the EU, with additional funds channelled through the Community Relations Council and charitable and philanthropic organisations such as the Joseph Rowntree Trust or Atlantic Philanthropies (Cochrane and Dunn, 2002). Most of this work is funded as project based and is now finishing the second EU funding cycle. It is widely acknowledged that Protestant groups were not as effective at accessing money as Catholic groups; the Office of First and Deputy First Minister was actively trying to rectify this disparity, while Intermediary Funding Bodies, which were used to distribute PEACE money, ringfenced specific money for areas with 'weak community infrastructure', which usually meant rural Protestant communities. It is difficult to measure the culpability of political parties in this state of affairs.

While most of this work has occurred outside the political leadership, Unionist political parties have been slow to see the full value of civil society activity in solving the political problems of Northern Ireland. The manner in which Direct Rule operated usually meant bypassing elected representatives and using civil society as a source of advice and administration, through Quangos. The institutionalisation of the Agreement involved altering that state of affairs and investing more power and responsibility in the hands of politicians. This was a fundamental alteration in the relationship between party politics and civil society, with the latter having to adjust (and at times reluctantly). The most significant section of civil society in Northern Ireland is the community sector, which has accessed most of the Peace and Reconciliation money from the EU; its importance was reflected in the large number of representatives that it was given on the Civic Forum. However, Unionist political parties have not endorsed this interpretation and are more likely to mention the business sector or the churches as the most important constituent elements of civil society. Some of the dynamics of this relationship stem from the legitimate question as to democratic accountability; civil society is more likely to stress a participative mode of democracy, whereas political parties stress a more representative mode (Farrington, 2004b). Unionists, who have a more state-centred approach to politics, are less receptive to those claims than Nationalists and, especially, Republicans, whose experience of politics has been a community- and civil society-based one, usually conceived in opposition to the British state in Northern Ireland. The dismissive attitude of both the UUP and the DUP towards the Civic Forum is illustrative of this but even beyond the suspicions of a potentially threatening second chamber, which was how some erroneously interpreted its role, there is hostility towards the perceived agenda of civil society.

It should be stated that this is a more generalised argument about some of the more powerful organisations within civil society and there is usually nothing but praise and commendations for local community activists. However, civil society is seen as pro-Agreement and giving little room for anti-Agreement voices within its hierarchy. As a generalised argument about civil society in its entirety this is obviously incorrect, as civil society is as diverse as wider society, but, as one DUP politician stated:

> From a pro-Agreement point of view I think that civic society has provided some degree of arguing force for the agreement, although from a practical point of view I'm not altogether sure that in any practical sense that has swayed opinion . . . whatever card was played in 1998 was only able to be played once, which was sort of this impression that all society was behind the agreement. I think that probably did have a degree of impact on people, made people feel almost a little bit guilty about voting no, they were sort of opposing all the good and great of society. I think that, as disillusion has set in within the Unionist community, any attempts to play that card again, be it church leaders, be it business leaders, members of civic society has had less and less impact. I think it only tended to appeal to those people who are strongly committed to the agreement in the first place. (Interview with Peter Weir, 15 January 2004)

This could be seen as paranoia but Unionist unease at civil society's relationship with politics has a wide base.

Elements of civil society have been used as the Government's chosen vehicle for delivery of its community relations programme, and the funding programmes have been established in such a way as to make funding dependent on a progression to cross-community work (Community Relations Council, n.d.). In view of the slow engagement of the Protestant community and the widespread opinion that Protestants are not as ready as Catholics to engage with the other community, this development has thus linked a suspicion of the community sector with the wider problems in the development of policy in Northern Ireland.

These views can be seen in the response to the discussions on community relations and the consultation on the 'A Shared Future' document in 2004. The DUP was the only one of the five major political parties which did not make a submission to the consultation and this was linked to a general suspicion of Government motives in relation to community relations policy (Foley and Robinson, 2004, 45–6). Moreover, in discussions about community relations, it is clear that Unionist politicians prioritise single identity work and issues. For example, during the Northern Ireland Grand Committee debate on Community Relations policy, there was no Unionist who articulated a long-term vision for community relations, let alone an integrated future. Indeed, the concerns which were expressed included Orange marches, the idea of choice to live in single identity housing estates and political symbols; David Trimble articulated the underlying premise behind the position of both parties: 'We do not think it is desirable to try to homogenise society. We accept that there are differences. One has to encourage toleration and pluralism, but those terms sit rather uncomfortably with the Minister's objective of a more integrated society.'[13]

These three issues of policing, human rights and community relations exemplify a Unionist attitude towards the conflict and its resolution that was discussed in Chapter 4. Unionist insecurities about the Union have taken precedence over almost all other issues and have left Unionist politicians with few tools to take advantage of the opportunities which a changing society presented. This was evident in the performance of ministers in the Executive and the socio-economic policies of the Unionist parties. Despite the UUP's slogan in 2000, 'Making Government Work' (*Irish Times*, 9 October 2000), its 2003 manifesto was particularly weak on the details of policy beyond the constitutional question (Wilson and Fawcett, 2004, 24). There does not appear to be any particular reason for this; the party is a broad coalition of interests and it could be speculated that some of these issues could be divisive as, for instance, there are people both strongly for and against the abolition of the 11 + exam for transfer into post-primary education. The DUP manifestoes prioritised style but it has been more adept at cultivating a media image and developing policies than the UUP (Wilson and Fawcett, 2004, 25) and its ministers were considered among the most competent in the Executive.

Party politics

The 2003 Northern Ireland Assembly election seemed to confirm many theories of ethnic party politics (Horowitz, 1985, 291–364) when the anti-Agreement and 'extremist' DUP replaced the UUP as the largest Unionist party. There was an apparent linear progression from agreement with Nationalists by the UUP to the replacement of the UUP by the more dogmatic and belligerent DUP. However, this analysis is too simplistic and misses some of the important changes within Unionism and Unionist politics. The party system of the Republic of Ireland has always been considered distinctive, as its roots are not in the socio-economic cleavages in much of Europe (Coakley, 2003, 238). The party system of Northern Ireland, on the other hand, is usually not considered at all (and is actually frequently explicitly excluded) by the general political science literature on political parties. Even within the voluminous literature on Northern Ireland, there is very little sustained consideration of the party system or type of political parties and how this impacts upon Northern Irish politics. The main political cleavage in Northern Irish society is religious (Walker, 1996, 15–33) and Paul Mitchell has described the system as an 'ethnic dual party system'. Essentially, this means Northern Ireland has two-party systems – one for Unionists and one for Nationalists – operating in tandem (Mitchell, 1995). There are few floating voters in this system and only a minimal number of parties which have attempted to appeal to voters from either side of the communal divide. The bi-confessional parties at present have attracted around 10 per cent of the vote since the early 1980s but this is in decline. The overall pattern of Unionist and Nationalist electoral percentages is shown in Figure 5.1.

If we are to argue that the Northern Ireland party system is, in effect, two different party systems then we should be examining the nature of party competition in each individual system. We saw in the Introduction how the study of Unionism has so far focused on cultural divisions within Unionism as a whole and only recently have these divisions been mapped with political divisions (Farrington, 2001). The analysis of intra-system dynamics has been heavily influenced by the ethnic conflict paradigm, and the analyses of the DUP outlined in Chapter 3 link the DUP to identity politics. Indeed, the quantitative literature would tend to endorse such an argument. Analysts using statistical mapping techniques or social attitudes survey data have been unable to explain support for Unionist parties beyond the electorate's perceptions on the effectiveness of the party at defending the Union (Knox, McIlheney and Osborne, 1995; Evans and Duffy, 1997). The stagnation of the DUP's vote was explained by the perceived ineffectiveness of Paisley to bring any real advantages to the Unionist community (Mitchell, 1995, 785). Under this reading, the growth of the DUP is

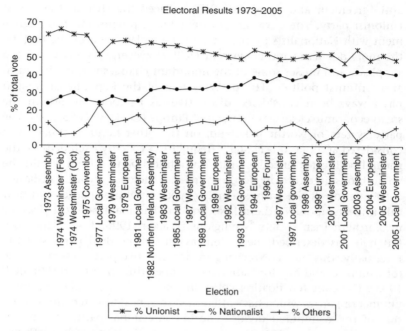

Figure 5.1   Unionist and Nationalist electoral performance 1973–2005.
Source: Derived from figures in Elliott and Flackes (1999) and www.ark.ac.uk/elections.

remarkably easy to explain: Unionists, uneasy with the political direction of Northern Ireland and particularly over the Agreement, have turned away from the moderate UUP towards the more reliable uncompromising DUP. The Unionist community thinks it can trust the DUP more than the increasingly fractured UUP and has endorsed its political message. This is highly plausible; support for the Agreement among Protestants has declined significantly and support for the DUP has grown and, as was noted earlier, a popular analysis in Northern Ireland is to explain the growth in the DUP vote in contingent terms, broadly explained by the direction of politics since the Agreement. In this reading, the growth of the DUP is the mirror of the growth of SF; both parties are seen as the most effective defenders of their community. However, the difficulty with these 'explanations' is that they are only partial explanations. In particular they do not explain the territorial differences in DUP vote, as we also encountered in Chapter 3, and they do not explain the timing of the growth in the DUP vote.

The DUP has overcome greater obstacles to achieve dominance in the Unionist bloc than SF have in the Nationalist bloc, which does not have a comparable party to the UUP, which has dominated the Unionist system since 1905 (Buckland, 1973; Jackson, 1989; Bew, Gibbon and Patterson, 1996; Walker, 2004a). Even a brief reflection on the state of the competition between the two parties shows that the Assembly election in 2003 requires explanation. Apart from European elections, which are contested by Ian Paisley primarily on a personality basis, the UUP has been eclipsed as the largest *party* in Northern Ireland on only two occasions since 1921. The first was the local government elections in 1981, where it was narrowly defeated by the DUP, and the second was the Assembly elections of 1998, where it gained a smaller number of first preference votes than the SDLP, although this translated into a larger number of seats. Throughout the 50 years of Stormont the UUP experienced very little electoral competition; it was the Northern Ireland Labour Party rather than any Nationalist party that provided the most effective challenge. O'Leary and McGarry have described this period as one of hegemonic rule because of the uncompetitive nature of the system and the various legal difficulties that the UUP erected for other parties (O'Leary and McGarry, 1996). The electoral hegemony of the UUP ended during the civil rights movement of the late 1960s and the Unionist party system entered a second phase. This phase saw a proliferation of Unionist parties and it was unclear which would survive the 1970s. Ultimately the only parties that did were the UUP and the DUP, partly by chance and partly by their organisational design. The UUP remained the dominant Unionist party until 2003.

The 2003 Assembly elections could therefore be seen as a temporary blip rather than a fundamental alteration in the political landscape. However, there are several important developments within the UUP system which indicate the latter interpretation. This is shown by an analysis of the electoral performances of the Unionist parties. The overall graph of electoral competition demonstrates some interesting trends. Figure 5.2 shows the percentage of the combined UUP and DUP vote from 1985; the combined UUP and DUP vote is used rather than the total Unionist vote because the proliferation of smaller Unionist parties and independents adversely affects the UUP, as is shown in Figure 5.3. Prior to 1996 such a graph showed very little; the peaks and troughs gave the impression of an electoral anarchy. The DUP peaks and UUP troughs are caused by European elections, which Paisley contests. However, with the addition of elections since 1996, the trends are clearer: there has been a convergence of the electoral performances

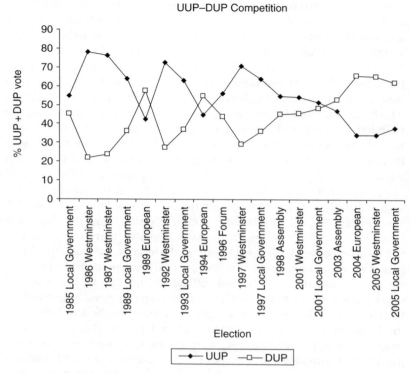

Figure 5.2   UUP–DUP Electoral competition.
Source: Derived from figures in Elliott and Flackes (1999) and www.ark.ac.uk/elections.

of the two parties. Part of this is explained looking exclusively at Westminster elections, as shown in Figure 5.4; the electoral pact of the AIA campaign disintegrated and the DUP have steadily contested more constituencies in Westminster elections, as also illustrated on the graph. There were still a number of reciprocal constituency pacts in place in 2001, particularly in the west of Northern Ireland in West Tyrone, Mid Ulster and Fermanagh and South Tyrone, and the DUP contested all constituencies in 2005. More interesting is a similar graph isolating elections held under the Single Transferable Vote system of Proportional Representation (Figure 5.5). This electoral system is used for all elections in Northern Ireland other than Westminster elections. The only exception was the Forum, which used a party list system, but which is still included here. This demonstrates that the DUP percentage of the total Unionist

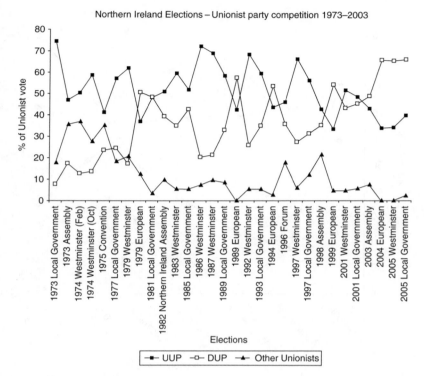

Figure 5.3 Unionist party competition 1973–2003.
Source: Derived from figures in Elliott and Flackes (1999) and www.ark.ac.uk/elections.

vote hovered between 33.1 per cent in 1989 and 35.4 per cent in 1998, despite the dramatic rise in the number of Unionist parties. In 1996, under the Entry to Negotiation Legislation, the Forum elections were held under party list system PR with an additional 20-member 'top-up' system; that is the top ten parties when the votes were collated across Northern Ireland would be given two seats each, thus enabling them to participate in the all-party talks, which eventually led to the Belfast Agreement of Good Friday 1998 (Mitchell and Gillespie, 1999, 80–2).

This system led to the creation of one new party, the Northern Ireland Women's Coalition (NIWC) (Fearon, 1999, 2–5) and also gave an electoral kick-start to several smaller Unionist parties: The Progressive Unionist Party (PUP), which is attached to the Ulster Volunteer Force (UVF), the Ulster Democratic Party (UDP), which is now no longer in existence but which was attached to the Ulster Defence Association

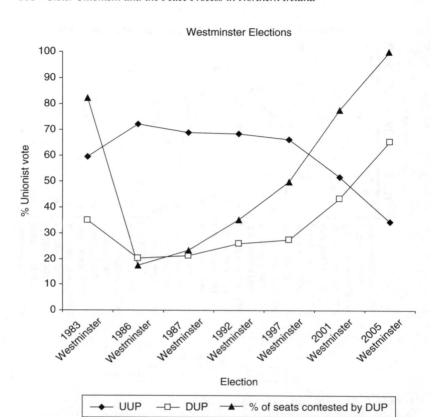

Figure 5.4   Electoral competition between the UUP and the DUP in Westminster elections.

Source: Derived from figures in Elliott and Flackes (1999) and www.ark.ac.uk/elections.

(UDA) and the Ulster Freedom Fighters (UFF) and the United Kingdom Unionist Party (UKUP), which was expanded from its base in North Down where its leader Robert McCartney was the sitting Westminster MP. With five-member constituencies only Robert McCartney could have had a realistic hope of securing a seat of any of these four parties but the top-up system encouraged these parties to contest all constituencies, as their aggregate votes would then, hopefully, push them into the top ten political parties. However, of the 18 constituencies in Northern Ireland, the UDP failed to achieve four-figure totals in eleven constituencies, the PUP in eight and the UKUP in six, which also did not contest a further three. Nevertheless, collectively, these parties and

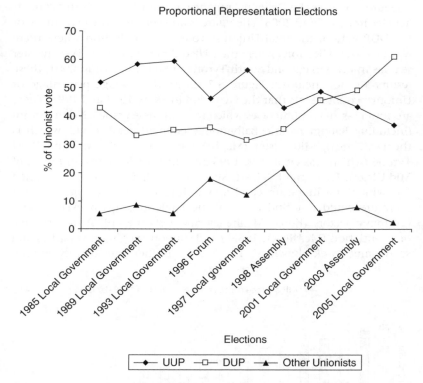

Figure 5.5 Unionist party competition in elections held using proportional representation (excluding European elections).
Source: Derived from figures in Elliott and Flackes (1999) and www.ark.ac.uk/elections.

a number of independents gained 17.9 per cent of the Unionist vote. A similar result was replicated in 1998, although there are a number of prominent individuals who were previously members of the UUP who effectively denied the UUP key seats, for example William Wright in North Antrim, Jim Dixon in Fermanagh and South Tyrone and Dennis Watson in Upper Bann. The overall effect was to fragment the UUP, but not the DUP, vote. Moreover, when these parties declined in significance, as Unionist voters returned to the two main parties, the votes which had seeped from the UUP did not return and instead were given to the DUP. Thus, it was only the double election of 2001 which saw the first real significant upward shift in the DUP share of the Unionist vote, which it then used to build on for the 2003 Assembly election.

Figure 5.6 ranks the DUP performance in the 18 Westminster constituencies from 1996 to 2003. The figure is an average of the percentage of the DUP vote of the total Unionist vote in each election where there was a contest. Therefore, where the DUP did not contest the Westminster seat, as in Fermanagh and South Tyrone or South Belfast in 2001, these results are not included. Figure 5.7 shows the average percentage of Unionist council seats that the DUP won in 1989, 1993 and 1997. There are a number of constituencies which recur in these graphs: North Antrim (including Ballymena and Ballymoney council areas), Foyle (which is the DCC area), Mid Ulster (Magherafelt and Cookstown) and West Tyrone (which was created in 1995 and includes Strabane and parts of Mid Ulster). These graphs clearly show results that need to be explained but which the literature cited above does not do. The quantitative literature could not find any statistical relationships between socio-economic factors (Knox, McIlheney and Osborne, 1995) or territorial differentiation (McAllister, 1983c) and support for Unionist parties and so we must look elsewhere. The ethnic conflict and identity politics

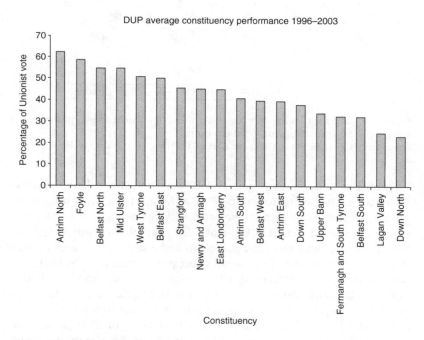

Figure 5.6   DUP constituency performance as percentage of the Unionist vote.
Source: Derived from figures in Elliott and Flackes (1999) and www.ark.ac.uk/elections.

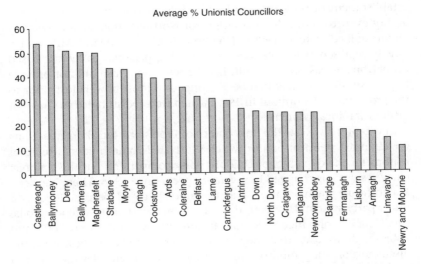

Average % Unionist Councillors

Figure 5.7 DUP's average percentage of Unionist councillors by local council area 1989–1997.
Source: Derived from figures in Elliott and Flackes (1999) and www.ark.ac.uk/elections.

literature above cannot explain why the DUP perform consistently well in Foyle and North Antrim but not in Lagan Valley or North Down. The figures presented since 1996 are not totally representative of DUP support prior to the peace process because electoral pacts reduced the number of intra-Unionist competitions and the relatively small number of PR elections exacerbated the effect of this. Thus, the two bastions of DUP support were presumed to have been East Belfast and North Antrim, the Westminster constituencies of Peter Robinson and Ian Paisley respectively. William McCrea also held the Mid Ulster constituency but this was the result of a split Nationalist vote and the UUP dropping out of the contest (this was reciprocated by the DUP in Fermanagh and South Tyrone, although Ken Maginnis did manage a straight plurality in this constituency on some occasions). The assumption behind all these analyses is that the Unionist party system is very traditional, static and has more to do with personal bailiwicks than competition, as McAllister observed in 1983 (McAllister, 1983b). Thus, the DUP strength in North Antrim and East Belfast is dependent on the personalities of Paisley and Robinson. This has a degree of truth to it but it cannot be totally explained in this way because politicians in Northern Ireland have had no executive power for the duration of the Troubles. Before the establishment of the Northern Ireland Select Committee in 1993 their ability even to scrutinise legislation for Northern Ireland was severely circumscribed (Greer, 1999). Therefore Northern Ireland MPs had a largely representative role, and constructing personal bailiwicks based on patronage was very difficult. Local government also did not provide any possibilities as they had been stripped of most powers just prior to the proroguing of Stormont in 1972, which were redistributed to Quangos rather than local councils.

In Chapter 3 we saw the importance of Protestant social organisations for Unionist political parties which illustrated some hidden structural reasons for the dynamics of Unionist party competition but the Unionist party system has changed in several respects since 1996. There has been a significant fragmentation and therefore it could be described as a multi-party system. However, these additional parties have tended to be small, lack a province-wide appeal and the evidence from 2003 and 2005 would indicate that they are temporary. The key indicator for the discussion on the Unionist party system here is their relevance. Sartori measures this based on the coalition or blackmail potential of the parties (Sartori, 1976, 122–4) but neither of these are of relevance in Northern Ireland, particularly in relation to the Northern Ireland Assembly because coalition formation is not determined by deals but by mathematical formula (Wilford and Wilson, 2003, 16–8) so smaller parties have no influence on that process. The consociational nature of the Assembly and Executive means that more parties actually damage the overall Unionist bloc; from 1998 to 2003 Unionists actually had one less ministerial position than their total numbers would have given them had they only been split between two rather than six parties (Whyte, 2003). It was unlikely that any of these parties would be able to challenge the predominance of the UUP or the DUP but this does not mean that there have been no changes in the relationship between the two larger parties. Throughout the Troubles the Unionist party system could have been described as a one-party dominant system. The UUP has consistently been the largest party, has the widest geographical support base and has been the most popular party in both elections and opinion polls. The only serious challenge to this position was in the 1970s when the UUP fragmented and lost leadership figures who then formed their own parties. During that period, and also during the first DUP challenge in 1979 and 1981, it staved off these electoral challenges by a series of electoral pacts, which stunted the growth of these smaller parties and, by eliminating competition, temporarily secured its own support base until the crisis was over. The current changes seem more significant.

The Unionist party system is now effectively a two-party system and the DUP appear to be able to compete on an equal basis with the UUP. This is a substantial change and can be attributed to several aspects of the politics of the peace process.

First, the peace process introduced a specific issue into Unionist party competition. If we accept that social and cultural divisions were the dominant political divisions within Unionism, it also has to be recognised that there was little competition for votes over these issues. Even if there was extensive competition, there is little evidence that voters were inclined to switch from one party to the other as a result of that competition. However, as we saw in Chapter 4, it is possible to distinguish policy positions on the Agreement – principles yes, pragmatic yes, pragmatic no, principled no – and these have altered how Unionist parties relate to one another and opened up the possibility for competition on issues. How this competition has occurred will be discussed below.

Secondly, the politics of the peace process has significantly increased the competitiveness of the party system, and not just between Unionist parties. Elections since 1985 have been remarkably predictable. In Westminster elections, incumbency was a high predictor of success. Seamus Mallon (SDLP) won a by-election in 1986 and, apart from death or retirement, from then until 1997 only West Belfast changed hands. The only change to this pattern in 1997 was Martin McGuinness' (SF) success in Mid Ulster when he defeated the DUP's William McCrea and Gerry Adams, who retook his West Belfast seat. This pattern was spectacularly disrupted in 2001 when eight constituencies changed hands. Local government elections, which were held under PR, also displayed a remarkable degree of stability and have not been particularly competitive either. In 1993, for instance, only four councils changed political allegiance and only one (Ballymena) changed between the DUP and the UUP (Knox, McIlheney and Osborne, 1995). The peace process has injected competition into these elections and also has produced its own series of elections, in 1996, 1998 and 2003, based on a PR voting system, which has enabled the DUP to compete with the UUP without any risk of splitting votes. This has, in turn, led to the DUP contesting, and winning, Westminster seats that it had not previously.

Thirdly, this competitiveness has changed how the Unionist political parties think about elections. Previously, the concern related to the possibility that a split vote would allow a Nationalist to win a seat because the electoral system encouraged such an attitude. In 2001 and 2005, however, this was only used as a rhetorical weapon by the Ulster Unionists. For the DUP, elections were no longer primarily about the

Unionist–Nationalist balance but about the intra-Unionist balance. Therefore, the electoral pact system within Unionism has been altered by changes in the electoral goals of the DUP. Until very recently, the predominance of the UUP meant that electoral pacts were good for it and not good for the DUP. In the 1970s and after the AIA, the DUP sacrificed its electoral goals for the 'greater cause of Unionism'. In the 1970s this involved aligning itself with the anti-power sharing elements of the UUP in the United Ulster Unionist Council. In 1986 the strategy of non-co-operation with sitting MPs was not universally welcomed within the party and led to the resignation of one of its most prominent politicians, Jim Allister (and several members in his constituency branch of Newtownabbey). During the peace process the DUP has not replicated these strategies. There has not even been speculation about the possibility of a pact with anti-Agreement Ulster Unionist representatives (although Martin Smyth in South Belfast was left uncontested in 2001) and even anti-Agreement electoral coalitions have been rhetorical. Anti-Agreement Unionists contested the 1998 Assembly elections under the banner of 'United Unionists' and produced joint election documents but there was little evidence, unlike in 1974 or in 1977, that this existed in the selection of candidates; at most it was a deal to tell supporters to transfer to other anti-Agreement Unionists. In 2003 there was no evidence of such alliances; indeed, it was DUP strategy to win the seats from those anti-Agreement Unionists who were not part of the DUP.

Fourthly, the political divisions within the UUP have been maintained in such a way so as to prevent the UUP from fragmenting into different parties. The Unionist political parties that contested the 1998 election had origins that pre-dated the Agreement. The PUP and UDP's origins and support base both lay within the Loyalist paramilitaries and therefore outside the two main parties. The UKUP contained members of both the UUP and the DUP but attracted them from the lower strata of the parties. Indeed, McCartney was reluctant to establish a party but under the Entry to Negotiation Legislation for the 1996 Forum needed a party to contest the election, which he felt compelled to do on the basis that as many Unionist parties as possible should occupy the top ten places in the top-up seats, which then gained him access to the negotiations (Interview with Robert McCartney, 19 September 2002). The UKUP then split over a number of issues ranging from an argument made by the party chairperson, Conor Cruise O'Brien, in his memoirs, to the personality of the leader, to party strategy in the Assembly. The four MLAs who split formed the Northern Ireland Unionist Party (NIUP), which then split again, and one of their MLAs joined the DUP. The UUP fragmentation did occur in 1998 but the tendency was to stand as individuals and some of these have since moved into the DUP. Moreover, the decision of Donaldson, Arlene Foster and Norah Beare to join the DUP clearly indicated that Unionism was moving into a two-party system.

Finally, the timing of the DUP growth requires explanation. The trend demonstrated by Figure 5.3 is that the DUP were unaffected by the growth in the number of Unionist parties and independents contesting elections; it is quite clear that it is the UUP vote which is reduced. It is also clear that the growth occurs between 1998 and 2001 and not in 1998. This would indicate, as is widely known, that the UUP lost out to smaller parties and defectors but did not regain those votes in 2001 and 2003; instead they went to the DUP. Moreover, the DUP are no longer confined to certain geographical areas and have witnessed a dramatic expansion in areas where they have previously been weak (Figure 5.8); it was the only party to win seats in every constituency in 2003.

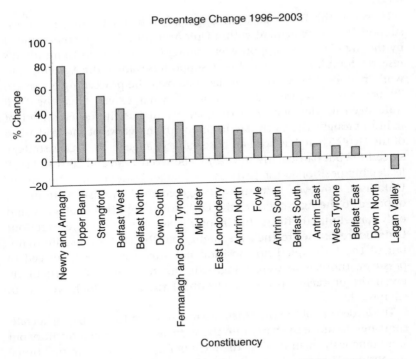

Figure 5.8   Percentage change in DUP vote by constituency 1996–2003.
Source: Derived from figures in Elliott and Flackes (1999) and www.ark.ac.uk/elections.

Models of competition between political parties have stressed a number of predictors of party behaviour and some important caveats which affect how parties pursue their goals (Ware, 1996, 318–30). First, political parties compete for the votes of electors and, in order to win as many as possible, seek to place the party's policies as close to the median voter as possible (Ware, 1996, 320–2). Throughout the period of direct rule, political parties had little influence over policy and it was therefore difficult to know what the median voter looked like, hence the stability in the system. However, political parties are not able to change their position radically in order to appeal to voters (Ware, 1996, 328) and this period was significant in building the reputations of the parties, which then affected how credible their position would be after the Agreement. Thus, the DUP's rhetoric and policy prior to all-party talks would have made it difficult for it to support the Agreement and retain credibility in the eyes of its electorate, given that it meant sharing power with SF, waiting for decommissioning and prisoner releases.

However, the DUP's position was made difficult because there *was* support for the Agreement within Unionism and this was compounded by the high levels of support even among DUP voters. As Colin Irwin's research found, 73 per cent of DUP supporters wanted the Agreement to work in 1999.[14] This figure has declined over the proceeding 6 years to 29 per cent,[15] raising the question, to what extent have the DUP influenced its electorate and to what extent has the development of politics brought the electorate in line with the views of the leadership of the DUP? There has been an observable change in the DUP's strategy since 1998 but particularly since 2001. Between 1998 and 2001 the DUP leadership positioned the party as the market leader in anti-Agreement Unionism. However, as many anti-Agreement Unionists were not as opposed to the Agreement as the DUP leadership, this strategy would only have limited effects. In Chapter 4, we saw how there were four Unionist responses to the Agreement, and the DUP leadership maintained the 'principled no' position but this was not guaranteed to persuade those who were 'pragmatic no' to vote DUP, particularly given the obstacles to the expansion of the DUP, which we saw in Chapter 3.

The leadership of the DUP then began a slow, and seemingly deliberate, campaign to move the party into the softer anti-Agreement territory but simultaneously maintaining their credibility among their traditional supporters. This was shown in a highly visual and symbolic way by the first direct media confrontation between a DUP and a SF representative on UTV's Insight programme on 10 October 2002. The programme was essentially two separate interviews, the first with Martin McGuinness and the second with Peter Robinson. Robinson walked into the studio a few minutes before the end of McGuinness' interview and his entrance was shown as the camera panned out. Robinson did not engage with McGuinness, despite his heckling, and maintained a dogmatic and belligerent attitude throughout. The message to the Unionist electorate was clear – the message had not changed but we are going to be pragmatic in other areas (*News Letter*, 11 October 2002). Slowly, however, the message altered; the DUP's campaign slogan in 2003 was 'It's time for a fair deal.'[16] The juxtaposition of a Unionist demand for a change in the Agreement with an indication that the DUP would pay some attention to Nationalist demands was a clever rhetorical device to show strength and flexibility. There was some kite-flying also, when William Hay suggested on RTE radio that the DUP would be prepared to work with SF, if they gave certain guarantees (*News Letter*, 8 January 2003).[17] Trimble's analysis demonstrated that he understood the DUP strategy:

> It is unlikely that the DUP would have got their head in front of us had they fought a simple 'No' campaign as in 2001. What may have made the difference were the hints of a new pragmatism summed up in the 'fair deal' slogan. Their manifesto, however, was a commitment-free zone without any specifics on what that deal might be. (Trimble, 2004b)

Despite understanding this, the UUP have been unable to withstand the challenge. The positioning of the DUP in the political spectrum of possible positions on the Agreement has made it the most likely party to pick up votes from other Unionist parties, in particular to eliminate the smaller anti-Agreement Unionist parties first, followed by anti-Agreement Ulster Unionist voters. This strategy was helped by the interjection of a First Past the Post Westminster election in 2001, which meant that the electorate only had two viable options – the UUP and the DUP. The success of the DUP in 2001 ensured that the UKUP, NIUP and UUAP were not viable options for Unionists dissatisfied with the Agreement in the 2003 Assembly elections. Therefore, as we can see from Figure 5.9, the DUP was playing the PR game, which allows more combinations of competitions with parties adjacent to each other on a policy spectrum (Katz, 1980). It had been moving towards the UUP to pick up the larger numbers of voters who are more ambivalent on the Agreement, while simultaneously it is the only competitor for the anti-Agreement

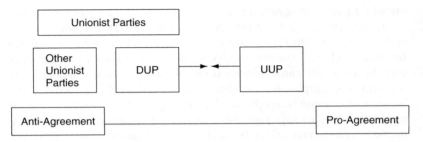

Figure 5.9   Diagram showing Unionist party competition.

vote. Therefore, we can talk meaningfully about a strategy based on policy positioning as being formulated and successful. This is perhaps the most significant effect of the peace process insofar as the previous explanations of the politics of the DUP, which were outlined above and in Chapter 3, are perhaps no longer applicable. It is not that the social networks have changed, although they have declined and the Orange Order has faced difficulties after the various crises at Drumcree in Portadown, but it is that the nature of the Unionist party system has altered from one where traditional elements, such as locality, were important to one where policy is salient. Socio-economic policy may not be the salient policy but the shift is evident.

Trimble's analysis of the changes in Unionist politics was set out clearly in his speech to the UUP annual conference in March 2004:

> The ground which the Ulster Unionist Party staked out in 1997/8 is now the ground upon which DUP stands today. For all of the rant and roar about our supposed treachery, they have, nevertheless, stolen our clothes – stolen them because they know that there is nothing else to fit the political realities. Read 'Devolution Now'. Among its proposals is the corporate Assembly, the 12-person Executive replaced by a 108-person Executive, but operating on all key matters on a cross community basis. They are in de facto negotiations with Sinn Féin. The DUP is champing at the bit to take office and co-operate with Sinn Féin in the day-to-day governance of Northern Ireland. The DUP has performed a triple somersault from the positions outlined in their election manifesto. (Trimble, 2004c)

The extent of the DUP changes is not as great as Trimble would have liked to believe. In contrast to the UUP, the DUP had managed its political changes carefully and gradually with concern both for grass-roots

Unionism and the party. Perhaps the clearest indication of the tensions between the thinking in the party and the knowledge that there were some practical realities to which they would have to agree was the DUP policy on power sharing in 2003, which was essentially no policy. The leadership refused to divulge whether the DUP would enter a power sharing executive on the basis that this would be a matter for negotiations and it was foolish to reveal party strategy before any such negotiations took place. This was a useful argument as there was division within the DUP over power sharing, and dodging the question enabled these divisions to remain hidden.

Of course, in this account, it should not be forgotten that the growth of the DUP has occurred at a moment when the UUP appeared to be disintegrating. We saw in Chapter 1 some of the unsuccessful attempts to strengthen the leadership and policy organs of the party. This was ultimately more important than might have been appreciated. When a relatively weak leadership was coupled with the divisions over the Agreement, the UUP began to tear itself apart with numerous challenges to the leader's policies and leadership challenges. Jonathan Tonge identified two camps within the UUC, the Orange sceptics and rational civics, and these two groups have been engaged in a protracted political struggle for control of the UUP (Tonge, 2005, 74–6). It is difficult to judge whether it has been a question about leadership or a question of policy. Those UUC delegates, led by David Burnside, Jeffrey Donaldson and Martin Smyth, avoided a leadership challenge until 2001 and the anti-Trimble elements in the party did not run a stalking horse until 2004. However, by this stage, Trimble had been working under what has become known as the 'Daphne principle', which stated that he would have a struggle at each stage of the process but would just get enough support to carry on (Miller, 2005, 165). The corollary of this was that his opponents would always get enough support to make a strong leadership impossible and would always get enough support to encourage them to come back for another attempt. Ultimately, this worked in favour of Trimble's leadership; when two stalking horses achieved 40 per cent of the UUC delegates in March 2004 (*News Letter*, 29 March 2004), he was able to ride out what was an indictment of his leadership on the basis that this figure was the well-established level of opposition that he had been dealing with for 6 years. However, it also signalled that Trimble was leading a divided party and had weak mandates for any decisions he took. There were rare occasions when Trimble led from the front, such as when he persuaded the UUP to enter a power sharing executive without prior decommissioning from the IRA, or when he defeated a

Burnside motion with one which allowed him tactical freedom to achieve decommissioning (*Irish Times*, 3 December 2001). However, it is in his party management where Trimble compares unfavourably with his predecessor, Jim Molyneaux. We saw Molyneaux's difficult handling of the debates on integration in 1987 in Chapter 2 but this was a temporary blip and the challengers were expelled over a more definite breach with the leadership, and Molyneaux understood the various factions within the party. When the UUP suffered defections to the DUP after Jeffrey Donaldson and Arlene Foster left the party in December 2003 and the Orange Order decided to break the link with the UUC in March 2005 (*Irish Times*, 14 March 2005) the damage had already been done. There was now the likelihood that Trimble would carry on as leader and that managing the party would be easier but there was less likelihood that he would be able to achieve anything. It was significant that it was his defeat by the electorate that led to his resignation rather than the defeat of the party under his leadership, which had occurred in 2003.

Conclusion

The changes in the party system could be temporary, such as they were in the 1970s; enough time has not passed for us to make any concrete analysis on that basis. However, there is enough evidence for us to assert that changes are taking place and that the DUP is evolving to become a more electorally focused and efficient party. If one of the defining features of a political party is a desire to hold elected office and exercise power then it is clear that this is an increasingly important goal of the DUP. It is also one that has not been in evidence over much of its history. Alvin Jackson described the DUP as 'the thought police of Unionism' (Jackson 1999, 409) and undoubtedly this was a role it played with aplomb. It was also one with which members of the UUP were frustrated. They frequently accuse the DUP of riding on their coat-tails but this just demonstrates the effectiveness of the DUP's timing. They have previously jeopardised their electoral position by entering into electoral pacts with the UUP. This has not happened since 1998 and it is on this crucial change that the future of the Unionist party system rests. It represents a fundamental shift in the power relationship between the two parties; the DUP no longer believe the best interests of Unionism are served by electoral pacts but by competition. This has severely affected the UUP's ability to try and reclaim some of the 'soft-no' voters who have been lost to the DUP. Any attempt by a pro-Agreement UUP leadership to move into space which has been occupied by the DUP, such as in the 2005 Westminster election when Trimble was advocating a voluntary coalition and the exclusion of SF for the long term (*News Letter*, 13 April 2005), was going to suffer from a lack of credibility, leaving the DUP as the strongest party in real and potential terms for most Unionist voters.

Conclusion: Questions of Unity

The Northern Ireland peace process has been a long and protracted affair and has involved addressing complicated and antagonistic relationships between parties which have spent many years demonising each other (Dixon, 2001a). For most of this process, Unionists have been seen as the reluctant participants. Unlike most claims in Northern Ireland, there is no Unionist counter-claim to Gerry Adams' statement that 'the IRA started this process' or the SDLP claim that the Agreement is the justification of its analysis. Indeed, it is difficult to construct a narrative of the process which gives ownership to Unionists. This book has sought to outline the origins of this reluctant engagement with the process but, simultaneously, point to those sections of Unionism who have attempted to problematise the simplistic view that Unionists are under siege, rely on force and bigotry and 'don't want a Catholic about the place', and suggest that this reluctance has its origins elsewhere. It has also argued that cultural and ideational factors, while important, should be understood in the context of politics in Northern Ireland. For example, while many Nationalists are scornful of the idea that the British Government has not supported Unionists, it is clear that the support of the British State is ambivalent, both in terms of actual policy and also in terms of ideology.

Thus, the picture that has been presented throughout this book has been of a largely passive Unionism. However, the peace process has not created as much division as it might be intuitively supposed. We have seen that in relation to both the AIA and the Agreement there is a common analysis. This is significant and needs to be factored into subsequent discussions on Unionism. How then have these divisions been perceived and operationalised by Unionists, in contrast to the explanations proffered by academics which were outlined in the introduction?

First, it is important to recognise that the discussions on this question within Unionism are not framed in the same manner as the academic debates on the subject, which tend to see division as natural, inevitable and almost insurmountable. Unionists frame the discussions in the context of a call to or for 'Unionist unity'. The divisions within Unionism are rarely thought of as politically constructive and the politically relevant question is: What is meant by Unionist unity and is this attainable? Moreover, when that analysis did lead to divergent opinion, these have been largely contained within the institutions of the political parties. The proliferation of parties between 1996 and 1998 can be partly attributed to the electoral system but the subsequent political debates and contests were conditioned by the two main political parties and this prevented a complete fracturing into the full range of political viewpoints. To put the point more strongly, the divisions between Unionists have been interpreted through the institutional lens of the political parties and it is through this lens that political actors have understood the unity/division dichotomy which they have constructed.

However, there *is* recognition of the diversity within Unionism, whether it is of a religious, class or political nature. The peace process has exemplified the difficulties of talking about *one* Unionist community by exposing the internal personality, institutional and policy tensions and this has dovetailed with academic research stressing the diversity within Unionism. Therefore unity does not mean uniformity. Instead it is a strategic question. The analysis which underpins the appeal of this strategy is common to both Unionists and Nationalists and states that Unionists are in a stronger position and better able to achieve strategic goals when they are united; basically the old dictum, 'united we stand, divided we fall'. Whether this holds objectively is another matter, and detailed consideration of this would require extensive theoretical experiments. Nevertheless, a long-running theme throughout the debates within Unionism after the fall of Stormont, through the debates on the AIA and through the peace process is that Unionism should avoid splits. Conversely, a long-running theme within Nationalism has been that it will be necessary to split Unionism in order to extract concessions for Irish Nationalists.

In July 1973, during the negotiations for the formation of the Executive and prior to the Sunningdale conference, the then Attorney General of the Republic of Ireland, Declan Costello, went on a fact-finding tour of various SDLP constituency associations around Northern Ireland. During one of these meetings, John Hume expressed concern that, if Faulkner was dropped as leader, this could result in Unionists uniting.[1]

Faulkner was seen as a divisive figure and thus Nationalists stood to get a better deal and more concessions under a divided Unionism. It should be noted that Faulkner was also one of the most progressive and accommodating Unionists at this time, in the same way that Trimble was to be 25 years later. Nevertheless, the same thinking can be seen behind parts of the AIA, as we saw in Chapter 2: in order to get an accommodation between Unionists and Nationalists, it was necessary to split Unionism. Again, in 1996, when the UKUP and the DUP walked out of the all party talks, this was seen by key figures as a useful development; as George Mitchell remarks: 'Reaching agreement without their presence was extremely difficult; it would have been impossible with them in the room' (Mitchell, 1999, 110).

The question has to be asked: Why is a divided and fragile Unionism seen as a necessary part of political progress in Northern Ireland? Why is it assumed that the broader Unionist community will not buy a deal with Nationalism and that Unionist leaders have to be coerced or tricked into making one? This book concurs with much recent research that essentialist assumptions about Unionism are misguided and yet these dominate much of the writings about the peace process, which seek to explain the conclusion of the Belfast Agreement by recourse to agential explanations stressing the role of a small number of political elites. These accounts fail to provide us with the tools to ask important questions of the peace process which interrogate our assumptions about the types of arguments which are used. For example, if we accept Trimble's argument that the conclusion of the 1998 Agreement was an attempt to break loose from defeatist Unionism, we also have to acknowledge that his argument is merely one possible solution. Trimble's arguments underpin the prevalent assumptions within writings on Unionism. His emphasis on consent and his analysis of the defeatist attitude of Unionists have shaped how we think about the battles within Unionism. However, the electoral growth of the DUP compels us to question these assumptions. Is consent the most important issue, if we agree with Jim Wells' argument?

> Only an Irishman could flog the same horse six times over. Every agreement this [consent] has been trotted out as being the one great concession to Unionism that they have a right to decide their future. Of course they've a right to decide their future but that is not something of a concession, that is our inalienable right in any democratic society but what they do is: we will give you your right to determine where you will go constitutionally, we've given you that in the

Anglo-Irish Agreement, we're going to give it to you in the Good Friday Agreement, we'll give it to you at Sunningdale but to balance that out we will give a whole raft of concessions to the IRA. Now the point is, whether that's enshrined in legislation or not is academic, the Protestant Unionist community will decide where they're going to go constitutionally... at the end of the day you cannot run a million Unionists into a united Ireland against their will so therefore that is no concession. (Interview with Jim Wells, 7 November 2002)

Has Trimble overcome defeatism or has he exacerbated it by embarking on a strategy which has divided Unionism more than ever and resulted in internecine squabbles between Unionists? If so, was this foreseeable and should he have embarked on this course of action?

We also take the existence of the two Unionist parties as established fact and interpret the political arena through this prism, when we should be taking them as contingent factors, although many Unionists also interpret the political arena in the same way. This is clear in the manner in which this strategic 'unity' has been operationalised through coalitions rather than consensus. Thus the formation of the UUC in 1905 was a coalition of Protestant organisations and political parties; the Ulster Vanguard Movement established itself in 1972 as an organisation to bring together all Loyalists (*Irish Times*, 10 February 1972); the campaign against the AIA was a coalition between the UUP and the DUP; and the anti-Agreement campaign in 1998 was a coalition of political parties. The maintenance of these coalitions takes on a dynamic of its own and there is always a sense, reflected in journalists' commentary, that they are fragile and transitory. The idea of a consensus is not prominent within Unionist discussions and yet it is possible that this will be an unforeseen result of the electoral changes within Unionism. This can be seen in the changing thinking of David Burnside. In September 2002 he advocated a United Unionist Convention (a coalition) to agree a bottom line for the renegotiation of the Agreement, whereas in 2005 he was advocating one Unionist party (a consensus) (*The Orange Standard*, September 2002; *News Letter*, 14 April 2005).

In Chapter 5 we saw the DUP counterargument to the Trimble project and the DUP electoral strategy since 1998 and, in particular, the victory speeches of DUP candidates in the 2005 Westminster election confirmed this as a general theme. The DUP have clearly rejected coalition as a viable strategy for Unionism. We noted in Chapter 1 how the DUP did not have the same traditions of debate within the party as the UUP and it is possible that the DUP is more able to offer the possibility of consensus by way of a centralised and coherent leadership. If this does happen, it will mark a significant change in how Unionists relate to their political parties and in how Unionists relate to political developments in general. It also raises questions relating to the possibility of the successful conclusion and implementation of a deal between Unionists and Nationalists. Most of the media opinion has interpreted the electoral growth of SF and the DUP as bad for the restoration of a power sharing Executive. However, there is an alternative reading of the situation. Nationalists have accused Trimble of not 'selling' the Agreement but Trimble's real problem lay in the patterns of UUP politics, which encouraged dissent and debate and were suspicious of centralised leadership. Part of the DUP appeal is in the contrasting leadership institutions and the way in which the party grass roots respond to that leadership. This offers more hope for the longevity of any deal that the DUP strike. When Trimble put the Belfast Agreement to the UUC, he was unsure as to the exact level of its support; it would seem unlikely that the DUP leadership would agree to a deal that they did not think would carry convincingly with the party members.

The peace process has obviously changed the parameters for how Unionists think about consensus and coalitions and thus, by extension, unity and division. We saw in Chapter 4 how Unionists related to the *process* in the same way, regardless of their opinion on the Agreement. However, it is also clear that their opinion on the Agreement determines, to a large degree, how they have interacted with each other politically since 1998. We saw the extent of the changes in the Unionist party system in Chapter 5 and it seems clear from a comparison with the period immediately following the AIA that the peace process altered the dynamics of Unionist party competition. To put the point more strongly: it would be impossible to arrive at the same conclusions about divisions within Unionism in 2005 and 1985. That is the measure of the type of changes that have occurred. This is not to say that the divisions identified in, say, 1985 do not currently exist, but merely that they have been overtaken by other issues and are not politically salient.

If the peace process has had such profound effects on the political divisions within Unionism, what conclusions can we draw concerning the second debate which framed this book, the debate over definition? It should be clear that definition has not been as much of an immediate issue over the course of this study than divisions. We saw how Unionists discussed this issue (Chapter 1) and at various points after the AIA and DSD how Unionists critiqued the direction of policy on the basis that it wrongly defined Unionists or presupposed symmetrical relationships between the two communities in Northern Ireland and their respective state and nation. However, because the talks process was established in such a way as to give a veto to Unionists (as well as Nationalists) the question seems to have receded in importance. Nevertheless, there is still an Irish-centric approach to thinking about Ulster Unionism and this is shown by many of the dominant intellectual and political discourses on the island. Within more general public debate, the John Hume thesis, which states that unity will be achieved by reconciliation, is still dominant and sustains the support for the 1998 Agreement in Southern Ireland and this raises questions as to whether there is a true acceptance of Unionists as anything other than Irish. The peace process confirmed this line of thinking by narrowing the number of viable potential 'solutions'. Northern Ireland would have a devolved assembly with a variety of inter-governmental institutions attached and would be governed according to strict equality and human rights provisions. In the long term, the options were either union with Britain or a united Ireland. Thus, the question of the inevitability of Irish unity is unlikely to disappear. Whether this question of long-term unity should be the most pressing one which preoccupies Unionist intellectual energies is something which Unionists should address. One of John Hume's most successful rhetorical devices was to detach the question of unity from the practicalities of reconciliation. As we saw in Chapter 4, Unionists have a tendency to qualify the desire for peace and, as we saw in Chapter 5, they have a tendency to qualify the desire for reconciliation. These issues are not detached from the two big questions of unity. Conflict resolution processes the world over have needed to address the relationships between the conflicting parties but when Unionists view their participation in the conflict as a reactionary response to Republican and Nationalist violence and agitation, thereby questioning their role in responsibility for the conflict, and then combine this with a qualified view of the desirability of reconciliation and a defence of segregated housing and education policies on the basis of individual choice, there is little reason to question why Unionists do not see even a pragmatic utility in a short-term accommodation with Nationalism.

Nevertheless, it is relatively easy to argue that Irish unity is at best a remote prospect and will perhaps never happen: opinion polls consistently show a large support for the maintenance of the Union; even if Catholics were united in their political options, demographic trends would seem to indicate that it will be at least decades before there is a Catholic majority in Northern Ireland; the Republic of Ireland has no particular designs over Northern Ireland and there is a widespread indifference about the idea of Irish unity among the population; even if there was a desire for unity, there are many questions about economic differentials and the cost of unification. However, the Agreement did not close the question of long-term constitutional change and this was a constant theme of the debates about the Agreement. Pro-Agreement Unionists argued that the Agreement was a settlement, rather than the Republican interpretation which was that it was transitionary. More importantly, many of the Unionist arguments concerning political institutions arising from the DSD, the Framework Documents and the Agreement are premised on the idea that there is an institutional logic which will tie Unionists to a situation over which they have no control. Thus, the North–South bodies will tie Unionists to an all-Ireland framework and will remove the need for Unionist consent to unity, as that will have already been achieved in practice.

The second theme of these arguments relates to the policy of the British Government. McCartney in particular has been prominent in arguing that the 'peace process' is a process of disengagement by the British Government and that the Government has been more concerned with ending Republican violence on mainland Britain than in the interests of peace and democracy in Northern Ireland. This is an exceptionally pessimistic argument and was one of the key points of difference between Trimble and the anti-Agreement Unionists. Trimble took a more benign view of British policy and had greater belief in Tony Blair's Unionism (Godson, 2004). Nevertheless, the argument carries much weight and it is the implications of this argument which are significant. McCartney has not followed the argument through to its logical conclusion that if Unionists can have no confidence in anything that the British Government does, then they have to find a way in which they can have control over their own affairs. The two options are either a UDI, which was floated during the reaction to the proroguing of Stormont, or to negotiate a united Ireland on favourable terms with the Republic of Ireland. Thus, Conor Cruise O'Brien's articulation of negotiated unity (O'Brien, 1998) is not necessarily the logic of O'Brien's arguments about the nature of the peace process but it is the logic of McCartney's arguments about British Government policy.

We can critique the arguments of McCartney and others on empirical grounds: Is the British Government disengaging from Northern Ireland through a process of appeasing terrorists? Is a neo-functionalist reading of North–South institutions credible when it has been discredited in relation to the institutions of the EU? These are empirical questions and require more space than is available here to fully address but it is more important to recognise the extent to which these arguments have become internalised within the Unionist lexicon. One of the recurring themes of this book has been the manner in which Unionists have attempted to challenge a defeatist mentality about the inevitability of unity but it is not whether the prospect of Irish unity is likely, or whether the form of that unity will provide safeguards for the Unionist position that is important. Instead, the important factor is the dominant frameworks which operate on the island and which all point to an all-Ireland reconciliation, without reference to the archipelagic context.

This has affected how political change within Unionist politics has been examined. The extent of that change is infrequently acknowledged and, in many ways, has been disguised by post-Agreement politics. This book has charted how Unionists have reacted to and attempted to shape ideas of change from both within and without since the AIA. The most obvious changes have taken place at an ideational and party political level but this book has examined how these changes have interacted with political change instigated by other actors and communities. However, it is essential to understand the political arguments of those sections of Unionism which have been unfairly labelled 'extremists' and 'rejectionists' and integrate them into the analysis. This can pose uncomfortable questions about the standard interpretations and standard paradigms and also leads to a more complex understanding of events.

Notes

Introduction

1. For example, before Walker (2004a) the last book that was written on the UUP was by John Harbinson (1973). Hume (1996) also contains some interesting data but is far from comprehensive. The DUP has had more recent analysis but Bruce (1989) and Smyth, C. (1987) are now over fifteen years old and the party has developed significantly since those books were written.

Chapter 1

1. Alvin Jackson has encountered similar difficulties in analysing Unionist historiography. He made the distinction between 'Unionist historians' and 'Historians of Unionism'; one of the key distinctions was a declaration of interest (Jackson, 1996, 121).
2. He cites Ronan Bennett and Robert Ballagh, although these are not the only examples that could be utilised, and Ruth Dudley Edwards quotes prominent journalist and writer Tim Pat Coogan as remarking at a conference that Unionists had no culture (Dudley Edwards, 2000, 351).
3. Advert in back of Hume (1996).
4. *Ulster Review*, Issue 18, Winter 1995/1996.
5. Although one Unionist called his book 'intellectual Lundyism', Alex Kane quoted in Jardin (1997).
6. The book won the prestigious Christopher Ewart-Biggs Memorial Prize.
7. See http://www.sluggerotoole.com/archives/2005/05/david_trimbles.php and http://www.sluggerotoole.com/archives/2005/05/uup_insiders_pl.php accessed 13 May 2005.

Chapter 2

1. This would appear to have been at the request of the British, and not Irish, government. See Cochrane (1997, 129–31) for a discussion on an offer made to Molyneaux on Privy Council terms to sign the Agreement in August 1985.
2. For the classic account of Unionist resistance to the third Home Rule bill, see Stewart (1967).
3. The Manifesto said: 'In the absence of devolved government, we will seek to establish one or more elected regional councils with a wide range of powers over local services.' http://www.psr.keele.ac.uk/area/uk/man/con79.htm#ni, accessed on 5 May 2005.
4. The UUUC was formed in January 1974 by the DUP, UUP and VUPP to oppose the Sunningdale Agreement and collapsed following the unsuccessful 1977 strike.

5. North Down Association selected him as a candidate in direct violation of Executive orders.
6. Allister is now a DUP MEP.
7. In January 1988, amid allegations of conspiracy and new scientific evidence, the Court of Appeal in London upheld the convictions of the Birmingham Six, who had been convicted of the 1974 Birmingham pub bombings.
8. In March three IRA members are shot dead by the SAS in Gibraltar. The British claim they were planting a bomb but they were unarmed and no explosives were found in the car, although there was other evidence of a plan. The issue is still clouded with controversy today.
9. In late February the Irish government launched an investigation into the killing of Aiden McAnespie who had been killed by the British army on the Northern Irish side of the border and this prompts controversy as the British claim they have sole rights over such an investigation, which concluded that he was killed by a ricochet.
10. In January the then Attorney General Patrick Mayhew announced there would be no prosecutions from the 'shoot to kill' inquiry headed by John Stalker and John Sampson. At the beginning of February there was more controversy as John Stalker alleged he was removed from the inquiry team because the report was about to cause controversy and lead to resignations of senior officials.
11. Further details can be found in Bew and Gillespie (1999, 212–4).

Chapter 3

1. Information from www.nilga.org/con_map.php, accessed 20 April 2005.
2. Derived from results on http://www.ark.ac.uk/elections/flg01.htm, accessed on 5 May 2005.
3. For example, in 1985 Carson Tweedie (UUP) and Dan Murphy (SDLP) both did not stand on this basis (*Lurgan and Portadown Examiner*, 17 January 1985; *Lurgan Mail*, 28 March 1985).
4. The reference is to Conor Cruise O'Brien, Irish politician, diplomat and journalist, whose career has taken him to a position where he has publicly embraced Unionism in his journalism and, most obviously, by joining the UKUP as Chairman.
5. See Ballymena Borough Council, Minutes of the Monthly Meeting of the Council held on Monday 2 December 1996 at 7.30pm in the Council Chamber, Town Hall, Ballymena.

Chapter 4

1. For examination of the tactical nature of the divisions within Unionism over the Agreement, see Farrington (2001). Porter argues that pro-Agreement Unionists do not have an interpretative framework that differs markedly from anti-Agreement Unionists but I argue that they share an interpretative framework (Porter, 2003, 208).
2. For a general synopsis of Protestant unease with the direction of politics in Northern Ireland, see Dunn and Morgan (1994).

3. This is a slightly expanded taxonomy of my analysis in 2001.
4. Shipley-Dalton has frequently dissented from UUP policy and was the foremost Unionist advocate of the Agreement, (see 2002a, b).
5. However, Malachi O'Doherty argues that the coupling of a constitutional agreement and peace was part of Republican's political strategy and that should not necessarily be seen as one and the same (O'Doherty, 1998, 161–2).
6. For example, Jim Nicholson is typical of most Unionists involved in the talks: 'What actually jettisoned them in my opinion out of the water was when John Hume decided he didn't want an agreement between constitutional nationalism and Unionism and went out and had his famous *tête a tête* with Gerry Adams and the agreement on an envelope.' Interview with Jim Nicholson, 4 October 2002.
7. Although see Moloney (2002) for what seems a tenuous account that Adams and Father Alex Reid were the initiators in these changes even before the AIA.
8. Unionists are not without reason for this interpretation; Brian Girvin has termed the DSD as 'passive rather than active support for the Union' (Girvin, 2000).
9. Patrick Roche describes 'an increasing exclusion of the pro-Union electorate of Northern Ireland from the bonds of national solidarity' (1998, 6).
10. Perhaps surprisingly, what sounds like a conspiracy theory actually has a large element of truth. The DSD was building on the Hume–Adams document, although this was not evident at the time because, in the words of Sean Duignan, aide to Albert Reynolds, 'they were declaring Hume–Adams dead in order to keep it alive'. (Quoted in Mallie and McKittrick, 2001, 130).
11. Part 2 of the *Declaration and Pledge of the United Unionists*, 1998.
12. De Bréadún also quotes a speech at the National Press Club in Washington where Trimble said that after 1921, when Unionists won all the elections, that was 'fine for us but not so fine for other people', (2001, 228).

Chapter 5

1. Northern Ireland Assembly debates, 15 February 1999, accessed on 26 April 2005. http://www.niassembly.gov.uk/record/reports/990215.htm.
2. See the TUAS document at http://cain.ulst.ac.uk/othelem/organ/ira/tuas94.htm, accessed on 21 April 2004.
3. See http://www.sluggerotoole.com/archives/2005/03/post_1.php, accessed on 25 April 2005.
4. See the comments of Willie O'Dea on RTE 1, Questions and Answers, 7 February 2005, available at http://www.rte.ie/news/2005/0207/qanda.html, accessed on 25 April 2005.
5. See, for example, the *Irish Independent* 4 February 2005, which ran the headline 'Now Provos put a gun to our heads.'
6. See poll 5 conducted in March 1998, available at www.peacepolls.org, accessed on 22 April 2005.
7. The question asked was: Looking back on the proposals contained in the Good Friday Agreement, could you tell me how you now feel about each of these? The creation of North–South bodies. Available at: http://www.ark.ac.uk/nilt/2000/Political_Attitudes/GFAPROP2.html, accessed on 22 April 2005.

8. See Colin Irwin's poll 5, www.peacepolls.org, accessed on 22 April 2005.
9. The report can be found at: http://cain.ulst.ac.uk/issues/police/patten/patten99.htm, accessed on 22 April 2005.
10. NI Grand Committee debates, 8 February 2001, http://www.publications.parliament.uk/pa/cm200001/cmstand/nilrelg/cmnirel.htm, accessed on 22 April 2005.
11. See the arguments of Jeffrey Donaldson and Roy Beggs in Northern Ireland Grand Committee debates; Morgan, Austen, 'How to get down the Garvaghy Road' http://www.austenmorgan.com/journal.htm, accessed on 22 April 2005.
12. See the arguments of Beggs in the Northern Ireland Grand Committee debates.
13. Northern Ireland Grand Committee Debates, 17 June 2004, Col 036, available at: http://www.parliament.the-stationery-office.co.uk/pa/cm200304/cmstand/nilrelg/st040617/40617s13.htm, accessed on 22 April 2005.
14. See poll six published in March 1999, available at www.peacepolls.org, accessed on 22 April 2005.
15. See poll 9, published in February 2003, www.peacepolls.org, accessed on 22 April 2005.
16. Available at: http://cain.ulst.ac.uk/issues/politics/election/manifestos.htm, accessed on 25 April 2005.
17. See also Iris Robinson's speech, *News Letter*, 22 May 2003.

Conclusion

1. Report on meeting with SDLP on 28 and 29 July 1973, Department of Taoiseach 2004/21/624, National Archives, Ireland.

Bibliography

Allen, J., R. Beggs, W. Bleakes, J. Burchill, D. Dunlop, R. McCartney, F. Millar and W.M. Smyth (1984) *Devolution and the Northern Ireland Assembly: The Way Forward, a discussion paper presented by the Ulster Unionist Assembly Party's Report Committee* (Belfast: Ulster Unionist Council).

Alter, P. (1994) *Nationalism*, 2nd edition (London: Arnold).

Anderson, B. (1991) *Imagined Communities: Reflections on the Origin and Spread of Nationalism* (revised edition) (London: Verso).

Arthur, P. (1999a) 'Anglo-Irish Relations and Constitutional Policy', in P. Mitchell and R. Wilford (eds), *Politics in Northern Ireland* (Boulder: Westview Press).

Arthur, P. (1999b) 'Quiet diplomacy and personal conversation: Track two diplomacy and the search for a settlement in Northern Ireland', in J. Ruane and J. Todd (eds), *After the Good Friday Agreement: Analysing Political Change in Northern Ireland* (Dublin: UCD Press).

Ascherson, N. (2002) *Stone Voices: The Search for Scotland* (London: Granta).

Aughey, A. (1989) *Under Siege: Ulster Unionism and the Anglo-Irish Agreement* (Belfast: Blackstaff Press).

Aughey, A. (1995a) *Irish Kulturkampf* (Belfast: Ulster Young Unionist Council).

Aughey, A. (1995b) 'The Idea of the Union', in J.W. Foster (ed.), *The Idea of the Union: Statements and Critiques in Support of the Union of Great Britain and Northern Ireland* (Vancouver: Belcouver Press).

Aughey, A. (1997) 'The Character of Ulster Unionism', in P. Shirlow and M. McGovern (eds), *Who are the People? Unionism, Protestantism and Loyalism in Northern Ireland* (London: Pluto Press).

Aughey, A. (1999) 'A new beginning? The prospects for a politics of civility in Northern Ireland', in J. Ruane and J. Todd (eds), *After the Good Friday Agreement: Analysing political Change in Northern Ireland* (Dublin: UCD Press).

Aughey, A (2001a) 'Unionism, Conservatism and the Anglo-Irish Agreement', in D.G. Boyce and A. O'Day (eds), *Defenders of the Union: A Survey of British and Irish Unionism Since 1801* (London: Routledge).

Aughey, A. (2001b) 'A question of degree? The Union, Unionism and the Belfast Agreement', in R. Hanna (ed.), *The Union: Essays on Ireland and the British Connection* (Newtownards: Colourpoint).

Aughey, A. (2001c) 'Learning from the Leopard', in R. Wilford (ed.), *Aspects of the Belfast Agreement* (Oxford: Oxford University Press).

Aughey, A. (2005) *The Politics of Northern Ireland: Beyond the Belfast Agreement* (London: Routledge).

Bew, P. (1994) *Ideology and the Irish Question: Ulster Unionism and Irish Nationalism 1912–1916* (Oxford: Clarendon Press).

Bew, P. (1998a) 'The Unionists have won, they just don't know it', *Sunday Times*, 17 May 1998.

Bew, P. (1998b) 'Consent is the key', *The Times Literary Supplement*, 24 April 1998.

Bew, P. (2001) 'The Union: A concept in terminal decay?' in D.G. Boyce and A. O'Day (eds), *Defenders of the Union: A Survey of British and Irish Unionism Since 1801* (London: Routledge).

Bew, P. and G. Gillespie (1999) *Northern Ireland: A Chronology of the Troubles 1968–1999* (Dublin: Gill and Macmillan).

Bew, P., P. Gibbon and H. Patterson (1996) *Northern Ireland 1921–1996: Political Forces and Social Classes* (London: Serif).

Bew, P., H. Patterson and P. Teague (1997) *Between War and Peace: The Political Future of Northern Ireland* (London: Lawrence and Wishart).

Bew, P. and H. Patterson (1987a) 'The New Stalemate: Unionism and the Anglo-Irish Agreement', in P. Teague (ed.), *Beyond the Rhetoric: Politics, the Economy and Social Policy in Northern Ireland* (London: Lawrence and Wishart).

Bew, P. and H. Patterson (1987b) 'Unionism: Jim leads on', *Fortnight*, November 1987, no. 256.

Billig, M. (1995) *Banal Nationalism* (London: Sage).

Birnie, E. and P. Roche (1995) 'The Economic Consequences of Albert, John and Gerry', *Ulster Review*, Winter 1995.

Birnie, E. and P. Roche (1997) 'The Celtic Pussy Cat', *Ulster Review*, Spring 1997, Issue 22.

Birrell, D. and A. Hayes (1999) *The Local Government System in Northern Ireland* (Dublin: Institute of Public Administration).

Birrel, D. and A. Murie (1980) *Policy and Government in Northern Ireland: Lessons of Devolution* (Dublin: Gill and Macmillan).

Bloomfield, D. (1997) *Peacemaking Strategies in Northern Ireland: Building Complentarity in Conflict Management Theory* (Basingstoke: Macmillan).

Bloomfield, D. (1998) *Political Dialogue in Northern Ireland: the Brooke Initiative, 1989–1992* (Basingstoke: Macmillan).

Boal, F., J.A. Campbell and D.N. Livingstone (1991) 'The Protestant mosaic: A majorities of minorities', in P. Roche and B. Barton (eds), *The Northern Ireland Question: Myth and reality* (Aldershot: Avebury).

Boal, F., M. Keane and D.N. Livingstone (1997) *Them and Us? Attitudinal Variation Among Churchgoers in Belfast* (Belfast: Institute of Irish Studies).

Buckland, P. (1973) *Irish Unionism 2: Ulster Unionism and the Origins of Northern Ireland* (Dublin: Gill and Macmillan).

Breen, R. (1996) 'Who wants a united Ireland? Constitutional preferences among Catholics and Protestants', in R. Breen, P. Devine and L. Dowds (eds), *Social Attitudes in Northern Ireland: The Fifth Report* (Belfast: Appletree Press).

Brown, D. (1999) 'Are there good and bad nationalisms?' *Nations and Nationalism*, vol. 5, no. 2, 281–302.

Brown, K. and C. Hauswedell (n.d.) *Brief 22: Burying the Hatchet: The Decommissioning of Paramilitary Arms in Northern Ireland* (Bonn International Centre for Conversion and INCORE).

Brown, T. (1992) 'British Ireland', in Edna Longley (ed.), *Culture in Ireland: Division or Diversity* (Belfast: Institute of Irish Studies).

Bruce, S. (1987) 'Ulster Loyalism and Religiosity', *Political Studies*, vol. 35, no. 4, 643–648.

Bruce, S. (1989) *God Save Ulster! The Religion and Politics of Paisleyism* (Oxford: Oxford University Press).

Bruce, S. (1994) *The Edge of the Union: The Ulster Loyalist Political Vision* (Oxford: Oxford University Press).

Bryan, D. (1998) ' "Ireland's very own Jurassic Park": The mass media, Orange parades and the discourse on tradition', in A.D. Buckley (ed.), *Symbols in Northern Ireland* (Belfast: Institute of Irish Studies).

Bryan, D. (2000a) *Orange Parades: The Politics of Ritual, Tradition and Control* (London: Pluto Press).

Bryan, D. (2000b) 'Drumcree and the "right to march": Orangeism, ritual and politics in Northern Ireland' in T.G. Fraser (ed.), *The Irish Parading Tradition: Following the Drum* (Basingstoke: Macmillan).

Burnside, D. (1995) 'A Positive Unionism in Great Britain', in A. Aughey, D. Burnside, J. Donaldson, E. Harris and G. Adams (eds), *Selling Unionism: Home and Away* (Belfast: Ulster Young Unionist Council).

Burnside, D. (1996) 'Professionalising Unionism', *Ulster Review*, Spring 1996.

Burnside, D. and I. Watson (1996) 'A Union under threat', *The Unionist*, Autumn 1996.

Cadogan Group (1992) *Northern Limits: The Boundaries of the Attainable in Northern Ireland politics* (Belfast: The Cadogan Group).

Campbell, G. (1994) *Ulster's Verdict on the Joint Declaration* (n.p.).

Coakley, J. (2003) 'The election and the party system', in M. Gallagher, M. Marsh and P. Mitchell (eds), *How Ireland Voted 2002* (Basingstoke: Palgrave Macmillan).

Cochrane, F. (1994) 'Any Takers? The isolation of Northern Ireland', *Political Studies*, vol. 42, no. 3, 378–395.

Cochrane, F. (1997) *Unionist Politics and the Politics of Unionism Since the Anglo-Irish Agreement* (Cork: Cork University Press 1997).

Cochrane, F. and S. Dunn (2002) *People Power? The Role of the Voluntary and Community Sector in the Northern Ireland Conflict* (Cork: Cork University Press).

Colley, L. (1992) *Britons: Forging the Nation 1707–1837* (London: Vintage).

Community Relations Council (n.d.) *Single Identity Work: A Brief Guide*.

Connolly, M. and C. Knox, (1988) 'Recent political difficulties of local government in Northern Ireland', *Policy and Politics*, vol. 16, no. 2, 89–97.

Connor, W. (1994) *Ethnonationalism: The Quest for Understanding* (Princeton: Princeton University Press).

Copus, C. (2004) *Party Politics and Local Government* (Manchester: Manchester University Press).

Coulter, C. (1994) 'The character of Unionism', *Irish Political Studies*, vol. 9, 1–24.

Coulter, C. (1996) 'Direct Rule and the Unionist Middle Classes', in R. English and G. Walker (eds), *Unionism in Modern Ireland: New perspectives on Politics and Culture* (Basingstoke: Macmillan).

Coulter, C. (2000) ' "A miserable failure of a state": Unionist intellectuals and the Irish Republic', in R. Ryan (ed.), *Writing in the Irish Republic: Literature, Culture, Politics 1949–1999* (Basingstoke: Macmillan).

Coulter, C. (2001) 'The Origins of the Northern Ireland Conservatives', *Irish Political Studies*, vol. 16, 29–48.

Cox, W.H. (1987) 'Public opinion and the Anglo-Irish Agreement', *Government and Opposition*, vol. 22, 336–351.

Cox, W.H. (2002) 'Keeping going: Beyond Good Friday', in M. Elliott (ed.), *The Long Road to Peace in Northern Ireland: Peace Lectures from the Institute of Irish Studies at Liverpool* (Liverpool University Press).

Cox, M. (1997) ' "Bringing in the international": The IRA ceasefire and the end of the Cold War', *International Affairs*, vol. 73, no. 4, 671–693.

Crick, B. (1988) 'The Concept of consent and the Agreement', in C. Townshend (ed.), *Consensus in Ireland: Approaches and Recessions* (Oxford: Clarendon Press).

Cunningham, M. (1995) 'Conservative Dissidents and the Irish Question: The pro-Integrationist lobby 1973–1994', *Irish Political Studies*, vol. 10, 26–42.

Cunningham, M. (1997) 'The political language of John Hume', *Irish Political Studies*, vol. 12, 13–22.

De Bréadún, D. (2001) *The Far Side of Revenge: Making peace in Northern Ireland* (Cork: The Collins Press).

Dickson, B. (2003) 'An answer to Arlene', *Fortnight*, March 2003, no. 412.

Dixon, C. (1997) 'Humeocracy', *Ulster Review*, Spring 1997, Issue 22.

Dixon, P. (1995) 'Internationalization and Unionist isolation: A response to Feargal Cochrane', *Political Studies*, 1995, vol. 43, no. 3, 497–505.

Dixon, P. (2001a) *Northern Ireland: The Politics of War and Peace* (Basingstoke: Palgrave).

Dixon, P. (2001b) 'British policy towards Northern Ireland 1969–2000: Continuity, tactical adjustment and consistent "inconsistencies" ', *The British Journal of Politics and International Relations*, vol. 3, no. 3, 340–368.

Dixon, P. (2002a) 'Political skills or lying and manipulation? The choreography of the Northern Ireland peace process', *Political Studies*, vol. 30, 725–741.

Dixon, P. (2002b) 'Northern Ireland and the International Dimension: The end of the Cold War, the USA and European integration', *Irish Studies in International Affairs*, vol. 13, 105–120.

Doherty, P. and M.A. Poole (1996) *Ethnic Residential Segregation in Northern Ireland* (Coleraine: University of Ulster).

Donaldson, J. (1995) 'The U.S.A. Effect', in A. Aughey, D. Burnside, J. Donaldson, E. Harris and G. Adams (eds), and *Selling Unionism: Home and Away* (Belfast: Ulster Young Unionist Council).

Donaldson, J. (1996) 'Building Blocks to Success', *Ulster Review*, Spring 1996.

Donaldson, J. (1999) *The Northern Ireland Peace Process: Blurring the Lines Between Democracy and Terrorism, the 9th Ian Gow Memorial Lecture*, 18 November 1999, http://www.unionist.org.uk/publications/donaldson.html accessed 5 May 2005.

Doyle, J. (1994) 'Workers and outlaws: Unionism and fair employment in Northern Ireland', *Irish Political Studies*, vol. 9, 41–60.

Dudley Edwards, R. (2000) *The Faithful Tribe: An Intimate Portrait of the Loyal Institutions* (London: Harper Collins).

Dunlop, J. (1995) *A Precarious Belonging: Presbyterians and the Conflict in Ireland* (Belfast: Blackstaff Press).

Dunn, S. and V. Morgan (1994) *Protestant Alienation in Northern Ireland: A Preliminary Survey* (Coleraine: University of Ulster).

DUP (1992) *A New Start*, paper submitted to the Mayhew talks 28 August 1992 (Belfast: Democratic Unionist Party).

DUP (1993) *Unionists Alienated – Answer Back! Get mad with Mayhew: Local government Manifesto and Policy Documents*, 1993 (Belfast: Democratic Unionist Party).

DUP (1994) *What's the British Government up to? Tampering with Northern Ireland's Constitutional Position* (Belfast: Democratic Unionist Party).

DUP (2003) *A Bill of Rights for Northern Ireland: A Unionist Vision* (no place: DUP).

Elliott, S. and W.D. Flackes (1999) *Northern Ireland: A Political Directory 1968–1999* (Belfast: Blackstaff Press).

English, R. (1995) 'Unionism and Nationalism: The notion of symmetry', in J.W. Foster (ed.), *The Idea of the Union: Statements and Critiques in Support of the Union of Great Britain and Northern Ireland* (Vancouver: Belcouver Press).

English, R. (1996) 'The same people with different relatives? Modern scholarship, Unionists and the Irish nation', in English and Walker (eds), *Unionism in Modern Ireland: New perspectives on Politics and Culture* (Basingstoke: Macmillan).

English, R. (1999) 'The state and Northern Ireland', in R. English and C. Townshend (eds), *The State: Historical and Political Dimensions* (London: Routledge).

English, R. (2003) *Armed Struggle: A History of the IRA* (Basingstoke: Macmillan).

English, R. and G. Walker (1996) 'Introduction', in R. English and G. Walker (eds), *Unionism in Modern Ireland: New Perspectives on Politics and Culture* (Basingstoke: Macmillan).

Evans, G. and M. Duffy (1997) 'Beyond the sectarian divide: The social bases and political consequences of Nationalist and Unionist Party competition in Northern Ireland', *British Journal of Political Science*, vol. 27, no. 1, 47–81.

Fair Employment Agency (1989) *Report of an Investigation into Derry City Council by the Fair Employment Agency for Northern Ireland* (Belfast).

Farrell, M. (1980) *Northern Ireland: The Orange State,* 2nd edition (London: Pluto Press).

Farren, S. (2000) 'The SDLP and the roots of the Good Friday Agreement', in M. Cox, A. Guelke and F. Stephen (eds), *A Farewell to Arms? From 'long war' to Long Peace in Northern Ireland* (Manchester: Manchester University Press).

Farrington, C. (2001) 'Ulster Unionist political divisions in the late twentieth century', *Irish Political Studies*, vol. 16, 49–72.

Farrington, C. (2003a) 'Ulster Unionism and the Irish historiography debate', *Irish Studies Review*, vol. 11, no. 3, 251–261.

Farrington, C. (2003b) 'Trimble can't expect to unite his party', *Fortnight*, February 2003a, no. 411.

Farrington, C. (2004a) 'We're not quite as interesting as we used to be: Conflicting interpretations of the international dimension among Northern Irish political elites', paper presented to 'Interpreting ongoing crises in the Northern Ireland peace process' conference, Belfast, 11 June 2004.

Farrington, C. (2004b) *Models of Civil Society and their Implications for the Northern Ireland Peace Process,* IBIS Working Paper No. 42.

Fay, M., M. Morrissey and M. Smyth (1999) *Northern Ireland's Troubles: The Human Costs* (London: Pluto Press).

Fearon, K. (1999) *Women's Work: The Story of the Northern Ireland Women's Coalition* (Belfast: Blackstaff Press).

Finlay, F. (2005) 'Gerry, for you it's a power process – not a peace process', *Irish Examiner*, 1 February 2005.

Foley, F. and G. Robinson (2004) *Politicians and Community Relations in Northern Ireland* (Coleraine: INCORE).

Foster, A. (1997) 'Promised Land', *Ulster Review*, Autumn 1997, Issue 23.

Foster, A. (2003) 'Protestants need rights explained to them', *Fortnight*, February 2003, no. 411.

Foster, J.W. (1991) *Colonial Consequences: Essays in Irish Literature and Culture* (Dublin: Lilliput Press).

Foster, J.W. (1995) 'The task for Unionists', in Foster, J.W. (ed.), *The Idea of the Union: Statements and Critiques in Support of the Union of Great Britain and Northern Ireland* (Vancouver: Belcouver Press).

Foster, J.W. (1996) 'Strains in Irish intellectual life', in L. O'Dowd (ed.), *On Intellectuals and Intellectual Life in Ireland: International, Comparative and Historical Contexts* (Belfast: Institute of Irish Studies/Royal Irish Academy).

Foster, J.W. (2002) 'Icy winds blow through Stormont', *Fortnight*, March 2002 no. 403.

Fukuyama, F. (1999) *The Great Disruption: Human Nature and the Reconstitution of Social Order* (London: Profile Books).

Gailey, A. (2001) 'The destructiveness of constructive unionism: Theories and practice, 1890s–1960s', in D.G. Boyce and A. O'Day (eds), *Defenders of the Union: A Survey of British and Irish Unionism since 1801* (London: Routledge).

Garvaghy Residents (1999) *Garvaghy: A Community Under Siege* (Belfast: Beyond the Pale Publications).

Gallagher, M. (1990) 'Do Ulster Unionists have a right to self-determination?' *Irish Political Studies*, vol. 5, 11–30.

Gilligan, C. (1997) 'Peace or pacification process? A brief critique of the peace process', in C. Gilligan and J. Tonge (eds), *Peace or War? Understanding the Peace Process in Northern Ireland* (Aldershot: Ashgate).

Girvin, B. (2000) 'The British State and Northern Ireland: Can the national question be reformed?' in P. Caterrall, W. Kaiser and U. Watton-Jordan (eds), *Reforming the Constitution: Debates in Twentieth Century Britain* (London: Frank Cass).

Godson, D. (2004) *Himself Alone: David Trimble and the Ordeal of Unionism* (London: Harpercollins).

Goodall, D. (1998) 'Actually it's all working out almost according to plan', *Parliamentary Brief*, vol. 5, no. 6, May/June 1998.

Goodall, D. (2002) 'Hillsborough to Belfast: Is it the last lap?' in M. Elliott (ed.), *The Long Road to Peace in Northern Ireland: Peace Lectures from the Institute of Irish Studies at Liverpool University* (Liverpool: Liverpool University Press).

Greer, A. (1999) 'Policymaking', in P. Mitchell and R. Wilford (eds), *Politics in Northern Ireland* (Boulder: Westview Press).

Gudgin, G. (1995) 'The economics of the Union: romance and reality', in Foster, J.W. (ed.), *The Idea of the Union: Statements and Critiques in Support of the Union of Great Britain and Northern Ireland* (Vancouver: Belcouver Press).

Gudgin, G. (1996) 'Northern Ireland: The economic reality', *The Unionist*, Autumn 1996.

Guelke, A. (1985) 'International legitimacy, self-determination and Northern Ireland', *Review of International Studies*, vol. 11, no. 1, 37–52.

Guelke, A. (1996a) 'Consenting to consent', *Fortnight*, September 1996 no. 353.

Guelke, A. (1996b) 'The influence of the South African transition on the Northern Ireland peace process', *South African Journal of International Affairs*, vol. 3, no. 2, 32–48.

Guelke, A. (2000) 'Ireland and South Africa: A very special relationship', *Irish Studies in International Affairs*, vol. 11, 137–146.

Guelke, A. (2003) 'Civil society and the Northern Ireland peace process', *Voluntas: International Journal of Voluntary and Nonprofit Organisations*, vol. 14, no. 1, 61–78.

Guibernau, M. (1999) *Nations without States: political communities in a global age* (Cambridge: Polity).

Hadden, T. and K. Boyle (1989) *The Anglo-Irish Agreement: Commentary, Text and Official review* (London: Sweet & Maxwell Ltd).

Harbinson, J.F. (1973) *The Ulster Unionist Party, 1882–1973: Its development and organisation* (Belfast: Blackstaff Press).

Harris, E. (1995) 'Why Unionists are not understood', in A. Aughey, D. Burnside, J. Donaldson, E. Harris and G. Adams (eds), *Selling Unionism: Home and Away* (Belfast: Ulster Young Unionist Council).

Harvie, C. (2004) *Scotland and Nationalism: Scottish society and politics 1707 to the present* (London: Routledge).

Hayes, B.C. and I. McAllister (2001a) 'Who voted for peace? Public support for the 1998 Northern Ireland Agreement', *Irish Political Studies*, vol. 16, 73–95.

Hayes, B.C. and I. McAllister (2001b) 'Sowing dragon's teeth: Public support for political violence and paramilitarism in Northern Ireland', *Political Studies*, vol. 49, no. 5, 901–922.

Hennessey, T. (1993) 'Ulster Unionist Territorial and National Identities 1886–1893: Province, Island, Kingdom and Empire', *Irish Political Studies*, vol. 8, 21–36.

Hennessey, T. (2000) *The Northern Ireland Peace Process: Ending the Troubles?* (Dublin: Gill & Macmillan).

Heslinga, M.W. (1979) *The Irish Border as a Cultural Divide: A Contribution to the Study of Regionalism in the British Isles* (Assen: Van Gorcum).

HMSO (1993) *Joint Declaration, Downing Street, 15 December 1993* (Belfast: HMSO).

HMSO (1998) *The Agreement: Agreement Reached in the Multi-party Negotiations* (Belfast: HMSO)

Holmes, R. (1995) 'SFUUP', *Ulster Review*, Spring 1995.

Horowitz, D.L. (1985) *Ethnic Groups in Conflict* (Berkeley: University of California Press).

Horowitz, D.L. (2001) 'Northern Ireland's Agreement: Clear, consociational and risky', in J. McGarry (ed.), *Northern Ireland and the Divided World: Post-Agreement Northern Ireland in Comparative Perspective* (Oxford: Oxford University Press).

Horowitz, D.L. (2002) 'Explaining the Northern Ireland Agreement: The sources of an unlikely constitutional consensus', *British Journal of Political Science*, vol. 32, no. 2, 193–220.

Hume, D. (1996) *The Ulster Unionist Party 1972–1992: A Political Movement in an Era of Conflict and Change* (Lurgan: Ulster Society).

Hume, J. (1993) 'A New Ireland in a new Europe', in D. Keogh and M. Haltzel (eds), *Northern Ireland and the Politics of Reconciliation* (Cambridge: Cambridge University Press).

Irwin, C. (2002) *The People's Peace Process in Northern Ireland* (Basingstoke: Palgrave).

Jackson, A. (1989) *The Ulster Party: Irish Unionists in the House of Commons, 1884–1911* (Oxford: Clarendon Press).

Jackson, A. (1996) 'Irish Unionism', in D.G. Boyce and A. O'Day (eds), *The Making of Modern Irish History: Revisionism and the Revisionist Controversy* (London: Routledge).

Jackson, A. (1999) *Ireland 1798–1998: Politics and War* (Oxford: Blackwell).

Jardin, G. (1997) 'A prophet without honour (and common sense)', *Ulster Review*, Spring 1997, Issue 22.

Katz, R.S. (1980) *A Theory of Parties and Electoral Systems* (Baltimore: The John Hopkins University).

Kaufmann, E. (2002) 'The Orange Order and British Protestant Ethnicity: A comparative perspective', paper presented to Orangeism and Protestant Politics Conference, University of Ulster, 8 November 2002.

Kearney, H. (1989) *The British Isles: A History of Four Nations* (Cambridge: Cambridge University Press).

Kearney, H. (1991) 'Four Nations or One?' in Crick, B. (ed.), *National Identities: The Constitution of the United Kingdom* (Oxford: Blackwell).

Keating, M. (2001) *Plurinational Democracy: Stateless Nations in a Post-sovereignty Era* (Oxford: Oxford University Press).

King, P. (1997a) 'The Selectively Democratic and Labour Party?' *Ulster Review*, Spring 1997, Issue 22.

King, P. (1997b) 'Consenting Adults', *Ulster Review*, Autumn 1997, Issue 23.

King, S. (1997) 'The Tragedy of Hume', *Ulster Review*, Spring 1997, Issue 22.

Knox, C. (1996) 'The emergence of power sharing in Northern Ireland: Lessons from local government', *The Journal of Conflict Studies*, vol. 16, no. 1, 7–29.

Knox, C. McIlheney, C. and B. Osborne (1995) 'Social and economic influences on voting in Northern Ireland', *Irish Political Studies*, vol. 10, 69–96.

Lijphart, A. (1977) *Democracy in Plural Societies: A Comparative Exploration* (New Haven: Yale University Press).

Longley, E. (1997) 'What do Protestants want?' *Irish Review*, no. 20, Winter/Spring 1997, 104–120.

MacGinty, R. (1997) 'American influences on the Northern Ireland peace process', *Journal of Conflict Studies*, vol. 17, no. 2, 31–50.

MacGinty, R. (2004) 'Unionist political attitudes after the Belfast Agreement', *Irish Political Studies*, vol. 19, no. 1, 87–99.

MacGinty, R., R. Wilford, L. Dowds and G. Robinson (2001) 'Consenting Adults: The principle of consent and Northern Ireland's constitutional future', *Government and Opposition*, vol. 36, no. 4, 472–492.

McAllister, I. (1983a) 'Class, region, denomination and Protestant politics in Ulster', *Political Studies*, vol. 31, no. 2, 275–283.

McAllister, I. (1983b) 'Political Parties: Traditional and modern', in J. Darby (ed.), *Northern Ireland: The background to the conflict* (Belfast: The Appletree Press).

McAllister, I. (1983c) 'Territorial differentiation and party development in Northern Ireland', in T. Gallagher and J. O'Connell (eds), *Contemporary Irish Studies* (Manchester: Manchester University Press).

McAuley, J.W. (2003) 'The emergence of new Loyalism' in J. Coakley (ed.), *Changing Shades of Orange and Green: Redefining the Union and the Nation in Contemporary Ireland* (Dublin: UCD Press).

McBride, I. (1996) 'Ulster and the British problem', in R. English and G. Walker (eds), *Unionism in Modern Ireland: New Perspectives on Politics and Culture* (Basingstoke: Macmillan).

McCartney, R. (n.d.) *The McCartney Report on consent* (n.p.;n.d but reprinted in *Reflections on Liberty, Democracy and the Union* (Dublin: Maunsel and Company, 2001)).

McCartney, R. (1981) *The Case for the Unionists* (originally 1981, copy supplied to the author 2002 reprint).

McCartney, R. (1986) *The Case for Integration* (Belfast: Ulster Unionist Party Policy Committee).

McCartney, R. (1999) UKUP Conference Speech, 6 February 1999.

McCartney, R. (2001) *Reflections on Liberty, Democracy and the Union* (Dublin: Maunsel and Company).

McCrone, D. (1992) *Understanding Scotland: The Sociology of a Stateless Nation* (London: Routledge).

McCrone, D. (1997) 'Unmasking Britannia: The rise and fall of British national identity', *Nations and Nationalism*, vol. 3, no. 4, 579–596.

McDowell, D. (1995/96) 'Lessons from Labour', *Ulster Review*, Issue 18, Winter 1995/96.

McFarland, A. (1995/96) 'Strategic Signposts', *Ulster Review*, Issue 18, Winter 1995/96.

McGarry, J. (1988) 'The Anglo-Irish Agreement and the prospects for power-sharing in Northern Ireland', *Political Quarterly*, vol. 59, no. 2, 236–250.

McGarry, J. and B. O'Leary (eds) (1990) *The Future of Northern Ireland* (Oxford: Clarendon Press).

McGarry J. and B. O'Leary (1995) *Explaining Northern Ireland: Broken Images* (Oxford: Blackwell).

McGarry, J. and B. O'Leary (2004) *The Northern Ireland Conflict: Consociational Engagements* (Oxford: Oxford University Press).

McIntosh, G. (1999) *The Force of Culture: Unionist Identities in Twentieth Century Ireland* (Cork: Cork University Press).

McIntyre, A. (1995) 'Modern Irish Republicanism: The product of British state strategies', *Irish Political Studies*, vol. 10, 97–122.

McKay, M. and G. Irwin (1995) *Local Government Power-Sharing: A Study of District Councils in Northern Ireland* (Belfast: Institute of Irish Studies).

Mallie, E. and D. McKittrick (1996) *The Fight for Peace: The Secret Story Behind the Irish Peace Process* (London: Heinemann).

Mallie, E. and D. McKittrick (2001) *Endgame in Ireland* (London: Hodder and Stoughton).

Mansergh, M. (1997) 'Real stumbling blocks: decommissioning and the principle of consent', *études Irlandaises*, vol. 22, no. 2, 19–35.

Mansergh, M. (2002) 'Mountain Climbing Irish style: The hidden challenges of the peace process', in M. Elliott (ed.), *The Long Road to Peace in Northern Ireland* (Liverpool: Liverpool University Press).

Miller, D.W. (1978) *Queen's Rebels: Ulster Loyalism in Historical Perspective* (Dublin: Gill and Macmillan).

Miller, F. (2005) *David Trimble: The price of peace* (Dublin: Liffey Press).

Mitchell, G. (1999) *Making Peace* (London: William Heinemann).

Mitchell, P. (1995) 'Party competition in an ethnic dual party system', *Ethnic and Racial Studies*, vol 18, no. 4, 773–796.

Mitchell, P. and G. Gillespie (1999) 'The electoral systems', in P. Mitchell and R. Wilford (eds), *Politics in Northern Ireland* (Boulder: Westview Press).

Moloney, E. (2002) *A Secret History of the IRA* (London: Allen Lane).

Moloney, E. and A. Pollak (1986) *Paisley* (Swords: Poolbeg).

Molyneaux, J. (1991) *Submission by the Rt Hon J H Molyneaux at the first plenary session of strand 1 talks*, Stormont, 18 June 1991 (Belfast: Ulster Unionist Party).

Moxon-Browne, E. (1983) *Nation, Class and Creed in Northern Ireland* (Aldershot: Gower).

Mulholland, M. (2000) *Northern Ireland at the Crossroads: Ulster Unionism in the O'Neill years 1960–9* (Basingstoke: Macmillan).

Myers, K. (2000) *From the Irish Times Column 'An Irishman's Diary'* (Dublin: Four Courts Press).

Nairn, T. (2000) 'Ukania under Blair', *New Left Review*, Jan/Feb 2000, no. 1, 69–103.

Nairn, T. (2001) 'Farewell Britannia', *New Left Review*, Jan/Feb 2001, no. 7, 55–74.

Nesbitt, D. (1995) *Unionism Restated: An analysis of the Ulster Unionist Party's 'Statement of Aims'* (Belfast: Ulster Unionist Information Institute).

Nesbitt, D. (2002) 'Redefining Unionism' in J. Coakley (ed.), *Changing Shades of Orange and Green: Redefining the Union and the Nation in Contemporary Ireland* (Dublin: UCD Press).

New Ireland Forum (1984) *Report* (Dublin: The Stationary Office).

Northern Ireland Charter Group (1986) *A Northern Ireland Charter: A Set of Three Proposals*, 5 March 1986.

O'Brien, C.C. (1994) *Ancestral Voices: Religion and Nationalism in Ireland* (Dublin: Poolbeg).

O'Brien, C.C. (1998) *Memoirs: My Life and Themes* (Dublin: Poolbeg).

O'Clery, C. (1996) *The Greening of the White House: The Inside Story on How America Tried to Bring Peace to Ireland* (Dublin: Gill and Macmillan).

O'Doherty, M. (1998) *The Trouble with Guns: Republican Strategy and the Provisional IRA* (Belfast: Blackstaff Press).

O'Donnell, C. (2004) *'Standing Idly By'? Fianna Fáil, Irish Republicanism and the Northern Ireland Troubles, 1968–2002*, Unpublished PhD thesis, Queen's University Belfast, 2004.

O'Dowd, L. (1991) 'Intellectuals and political culture: a unionist – nationalist comparison', in E. Hughes (ed.), *Culture and Politics in Northern Ireland 1960–1990* (Milton Keynes: Open University Press).

O'Dowd, L. (1998a) 'Constituting Division, Impeding Agreement: The neglected role of British Nationalism in Northern Ireland', in J. Anderson and J. Goodman (eds), *Dis/Agreeing Ireland: Contexts, Obstacles, Hopes* (London: Pluto Press).

O'Dowd, L. (1998b) 'New Unionism, British Nationalism and the prospects for a negotiated settlement in Northern Ireland', in D. Miller (ed.), *Rethinking Northern Ireland: Culture, Ideology and Colonialism* (London: Longman).

O'Dowd, N. (2002) 'The Awakening: Irish America's key role in the Irish peace process', in M. Elliott (ed.), *The Long Road to Peace in Northern Ireland: Peace Lectures from the Institute of Irish Studies at Liverpool* (Liverpool: Liverpool University Press).

O'Duffy, B. (1993) 'Containment or Regulation? The British approach to ethnic conflict in Northern Ireland', in J. McGarry and B. O'Leary (eds), *The Politics of Ethnic Conflict Regulation: Case Studies of Protracted Ethnic Conflicts* (London: Routledge).

O'Halloran, C. (1987) *Partition and the Limits to Irish Nationalism: An Ideology Under Stress* (Dublin: Gill and Macmillan).

O'Leary, B. (1987) 'The Anglo-Irish Agreement: Meanings, Explanations, Results and a Defence', in P. Teague (ed.), *Beyond the Rhetoric: Politics, the Economy and Social Policy in Northern Ireland* (London: Lawrence and Wishart).

O'Leary, B. (1997) 'The Conservative stewardship of Northern Ireland 1979–97: Sound-bottomed contradictions or slow learning?' *Political Studies*, vol. 45, no. 4, 663–676.

O'Leary, B. (1999) 'The Nature of the British – Irish Agreement', *New Left Review*, 233, 66–96.

O'Leary, B. and P. Arthur (1990) 'Introduction: Northern Ireland as a site of state- and nation-building failures', in J. McGarry and B. O'Leary (eds), *The Future of Northern Ireland* (Oxford: Clarendon Press).

O'Leary, B. and J. McGarry (1996) *The Politics of Antagonism: Understanding Northern Ireland*, 2nd edition (London: Athlone Press).

O'Leary, C., S. Elliott and R. Wilford (1988) *The Northern Ireland Assembly 1982–1986: A Constitutional Experiment* (London: C Hurst & Co).

O'Malley, P. (1990) *Northern Ireland: Questions of Nuance* (Belfast: Blackstaff Press).

O'Neill, S. (1994) 'Pluralist justice and its limits: the case of Northern Ireland', *Political Studies*, vol. 42, no. 3, 363–377.

O'Neill, S. (1996) 'The idea of an over-lapping consensus in Northern Ireland: Stretching the limits of liberalism', *Irish Political Studies*, vol. 11, 83–102.

O'Neill, S. (2000) 'Liberty, equality and the rights of cultures: the marching controversy at Drumcree', *The British Journal of Politics and International Relations*, vol. 2, no. 1, 26–45.

O'Toole, F. (1998) *The Lie of the Land: Irish Identities* (Dublin: New Island Books).

Owen, A.E. (1994) *The Anglo-Irish Agreement: The First Three Years* (Cardiff: University of Wales Press).

Paisley, I. (1991) *Dr Paisley's Opening Speech at the Brooke Talks – Stage One* (Belfast: Democratic Unionist Party).

Parekh, Bhikhu (2002) 'Being British', *Government and Opposition*, vol. 37, no. 3, 301–316.

Parkinson, A.F. (1998) *Ulster Loyalism and the British Media* (Dublin: Four Courts Press).

Parkinson, A.F. (2001) 'Bigots in Bowler Hats? The presentation and reception of the loyalist case in Great Britain', in D.G. Boyce and A. O'Day (eds), *Defenders of the Union: A survey of British and Irish Unionism since 1801* (London: Routledge).

Patterson, L. (1994) *The Autonomy of Modern Scotland* (Edinburgh: Edinburgh University Press).

Pocock, J.G.A. (1975) 'British History: A Plea for a New Subject', *Journal of Modern History*, vol. 47, no. 4, 601–628.

Pollak, A. (ed.) (1993) *A Citizen's Inquiry: The Opsahl Report on Northern Ireland* (Dublin: The Lilliput Press).

Porter, N. (1996) *Rethinking Unionism: An Alternative Vision for Northern Ireland* (Belfast: Blackstaff Press).

Porter, N. (2003) *The Elusive Quest: Reconciliation in Northern Ireland* (Belfast: Blackstaff Press).

Putnam, R.D (2000) *Bowling Alone: the Collapse and Revival of American Community* (New York: Simon and Schuster).

Reid, J. (2001) *Becoming Persuaders – British and Irish identities in Northern Ireland*, http://www.nio.gov.uk/press/011121sos.htm, speech delivered to the Institute of Irish Studies, Liverpool, 21 November 2001.

Robbins, K. (1990) 'Varieties of Britishness' in M. Crozier (ed.), *Cultural Traditions in Northern Ireland: Varieties of Britishness* (Belfast: Institute of Irish Studies).

Roche, P.J. (1994) 'Northern Ireland and Irish Nationalism – A Unionist perspective', *The Irish Review*, no. 15, Spring 1994, 70–78.

Roche, P.J. (1996) 'Irish Nationalism', *The Salisbury Review: The Quarterly Magazine of Conservative Thought*, Winter 1996, 23–25.

Roche, P. (1997) 'John Hume: Architect of the Troubles?' *Ulster Review*, Spring 1997, Issue 22.

Roche, P. (1998) 'Unionism', *The Salisbury Review: The Quarterly Magazine of Conservative thought*, Winter 1998.

Roche, P.J. and Birnie, J.E. (1995) *An Economics Lesson for Irish Nationalists and Republicans* (Belfast: Ulster Unionist Information Institute).

Roche, P.J. and E. Birnie (1996) 'Irish Nationalism: Politics of the absurd', *Ulster Review*, Summer 1996.

Roche, P. and Birnie, E. (1997) 'Unionism and the Irish Dimension', *Ulster Review*, Autumn 1997, Issue 23.

Ross, Willie, (1986) *The Devolution/Integration Argument* (Belfast: Ulster Unionist Party Policy Committee).

Ruane, J. (1999) 'The end of (Irish) history: three readings of the current conjecture', in J. Ruane and J. Todd (eds), *After the Good Friday Agreement: Analysing political change in Northern Ireland* (Dublin: UCD Press).

Ruane, J. (2004) 'Contemporary Republicanism and the strategy of armed struggle', in J. Coakley and M. Bric (eds), *From Political Violence to Negotiated Settlement: The winding path to peace in twentieth-century Ireland* (Dublin: UCD Press).

Ruane, J. and J. Todd (1992) 'Diversity, division and the middle ground in Northern Ireland', *Irish Political Studies*, vol. 7, 73–98.

Ruane, J. and J. Todd (1996) *The Dynamics of the conflict in Northern Ireland: Power, conflict and emancipation* (Cambridge: Cambridge University Press).

Ruane, J. and J. Todd (2001) 'The politics of transition? Explaining political crises in the implementation of the Belfast Good Friday Agreement', *Political Studies*, vol. 49, no. 5, 923–940.

Ruane, J. and J. Todd (2004) 'The roots of intense ethnic conflict may not in fact be ethnic: Categories, communities and path dependence', *European Journal of Sociology*, vol. 45, no. 2, 209–232.

Ryder, C. and V Kearney (2001) *Drumcree: The Orange Order's Last Stand* (London: Methuen).

Sartori, G. (1976) *Parties and party systems: a framework for analysis* (Cambridge University Press).

Schultz, K.E. (1997) 'The Northern Ireland Political Process: A viable approach to conflict resolution', *Irish Political Studies*, vol. 12, 92–110.

SDLP (1993) *Progress through Partnership: Local Government election manifesto*, May 1993.

Shipley-Dalton, D. (2002a) 'A deal with Durkan can save the Agreement', *Fortnight*, October 2002, no. 407.

Shipley-Dalton, D. (2002b) 'If my party won't govern then go on without us . . .,' *Fortnight*, November 2002, no. 408.

Shirlow, P. and M. McGovern (1998) 'Language, discourse and dialogue: Sinn Féin and the Irish peace process', *Political Geography*, vol. 17, no. 2, 171–186.

Skelly, J.M. (1999) 'Appeasement in our time: Conor Cruise O'Brien and the peace process in Northern Ireland', *Irish Studies in International Affairs*, vol. 10, 221–236.

Smith, P. (1986) *Principles for Devolved Government* (Belfast: Ulster Unionist Party Policy Committee).

Smyth, C. (1986) 'The DUP as a politico-religious organization', *Irish Political Studies*, vol. 1, 33–43.

Smyth, C. (1987) *Ian Paisley: The voice of Protestant Ulster* (Edinburgh: Scottish Academic Press).

Smyth, M. (1986) *Another Way* (Belfast: Ulster Unionist Party Policy Committee).

Stewart, A.T.Q. (1967) *The Ulster Crisis: Resistance to Home Rule 1912–1914* (London: Faber and Faber).

Taylor, J. (1995) 'The New Unionist Approach', *Ulster review*, Summer 1995.

Taylor, R. (2001) 'Northern Ireland: Consociation or social transformation?' in J. McGarry (ed.), *Northern Ireland and the divided world: post-agreement Northern Ireland in comparative perspective* (Oxford: Oxford University Press).

Templegrove Action Research Limited (prepared by Marie Smyth) (1995) *Sectarian Division and Area Planning: a commentary on 'The Derry Area Plan 2011: Preliminary Proposals'* (Derry Londonderry: Templegrove Action Research Limited).

Todd, J. (1987) 'Two traditions in Unionist political culture', *Irish Political Studies*, vol. 2, 1–26.

Todd, J. (1989) 'The Limits of Britishness', *The Irish Review*, no. 5.

Todd, J. (1993) 'Unionist Political Thought, 1920–72', in D.G. Boyce, R. Eccleshall and V. Geoghegan (eds), *Political Thought in Ireland since the seventeenth century* (London: Routledge).

Todd, J. (1995a) 'Equality, plurality and democracy: justifications of proposed constitutional settlements of the Northern Ireland conflict,' *Ethnic and Racial Studies*, vol. 18, no. 4, 818–836.

Todd, J. (1995b) 'Beyond the community conflict: Historic compromise or emancipatory process?' *Irish Political Studies*, vol. 10, 161–178.

Tonge, J. (2005) *The New Northern Irish Politics?* (Basingstoke: Palgrave Macmillan).

Trimble, D. (1988) 'Initiatives for Consensus: a Unionist Perspective', in C. Townshend (ed.), *Consensus in Ireland: Approaches and Recessions* (Oxford: Clarendon Press).

Trimble, D. (1996) 'In Denial', *The Unionist*, Autumn 1996.

Trimble, D. (2001) *To raise up a new Northern Ireland: Articles and speeches 1998–2000* (Belfast: Belfast Press).

Trimble, D. (2004a) Statement by David Trimble (UUP) at the opening of the Review of the Agreement, 3 February 2004, available at: http://cain.ulst.ac.uk/issues/politics/docs/uup/uup030204.htm accessed 22nd April 2005.

Trimble, D. (2004b) Speech by David Trimble, then leader of the Ulster Unionist Party (UUP), at the UUP Annual Conference in the Slieve Donard Hotel, Newcastle, Saturday 13 November 2004, available at http://cain.ulst.ac.uk/issues/politics/docs/uup/dt131104.htm accessed 22nd April 2005.

Trimble, D. (2004c) Speech by David Trimble, then leader of the Ulster Unionist Party (UUP), at the UUP Annual Conference in the Ramada Hotel, Belfast, Saturday 27 March 2004, available at: http://cain.ulst.ac.uk/issues/politics/docs/uup/dt270304.htm accessed 22nd April 2005.

UK Group (1986) *No Longer a Place Apart*.

UUP (1986) Party Conference Agenda, 1986 (Belfast: Ulster Unionist Party).

UUP (1987) Party Conference Agenda, 1987 (Belfast: Ulster Unionist Party).

UUP (1989) *The Constitution and Rules of the Ulster Unionist Council adopted by the Council on 18 March 1989* (held in the Northern Ireland Political Collection of the Linenhall Library).

UUP (1992a) *A Question of Identities? A statement by the Ulster Unionist Party*, Brooke talks, 7 May 1992.

UUP (1992b) *Manifesto: The people's choice, General Election*, 9 April 1992 (Belfast: Ulster Unionist Party).

UUP (1994) *A Blueprint for Stability*, 1994 (Belfast: Ulster Unionist Party).

UUP (1995) *A Practical Approach to Problem-Solving in Northern Ireland*, 1995 (Belfast: Ulster Unionist Party).

UUP (1998) *Understanding the Agreement*, 1998 (Belfast: Ulster Unionist Party).

UUP and DUP (1987) *To put right a great wrong, Joint Unionist Manifesto*, 1987 (Belfast: Ulster Unionist Party/Ulster Democratic Party).

Walker, B. (1996) *Dancing to History's Tune: History, myth and politics in Ireland* (Belfast: Institute of Irish Studies).

Walker, G. (1995) *Intimate Strangers: Political and cultural interaction between Scotland and Ulster in modern times* (Edinburgh: John Donald Publishers Ltd).

Walker, G. (2004a) *A History of the Ulster Unionist Party: Protest, pragmatism and pessimism* (Manchester: Manchester University Press).

Walker, G. (2004b) 'The Ulster Unionist Party and the Bannside by-election 1970', *Irish Political Studies*, vol. 19, no. 1, 59–73.

Ware, A. (1996) *Political Parties and Party Systems* (Oxford: Oxford University Press).

Waterside Think Tank (1999) *Are We not Part of this City Too?* (Newtownabbey: Island pamphlets).

Whyte, J. (1990) *Interpreting Northern Ireland* (Oxford: Clarendon Press).

Whyte, N. (2003) 'Election Predictions', *Fortnight*, December 2003, no. 420.

Wilford, R. and R. Wilson (2003) *A route to stability: the review of the Belfast Agreement* (Belfast: Democratic Dialogue).

Wilson, A. (1995) *Irish America and the Ulster Conflict 1968–1995* (Belfast: Blackstaff Press).

Wilson, A. J. (2000) 'The Ulster Unionist Party and the U.S. role in the Northern Ireland peace process, 1994–2000', *Policy Studies Journal*, vol. 28, no. 4, 858–874.

Wilson, R. and L. Fawcett (2004) *The Media Election: Coverage of the 2003 Northern Ireland Assembly poll* (Belfast: Democratic Dialogue).

Index